TOCQUEVILLE: THE ANCIEN RÉGIME AND THE FRENCH REVOLUTION

This new translation of an undisputed classic aims to be both accurate and readable. Tocqueville's subtlety of style and profundity of thought offer a challenge to readers as well as to translators. As both a Tocqueville scholar and an award-winning translator, Arthur Goldhammer is uniquely qualified for the task. In his Introduction, Jon Elster draws on his recent work to lay out the structure of Tocqueville's argument. Readers will appreciate *The Ancien Régime and the French Revolution* for its sense of irony as well as tragedy, for its deep insights into political psychology, and for its impassioned defense of liberty.

JON ELSTER has taught at the Université de Paris VIII, the University of Oslo, the University of Chicago, Columbia University, and the Collège de France. He is the author of twenty-three books translated into seventeen languages, including *Ulysses and the Sirens* (1979), *Sour Grapes* (1983), *Making Sense of Marx* (1985), *Alchemies of the Mind* (1999), *Explaining Social Behavior* (Cambridge 2007), *Le désintéressement* (2009), *Alexis de Tocqueville: The First Social Scientist* (Cambridge 2009), and *L'Irrationalité* (2010). Professor Elster is a member of the American Academy of Arts and Sciences, the Norwegian Academy of Science, and Academia Europaea and is a Corresponding Fellow of the British Academy.

ARTHUR GOLDHAMMER has translated more than a hundred works from French, including Tocqueville's *Democracy in America*. He is a three-time recipient of the French-American Foundation translation prize. France made him a Chevalier de l'Ordre des Arts et des Lettres, and the Académie Française awarded him its Médaille de Vermeil.

T0345966

CAMBRIDGE TEXTS IN THE HISTORY OF POLITICAL THOUGHT

Series Editors

RAYMOND GEUSS
Professor of Philosophy, University of Cambridge

QUENTIN SKINNER
Barber Beaumont Professor of the Humanities, Queen Mary, University of London

Cambridge Texts in the History of Political Thought is now firmly established as the major student textbook series in political theory. It aims to make available to students all of the most important texts in the history of Western political thought, from ancient Greece to the early twentieth century. All the familiar classic texts will be included, but the series seeks at the same time to enlarge the conventional canon by incorporating an extensive range of less-well-known works, many of them never before available in a modern English edition. Wherever possible, texts are published in a complete and unabridged form, and translations are specially commissioned for the series. Each volume contains a critical introduction together with chronologies, biographical sketches, a guide to further reading, and any necessary glossaries and textual apparatus. When completed, the series will offer an outline of the entire evolution of Western political thought.

For a list of titles published in this series, please see end of book.

Tocqueville: The Ancien Régime and the French Revolution

TRANSLATED BY
ARTHUR GOLDHAMMER

EDITED WITH AN INTRODUCTION BY
JON ELSTER
Columbia University

CAMBRIDGE
UNIVERSITY PRESS

CAMBRIDGE
UNIVERSITY PRESS

32 Avenue of the Americas, New York NY 10013-2473, USA

Cambridge University Press is part of the University of Cambridge.

It furthers the University's mission by disseminating knowledge in the pursuit of education, learning and research at the highest international levels of excellence.

www.cambridge.org
Information on this title: www.cambridge.org/9780521718912

© translation, Introduction, and editorial matter Cambridge University Press 2011

First published 2011

A catalogue record for this publication is available from the British Library

Library of Congress Cataloguing in Publication data
Tocqueville, Alexis de, 1805–1859.
[Ancien régime et la Révolution. English]
Tocqueville : the Ancien Régime and the French Revolution / Jon Elster ; Arthur Goldhammer.
p.   cm. – (Cambridge Texts in the History of Political Thought)
Includes bibliographical references and index.
ISBN 978-0-521-88980-3 – ISBN 978-0-521-71891-2 (pbk.)
1. France – History – Revolution, 1789–1799 – Causes.   I. Elster, Jon,
1940– editor.   II. Goldhammer, Arthur, 1946– translator.   III. Title.
DC138.T6313   2011
944.04–dc22   2010046536

ISBN 978-0-521-88980-3 Hardback
ISBN 978-0-521-71891-2 Paperback

With grateful acknowledgment to Jon Elster, who read the entire text of the translation and improved it immeasurably. – AG

Contents

Contents

Contents

Introduction

The Ancien Régime and the French Revolution (*AR*) is one of the best and best-known works of history ever written. Some might object that it does not really belong to the genre of history, as it contains no narrative. In the opening sentences of the work, Tocqueville himself asserts, "This book is not a history of the French Revolution, which has been recounted too brilliantly for me to contemplate doing it again. It is rather a study of that Revolution." As he also explains in the Foreword, he intended to write a second volume that would include a narrative of the Revolution itself. His drafts for that volume are absorbingly interesting, and I shall say a bit about them later.

The possible objection can be sustained only if one has a needlessly purist conception of historical writing. French historians in the twentieth century often contrasted the *histoire de la longue durée* with the *histoire événementielle*, the long-term study of institutional and cultural change with the short-term narrative of actions and events. *AR* certainly spans a long period, from Charles VII in the fifteenth century to the years immediately before the Revolution. Tocqueville shows, for instance, how a resourceful *nobility* slowly turned into an impotent *aristocracy*, and how the towns gradually lost their independence until only a hollow shell remained.

In addition to being a study of the *longue durée*, *AR* can be read as a work of *structural analysis* and as *social science*. Since the expression "structural analysis" can be understood in many ways, I need to explain how I use it. Imagine a house of cards subject to occasional gusts of wind. Although one cannot tell *when* a gust will be strong enough to make the structure crumble, nor *which* card will be the first to fall, one can say with "moral certainty," beyond a reasonable doubt, *that* the house will fall.

Similarly, it has been said that the 2007 subprime mortgage crisis was "an accident waiting to happen." We can understand the title of the final chapter of *AR* – "How the Revolution Emerged Naturally from the Foregoing" – along the same lines. As I shall explain, Tocqueville argued that the absolute monarchy had, in fact, become a house of cards. The exact trigger of its collapse was contingent, but by (say) 1750 the occurrence of *some* triggering event was a moral certainty.

In a letter to W. Borgius from 1894, Friedrich Engels wrote, naively, "That Napoleon, just that particular Corsican, should have been the military dictator whom the French Republic, exhausted by its own war, had rendered necessary (*nötig*), was an accident; but that, if a Napoleon had been lacking, another would have filled the place, is proved by the fact that the man has always been found as soon as he became necessary: Caesar, Augustus, Cromwell, etc." Tocqueville did not espouse this teleological form of necessity. Had he written in German, he would have said that the occurrence of some event that would trigger the Revolution was *notwendig* rather than *nötig* – causally necessary rather than needed. At the same time, he intended to go on, in the second volume, to study the particular triggering events.

As does any work of history, *AR* invites the question: Did the author *get it right?* On a number of specific factual matters, he did not. As Gilbert Shapiro and John Markoff show in *Revolutionary Demands: A Content Analysis of the Cahiers de Doléance of 1789*, Tocqueville offered many unsupported generalizations about the grievance books that the three estates prepared on the eve of the Revolution. In his essay on Tocqueville in *Interpreting the French Revolution*, François Furet finds many sins of commission and omission in Tocqueville's treatment of the period before 1750, but endorses the famous "Tocqueville effect" (see the following paragraph) regarding the immediate prerevolutionary period. As he observes, Tocqueville was simply much more knowledgeable about the recent past than about the distant past.

Be this as it may, we can benefit immensely from *AR* because of its powerful causal arguments, which transcend the specific time and place to which Tocqueville applied them. It is, in fact, a work of social science. As is true of other classical works of history, such as the *Protestant Ethic and the Spirit of Capitalism* by Max Weber or *Bread and Circuses* by Paul Veyne, it offers *exportable causal mechanisms* that are by now part of the toolbox of the social scientist. The best known is probably the "Tocqueville effect" – revolutions occur when conditions are improving, not (as Marx sometimes asserted) when they are going from bad to worse. A related fruitful idea is that of the ineffectiveness of both moderate repression and moderate concessions as responses to social unrest. Equally important in a more general perspective is the idea of "pluralistic ignorance" – the apparent consensus that arises when few people believe in a given doctrine, but most people believe that most people believe it. (This idea was already present in *Democracy in America*.) Finally, one can cite the idea of "second-best" political systems – one evil can offset another, so that if one of them is removed, the overall performance of the system will suffer. I shall return to the way these ideas are deployed in *AR*.

If we read *AR* as a work of social science, it is tempting to ask some slightly anachronistic questions. Was Tocqueville a rational-choice theorist? Was he a functionalist? Did he espouse methodological individualism or holism? How can we situate him with respect to other great social thinkers such as Marx, Durkheim, or Weber? Although one could probably give reasonably meaningful answers to these questions, I shall address them only indirectly. In my opinion, the central task Tocqueville set for himself in *AR* was to explain the Revolution in terms of the *political psychology of the class struggle*. In his analysis of the run-up to the Revolution, Tocqueville, like many Marxist writers, emphasized the triangular struggle among nobility, peasantry, and bourgeoisie. Unlike them, however, he gave center place to symbolic and subjective aspects of the conflicts rather than to objective economic relations. I cite some examples in the next section.

AR is also a work of social science in its extensive use of the comparative method. Tocqueville wanted to explain not only why the Revolution occurred in France but also why no similar upheaval took place in England and Germany. Within France, he wanted to understand why it first erupted in the region around Paris rather than elsewhere. In his cross-country as well as within-country analyses, he deploys the psychological method just described to argue that even though exploitation and oppression were objectively lighter in the revolutionary areas, the burdens were *perceived* to be heavier in these regions.

To set out the structure of *AR* and its relation to the planned second volume, it may be useful to adopt Lawrence Stone's terminology in *The Causes of the English Revolution*, where he distinguishes *preconditions*

(1529–1629), *precipitants* (1629–39), and *triggers* (1640–2). If we apply the schema to *AR*, we can say, in line with my earlier remarks, that the preconditions made the Revolution possible, while the precipitants made it necessary in the sense that some events or actions would predictably occur to trigger it. The preconditions, discussed in Book II, were established over the period from 1439 to 1750. The precipitants, the topic of Book III, developed from 1750 to 1787. The triggering events, discussed in the notes for the planned second volume, occurred from 1787 to 1789.

The preconditions of the Revolution can be summarized in some words spoken to Napoleon by the poet François Andrieux: "On ne s'appuie que sur ce qui résiste" (You can lean only on what offers resistance). In a nutshell, Tocqueville claimed that the successive French kings were so successful in reducing the nobility and the bourgeoisie to a state of political impotence that when Louis XVI needed their help to resist the Revolution, they had nothing to offer: "Nothing was left that could obstruct the government, nor anything that could shore it up" (p. 124). Only in the West of France, where the nobles had resisted the summons of the king to come to the court, did they come to his assistance: "The letter of one intendant who responded to the query has survived. He complains that the nobles of his province are pleased to remain with their peasants rather than fulfill their obligations at court. It is worth noting that the province in question was Anjou, later known as the Vendée. The nobles who are said to have refused to do their duty toward the king were the only ones in France who would later take up arms in defense of the monarchy" (pp. 113–14).

An important reason for the weakness of the nobles was their isolation from the bourgeoisie that followed from their tax exemption. Tocqueville claimed that "of all the ways of distinguishing men and marking class divisions, unequal taxation is the most pernicious and the most apt to add isolation to inequality, rendering both incurable" (p. 85). Because they were not subject to the same taxes, the two classes had few common interests and few occasions to take concerted action. Although Tocqueville does not use the phrase "divide and conquer," it is very clear from his analyses that this was the strategy he imputed to the kings: "Nearly all the unfortunate defects, errors, and prejudices I have just described owe either their origin, duration, or development to the skill that most of our kings have had in dividing men in order to govern them more absolutely" (p. 124).

Yet the fact that party C may benefit from a falling-out between parties A and B is not by itself proof of intentional *divide et impera*. There is always the possibility of an accidental third-party benefit, *tertius gaudens*.

In fact, Tocqueville does not offer any proof of the more intentional or Machiavellian thesis. His actual explanation of the origin of the tax exemption of the nobles relies on a quite different mechanism. He asserts that the "cowardly" nobility accepted tax exemption as a bribe to allow the king to impose new taxes without calling a meeting of the Estates General. "I dare to affirm that on the day the nation, tired of the interminable disorders that had accompanied the captivity of King John and the dementia of Charles VI, allowed kings to levy a general tax without its consent, and when the nobility was cowardly enough to allow the Third Estate to be taxed provided that it remained exempt – on that day the seed was sown of practically all the vices and abuses that ravaged the Ancien Régime for the remainder of its existence" (p. 94). As an additional explanatory factor, Tocqueville notes that when Charles VII first established the taille (a land tax) on a national basis, it would have been dangerous to impose it on the nobles: "When the king attempted to levy taxes on his own authority for the first time, he realized that it would be necessary initially to choose one that did not appear to fall directly on nobles, because in those days they constituted a class that stood as a dangerous rival to the monarchy and would never have tolerated an innovation so prejudicial to themselves. He therefore chose a tax from which they were exempt: the taille" (p. 95).

Moreover, one could hardly ask the nobles to pay a tax that was likely to be used against them. In his notes for the second volume, Tocqueville quotes from Turgot, the minister of Louis XVI: "Under Charles VII one began to mount a permanent paid militia, and it was in this period that the taille was established on a permanent basis." He adds that "since the purpose of the paid troops was to subdue the nobles or at least to circumvent them, it was quite natural that, in order to pave the way for the transition, they were not themselves asked to provide the money to be used against them." This straightforward explanation does not support the story according to which the kings granted tax exemptions to the nobles in order to undermine their political power. In fact, to complicate matters, Tocqueville at one point reverses the causal chain by asserting that the exemptions were a "consolation" for the loss of power: "In the eighteenth century in England, it was the poor man who enjoyed the tax privilege; in France it was the rich man. There, the aristocracy took the heaviest public responsibilities on itself so that it would be allowed to govern; here it retained the tax exemption to the end to console itself for having lost the government" (p. 94).

Even before being exempted from the taille, the nobles had enjoyed tax immunities. The novel element was that they were also exempted from the duty to raise troops that had justified the tax exemption. They were "relieved of the very onerous obligation to make war at their own expense, yet their immunity from taxation had been maintained and in fact expanded considerably. In other words, they retained the indemnity while shedding the burden" (pp. 77–8). This amounted to a breach of an *implicit contract*. Without the obligation of public service, the nobility lost its energy and became a mere ornament: "One might say that the limbs gained at the expense of the body. The nobility less and less enjoyed the right to command, but nobles more and more claimed the exclusive prerogative of being the principal servants of the master" (p. 84). The double exemption from raising troops and from paying taxes was a *poisoned gift* – with the added twist that its long-term effect was to harm the donor as well as the recipient, for "on ne s'appuie que sur ce qui résiste."

The public service that the nobles had traditionally performed included not only the raising of armies for the king but also the provision of public goods to the local peasantry, notably law, order, and famine relief. When they ceased to perform these tasks, they broke *a second implicit contract*, this time with the peasantry: "If the French peasant had still been subject to the administration of his lord, feudal dues would have seemed far less unbearable to him" (p. 37). Just as the royal militia replaced the nobles in their military function, so did the royal *intendant* and his *subdélégué* replace the *seigneur* in his administrative function. And just as the tax exemption fueled the envy of the bourgeois for the nobles, so did the withdrawal of the nobles from local administration fuel the hatred the peasantry felt for them.[1]

There is one gap in this otherwise admirably tight argument: Why, how, and when did the intendant (or his *subdélégué*) take the place of the seigneur in local administration? Virtually all references to the intendant in *AR* are to his functions in the eighteenth century, and there is no mention of the creation of the office in the sixteenth century. A divide-and-conquer explanation might be that the successive kings deliberately undermined the local power of the nobles by luring them to the court.

---

[1] The reader may be confused by Tocqueville's occasional tendency to use "hatred" and "envy" as if they refer to the same emotion. They do not: The urge of hatred is to destroy the hated person; that of envy is to destroy the envied object, not its possessor. In the analysis of a revolution that began by destroying privileges and ended by killing the privileged, this distinction is obviously important.

Tocqueville, however, explicitly rejects this idea. He notes that "the nobility's abandonment of the countryside has often been attributed to the specific influence of certain kings and ministers, notably Louis XIV and Richelieu" (p. 113), but objects that "We must nevertheless beware of attributing the desertion of the countryside by what was then the leading class of the nation to the direct influence of certain kings. The primary and persistent cause of this desertion was not the will of certain individuals but the slow and steady operation of certain institutions. Proof of this can be seen in the fact that when the government wanted to counter the evil in the eighteenth century, it could not even slow its progress. As nobles lost their political rights without acquiring others in their place, and as local liberties disappeared, the emigration of nobles increased. There was no longer any need to lure them from their homes because they no longer wished to stay in them. Country life had become insipid for them" (p. 114). The alleged "proof" is not one, however, since the fact that the kings tried unsuccessfully to reverse the trend later does not prove that the trend was not originally due to their initiative. In fact, the phrase that "there was no longer any need to lure them from their homes" implies that it had been necessary at some point in the past. The details of the process remain obscure, however.

Whatever ambiguity there may be concerning the importance of intentional royal action in Tocqueville's account of the decline of the nobility, there is none whatsoever in his explanation of the decline of the towns: "Louis XI had curtailed municipal freedoms because he feared their democratic character. Louis XIV did not fear them but destroyed them nonetheless. Proof that this was the case can be seen in the fact that he was willing to sell these freedoms back to any town that could pay for them. In fact, his intention was not so much to abolish as to trade in them, and if he did abolish them, it was done as it were inadvertently, as a purely expedient financial policy" (pp. 47–8). In other words, the king abolished municipal freedom by putting offices up for sale, but from his point of view the revenue he could raise from letting towns buy their freedom back was just as good. For the towns, the choice was between political decline and financial ruin. Make-believe autonomy did not work: "The people, who are less easily fooled by the mere semblance of freedom than one might imagine, everywhere lost interest in town affairs and lived as strangers within their own town walls" (p. 49).

In his analysis of the fragmentation of the prerevolutionary bourgeoisie, Tocqueville broke new ground. Referring to the obsessive striving for priority (*préséance*) in guilds and professions, he asserts that "each of the thousand small groups of which French society was composed thought only of itself.... What is stranger still, moreover, was that all these men who remained so aloof from one another had become so similar that, had they been forced to change places, they would have been unrecognizable. More than that, anyone capable of sounding the depths of their minds would have discovered that all the petty barriers that divided these very similar people from one another struck them as both inimical to the public interest and hostile to common sense; in theory they already adored unity. Each of them clung to his own particular status only because others distinguished themselves by theirs, but all were ready to meld into a single mass, provided that no one else could claim any advantage for himself or rise above the common level" (pp. 91–2). This illustrates the mechanism of pluralistic ignorance. The fragmentation of the bourgeoisie took place because each group believed, *wrongly*, that all others wanted only to promote their particular interests.

With the decline of the nobility and of the towns, and the isolation of the various bourgeois elements from one another, the preconditions for the Revolution were in place. Among the precipitants, the most important is encapsulated in the "Tocqueville effect," the idea that subjective discontent (and hence the likelihood of revolution or rebellion) and objective grounds for discontent can be inversely related to each other. Tocqueville offers two synchronic versions and one diachronic version of the paradox. At the beginning of Book II, he asks why the Revolution occurred in France rather than in Germany, given that feudal burdens were lighter in France. Somehow, "their yoke seemed most unbearable where in fact its burden was lightest" (p. 31). The resolution of the paradox is that in Germany the nobles still performed the administrative functions that justified their appropriation of feudal benefits.

In Book III, Tocqueville notes that another synchronic version of the paradox could be observed within France itself: "The parts of France that were to become the principal center of that revolution were precisely those where progress was most evident" (p. 156). The areas in Île-de-France where the Revolution would break out enjoyed greater personal freedom and lower taxes than the Western lands that would be the bastion of the counterrevolution: "If one studies what remains of the archives of the former Île-de-France district, it is easy to see that it was in the regions around Paris that the old regime reformed itself soonest and most profoundly.... Nowhere, by contrast, did the old regime maintain itself better than along the Loire, toward its mouth, in the marshes of Poitou and the moors of Brittany. It was precisely there that civil war flared up and spread and that the most durable and violent resistance to the Revolution occurred. Thus, one might say that the better the situation of the French became, the more unbearable they found it" (pp. 156–7).

The mechanism behind this synchronic paradox is not quite clear. As we saw, the nobles of Vendée were "pleased to remain with their peasants" and hence generated more loyalty than absentee landlords did. At the same time, the feudal burdens on the peasantry in these regions were heavier than in the Île-de-France. The net effect of these two mechanisms could presumably go either way. Yet I believe the reason why Tocqueville so unambiguously states that the better-off were more discontented is that he confused the synchronic and the diachronic paradoxes. In the continuation of the last-cited passage, he goes on to restate the paradox in what is probably the most famous statement in the whole work: "It is not always going from bad to worse that leads to revolution. What happens most often is that a people that put up with the most oppressive laws without complaint, as if they did not feel them, rejects those laws violently when the burden is alleviated. The regime that a revolution destroys is almost always better than the one that immediately preceded it, and experience teaches that the most dangerous time for a bad government is usually when it begins to reform" (p. 157).

This is obviously a diachronic statement, presented, misleadingly, as equivalent to the synchronic one that immediately precedes it. If we focus on the diachronic paradox, we can approach it as part of the larger question of how governments respond to an actual or predictable crisis. Broadly speaking, we may distinguish four responses: preemption, concession, moderate repression, and severe repression. Wisdom dictates preemption – meeting popular demands before they are formulated, or granting more than is demanded. In a letter to Lord Radnor on May 26, 1848, Tocqueville asserts that "the only way to attenuate and postpone [the] revolution, is to do, before one is forced to do it, all one can to improve the situation of the people." Both Louis XV and Louis XVI were sorely lacking in this quality of mind. Moreover, as we shall see shortly, even preemptive measures may backfire.

Severe repression, for its part, requires a decisiveness that was also absent. Although Tocqueville does not mention the well-known aversion of Louis XVI for spilling the blood of his subjects, he does cite the more general tendency of the eighteenth-century monarchy to be *fortiter in modo, suaviter in re*: "In the eighteenth-century monarchy, the forms of punishment were terrifying but the penalties was almost always moderate. One preferred to frighten rather than harm, or, rather, one was arbitrary and violent out of habit and indifference, and mild by temperament" (p. 169). Although the comment refers to criminal justice, it also applies to the preference for moderate over severe repression. The administration was left, therefore, with the alternatives of concession and moderate repression.

It is a fundamental Tocquevillian idea that *half-measures tend to work against their purpose*. When you try to get the best of both worlds you often get the worst of both. Consider first moderate repression: "At the beginning of a revolution such measures [granting no real liberties but only their shadow] always fail and merely inflame the people without satisfying them" (p. 133). Or again: "The half-measures that were imposed on the enemies of the Church at that time did not diminish their power but rather increased it.... Authors were persecuted just enough to elicit complaint but not enough to provoke fear. They were subjected to enough restraint to provoke resistance but not to the heavy yoke that might quell it" (p. 139).

Consider next concessions or moderate reform. As we saw, Tocqueville claims that a people "that put up with the most oppressive laws without complaint, as if they did not feel them, rejects those laws violently when the burden is alleviated." For each demand that is granted, more will spring up until the capacity of the system to absorb them is broken. Yet we have to ask: *Why* does one concession generate the demand for more? Generally speaking, it could be because it induces a change in the *beliefs* of the citizens, in their *preferences*, or in both.

On the one hand, the granting of a demand may provide new information about the resolve of the administration, and support the belief that further demands will also be met with a positive response. (For a contemporary example, consider how the nonintervention by the USSR after the first free elections in Poland in June 1989 signaled to the opposition in Hungary that intervention was unlikely there as well.) In *AR* Tocqueville does not appeal to this mechanism, but in the notes for the second volume he cites it to argue that the recall of the Parlement of Paris in September 1788 was a point of no return for the monarchy. "The king ... recalled parlement and rescinded the stamp law and the territorial tax.... If the king wished to remain the king of the old monarchy, this was precisely what he should not have done. From that moment on, all sorts of concessions were indispensable."

On the other hand, reforms that satisfy a given desire may at the same time cause dormant or latent desires to appear on the horizon. This was Tocqueville's main answer: "The evil that one endures patiently because it seems inevitable becomes unbearable the moment its elimination becomes conceivable. Then, every abuse that is eliminated seems only to reveal the others that remain, and makes their sting that much more painful. The ill has diminished, to be sure, but sensitivity to it has increased" (p. 157). Once the first evil has been removed, other evils will appear as removable and therefore as intolerable. A cognitive change (the evil is not inevitable) triggers a motivational change (it is intolerable). Although Tocqueville is often cited as arguing that the improvement of conditions cause subjective expectations to rise even faster, this is not an accurate rendering of his views. His argument was that an objective improvement today makes people feel subjectively worse off *today*, not that it generates expectations that will make them feel frustrated tomorrow.

Chapter 5 of Book III does not address the "Tocqueville paradox" as usually understood but another paradoxical effect of the initiatives of *AR*. Here Tocqueville discusses preemptive measures to alleviate the misery of the people in the years immediately before the Revolution. However wise the measures themselves may have been, the wisdom of the way they were proposed was highly questionable. The privileged classes publicly stated their own responsibility for the plight of the peasantry, as if their intention was to create disturbances rather than to prevent them: "This was to inflame each and every individual by enumerating his woes and pointing a finger of blame at those responsible, thereby emboldening the victims by revealing the small number of authors of their woes, piercing their hearts to the quick, and setting them ablaze with greed, envy, and hatred" (p. 164). Adding insult to the perception of injury, they also used contemptuous language when referring to the individuals they intended to help as if the latter were unable to understand what they were saying: "What is rather peculiar, moreover, is that, to the striking expressions of interest that the people inspired in them, they occasionally added public expressions of contempt.... The provincial assembly of Haute Guyenne, while warmly pleading the cause of the peasants, called them 'coarse and ignorant creatures, troublemakers, and uncouth, undisciplined characters.' Turgot, who did so much for the people, expressed himself in largely similar terms" (p. 163). The precipitants of the Revolution thus included preemptive no less than reactive attempts to improve the situation of the population.

As I noted, in *AR* Tocqueville does not discuss the triggers of the Revolution. In his notes for the second volume we find, however, a number of insightful comments on the dynamics of the Revolution. I shall briefly summarize three of them.

Tocqueville emphasized the enormous importance of events in the Dauphiné (around Grenoble). In 1788, the immensely influential assembly in Vizille achieved an unprecedented unity of action among the three orders: "The assembly of Vizille was in a sense a material and visible sign to all that this new union had taken place and showed what effects it might have. This was the last time that an event in a remote corner of a tiny province in the Alps proved decisive for all of France. It brought to the attention of all what had been visible to only a few, showed everyone where power lay, and thus decided the victory in an instant." An effect (or a sign) of their unity was the adoption of the system of "cross-voting" in electing deputies to the Estates General. In this system, deputies for a given order were chosen jointly by members of all three orders. Tocqueville asserts that the Estates General might have found it easier to agree if this electoral system had been universally adopted: "If the vote in common had to be adopted, it is unfortunate that what was done in Dauphiné was not done everywhere, because there the deputies of all three orders were chosen by all three orders, and this might have favored an accord." Yet the spearheading effect of the Dauphiné, though important, was blunted by the nonadoption of cross-voting in almost all other electoral districts.

In the notes for the second volume, Tocqueville argues, once again, that the half measures Louis XVI took against the courts of the Ancien Régime (the parlements) and the Estates General had the effect of accelerating the Revolution. In its struggle against the parlements, the government was "employing violence to the point of irritation but never pushing it to the point of fear." Tocqueville also refers to the "attitude of power mixed with incomplete violence and disdain." Fatally, "to raise hopes of voting by head [in the Estates General] and yet not authorize it was to spur the Third Estate to attack and allow the privileged to resist." As the king left the situation shrouded in uncertainty, each side could self-servingly and self-deceptively believe that it would be resolved in its favor. After the attempt on June 23, 1789, by Louis XVI to impose his will on the assembly, the latter "irritated and aroused rather than demoralized by this mild pressure from the government, increasingly adopted the attitude of being in charge."

Tocqueville also discusses the suicidal fragmentation of the elites. After citing complaints in the grievance books of the clergy over the trespassing of the lords on the property of their tenants, he adds that "several other grievance books [of the clergy were written] in the same spirit and with the same bitterness of peasants become curés. Later on we will see the clergy come in for similarly strong abuse from the nobility. The two orders had yet to learn to make common cause." In his notes to himself, Tocqueville wrote that "when I come to the era of class warfare, show clearly how dizzying the disintegration was. It was not just the bourgeoisie that made war on the nobility but the lesser nobility that attacked the greater, the lower clergy the higher." Whereas previously the conflicts within and between the privileged orders had benefited the government, they now became so virulent as to bring it down: "Nothing serves more to ... fuel despotism [than] the hatred [and] jealousy of the various classes. But with the proviso [that] this hatred and envy are nothing more than a bitter and tranquil emotion, just enough to prevent people from helping one another but not enough to spur them to fight. There is no government that will not collapse once violent clashes between the classes have begun."

The Ancien Régime and the French Revolution is not merely an historical study of the preconditions and the precipitants of a world-historical event. It is also the expression of Tocqueville's personal philosophy, notably his obsession with *liberty* as the overriding political value. Published in 1856, it was written under Louis Napoleon's Second Empire, which Tocqueville detested for its oppression of civil and political freedom. In the planned follow-up volume, Tocqueville also intended to discuss Louis Napoleon's uncle, the first Napoleon. Whereas Tocqueville felt only contempt for the nephew, he expressed both great admiration for Napoleon's gifts and utter revulsion for the ways he used them to crush liberty.

According to Benjamin Franklin, "Those who would give up essential liberty to purchase a little temporary safety deserve neither liberty nor safety." Substituting wealth for safety, Tocqueville would agree. He would also make a stronger statement: Those who give up liberty for the sake of wealth will *obtain* neither: "[I do not] think that a genuine love of liberty ever arises out of the sole prospect of material rewards, for that prospect is often barely perceptible. It is indeed true that in the long run liberty always brings comfort and well-being and often wealth to those who are able to preserve it. At times, however, it temporarily hinders the use of such goods. At other times despotism alone can ensure their fleeting enjoyment. Those who prize liberty only for the material benefits it offers have never kept it for long" (p. 151). The benefits of freedom are essentially by-products of the love of freedom for its own sake.

Tocqueville was acutely aware of this difference between universal rights and liberties on the one hand and irregular privileges on the other. Modern conceptions of rights imply that if anyone is free to do X or has the right to do X, then everyone has the right or freedom to do X. In the Ancien Régime, by contrast, one could enjoy only "a kind of irregular and intermittent liberty, always limited by class distinctions, always bound up with the idea of exception and privilege, which allowed people to defy the law almost as much as the exercise of arbitrary power and seldom went so far as to guarantee to all citizens the most natural and necessary rights" (p. 111). Although "limited and twisted ... disorderly and unwholesome" (p. 111), it was nevertheless a second-best defense against the arbitrary despotism of the royal administration. Albeit in perverse and pathological forms, the Ancien Régime did contain some checks on absolute power: "This bizarre and flawed constitution of public functions served as a substitute for any kind of political guarantee against the omnipotence of the central government. It was an irregular and badly constructed dike that dispersed the government's force and blunted its impact.... The irregular intervention of the courts in government, which often disrupted the orderly dispatch of the public's affairs, thus served at times to safeguard liberty. It was a great evil that limited a still greater one" (pp. 103, 108).

The Revolution broke down all these barriers to centralization and absolutism. After it had run its course, "centralization was salvaged from the ruins and restored. And because it was raised up again, while everything that had once kept it in check still lay in ruins, what suddenly emerged from the entrails of a nation that had just overthrown the monarchy was a power more extensive, more minute, and more absolute than our kings had ever exercised" (p. 183). The tragedy of the Revolution lies in the fact that its main actors, in their admirable struggle for freedom, created the conditions for a more repressive regime than the one they had brought down.

The fascination that Tocqueville's book will always exercise on readers owes a great deal to the seamless way in which the historical analysis is overlaid with this sense of tragedy. The attraction is further heightened by Tocqueville's exquisite use of irony. To bring home his point that the elites openly expressed their contempt for those whose woes they sincerely wished to alleviate, he cites "Mme Duchâtelet, who, according to Voltaire's secretary, was quite comfortable disrobing in front of her servants, in view of the absence of incontrovertible proof that valets were men" (p. 162). To illustrate the hypocrisy of the noblemen, he recounts that they "generally addressed the intendant simply as 'Monsieur,' but in their petitions I noted that they always addressed him as 'Monseigneur' (My Lord), just as the bourgeois did" (p. 169). The amused references to the indignation of the wigmakers at the award of priority to the bakers in the general assembly and to the willingness of the privileged orders to "forgo the benefits of unequal taxation" as long as they could maintain the "appearance" of exemption (p. 163) provide other examples among many. Moreover, the reader is constantly startled by the epigrammatic formulations in which Tocqueville often encapsulates key ideas. Reading him is a feast of the mind.

It remains to be said that Tocqueville also knew revolutions from the inside, as it were. During the 1830 July Revolution, he observed the revolutionary violence as a semiparticipant observer. Writing to his fiancée and future wife Marie Mottley on July 30, he expressed his horror at seeing "the French endlessly cutting each other's throats." Later, he played a very active political part during the Revolution of 1848. Although he had no military function, he was a close observer of the battles and skirmishes taking place in the streets and even inside parliament, as when the crowd invaded the Assemblée Nationale (of which he was a member) on May 15. His absorption in the events was existential. In March 1849, he complained to a friend that "now that properties and life are no longer at stake, I cannot interest myself in anything. This is the evil of revolutions, which, like gambling, create the habit of emotions and make us love them for their own sake, independently of the gain."

His *Recollections*, covering the period from 1848 to 1851, is chock full of vignettes and acute insights. Let me mention two of them. At one point, he notes that the revolutionary codes of honor "tolerate murder and allow devastation, but theft is strictly forbidden." Also, he observes that Lamartine tried "to dominate the Mountain without quenching the revolutionary fires, so that the country would bless him for providing security, but would not feel safe enough to forget about him."

Each observation has an echo in the notes for the second volume of *AR*. In the correspondence between the deputies from Anjou and their constituencies, on which he relied heavily (and perhaps too much), he notes the following statement from July 13, 1789: "In the tumult the prisoners of common crimes escaped; the people opposed their release, declaring that criminals were not worthy to mix with the makers of liberty.... If an armed man committed something vile, he was immediately taken to prison by his comrades." He comments that "this is particularly French." From the same correspondence, he cites another letter from July 1789 from the deputies to their constituents, saying that "we must temper the movement of the violent passions without smothering a salutary fermentation," as an illustration of his own claim that "the national assembly wanted to limit the fire and was afraid of extinguishing it."

There is little doubt that Tocqueville's personal exposure to revolutionary events shaped and informed his study of the Revolution. He probably had a better understanding of the dynamics of revolution than anyone before or since.

Bibliographical Note

Biographies of Tocqueville include André Jardin, *Tocqueville: A Biography* (Farrar, Strauss, and Giroux, 1988) and Hugh Brogan, *Alexis de Tocqueville: A Life* (Yale University Press, 2006). In his *Recollections* (Transaction Books, 1985) Tocqueville offers a striking self-portrait as well as an observer-participant account of the 1848 Revolution.

Tocqueville's first study of the French Revolution, "The social and political state of France before and after 1789," was translated by John Stuart Mill and published in the *London and Westminster Review* in 1836.

The French text of *The Ancien Régime and the French Revolution* can be consulted in the two major modern editions of Tocqueville's works: in Volume II.1 of the *Oeuvres Complètes* (Gallimard, 1953) and in Volume III of the *Oeuvres* (Éditions de la Pléiade, Gallimard, 2004). (It can also be found online at http://classiques.uqac.ca/classiques/De_tocqueville_alexis/ancien_regime/ancien_regime.html.) The former has a valuable Introduction by Georges Lefebvre, perhaps the preeminent historian of the Revolution. In Volume II.2 of the *Oeuvres Complètes* and in Volume III of the *Oeuvres*, readers can find slightly different versions of Tocqueville's notes for the planned second volume of the *AR*.

Tocqueville claimed that in preparing *AR* he had worked only with primary sources, because he found it painful to read what others had written on the subject. The best study of these sources is Robert T. Gannett, *Tocqueville Unveiled: The Historian and His Sources for The Old Regime and the Revolution* (University of Chicago Press, 2003). Tocqueville had, however, read the histories of the Revolution by Jules Michelet and by Adolphe Thiers. More important influences, because more

"Tocquevillian" in their approach to the Revolution through political psychology, were probably Joseph Droz, *Histoire du règne de Louis XVI* (1839) and Madame de Staël, *Considérations sur la Révolution Française* (published posthumously in 1818). Broader aspects of the genesis and the reception of the work are discussed in Françoise Mélonio, *Tocqueville and the French* (University Press of Virginia, 1998). A unique perspective on the work is offered in Robert Palmer, ed., *The Two Tocquevilles, Father and Son: Herve and Alexis De Tocqueville on the Coming of the French Revolution* (Yale University Press, 1997).

In *Interpreting the French Revolution* (Cambridge University Press, 1981), François Furet situates (as did Lefebvre) Tocqueville in the historiography of the Revolution. Some of Tocqueville's specific claims are assessed in John Markoff, *The Abolition of Feudalism* (Pennsylvania State University Press, 1996) and in Gilbert Shapiro and John Markoff, *Revolutionary Demands* (Stanford University Press, 1998).

Social scientists have also addressed Tocqueville's ideas in *AR*, notably "the Tocqueville effect." In "Toward a Theory of Revolution" (*American Sociological Review* 27, 1962), James Davies proposed a synthesis of Marx and Toqueville. Raymond Boudon offers a simple formal model of the Tocqueville effect in "The Logic of Relative Frustration," in *Rational Choice*, ed. Jon Elster (Blackwell, 1986). Tocqueville's pioneering insights into pluralistic ignorance are highlighted in Elisabeth Noelle-Neumann, *The Spiral of Silence* (University of Chicago Press, 1993).

Chronology

1805	Born in Paris on July 29.
1814/15	Restoration of the French monarchy.
1828	Meets Marie Mottley, whom he married in 1835.
1829	Attends lectures on French history by Guizot.
1830	July Revolution and accession of Louis Philippe.
1831–2	Travels in the United States with Gustave de Beaumont, officially to study the American penitentiary system.
1833	Publication of *Du système pénitentiaire aux Etats-Unis et de son application en France* (American translation published the same year).
1835	Publication of the first volume of *De la démocratie en Amérique* (English translation published the same year).
1835	Travels in England and Ireland.
1837	Runs for election to the Chamber of Deputies, but loses in the second round.
1838	Elected to the Académie des Sciences Morales et Politiques.
1839	Runs for election again and is elected in the first round. He will be constantly reelected until 1849.
1840	Publication of the second volume of *De la démocratie en Amérique* (English translation published simultaneously).
1841	Travels in Algeria.
1841	Elected to the Académie Française.
1846	Travels in Algeria.
1848	Predicts a revolution in a speech to the Chamber of Deputies on January 27.

1848	Outbreak of the February Revolution on February 22. Fall of the July Monarchy and creation of the Second Republic.
1848	Elected to the Constitutional Committee of the newly elected Constituent Assembly.
1848	Opposes Louis Napoleon in the presidential campaign. Louis Napoleon elected president with 74 percent of the vote.
1849	Appointed foreign minister in a cabinet presided over by Odillon Barrot. Louis Napoleon dismissed the cabinet after five months.
1850	First signs of tuberculosis. Begins working on his *Souvenirs* of the 1848 Revolution (first published in 1893).
1851	Louis Napoleon stages a military coup d'état on December 2. Tocqueville is arrested along with 200 protesting members of the National Assembly and held in jail for two days. He retires from politics.
1852	Louis Napoleon proclaims the Second Empire and takes the title of Napoleon III.
1852	Begins research and writing for *L'ancien régime et la Révolution*.
1856	Publication of *L'ancien régime et la Révolution* (English translation published simultaneously).
1859	Dies on April 16.

TOCQUEVILLE: THE ANCIEN RÉGIME AND THE FRENCH REVOLUTION

———

Foreword

This book is not a history of the French Revolution, which has been recounted too brilliantly for me to contemplate doing it again. It is rather a study of that Revolution.

In 1789 the French tried harder than any other people has ever done to sever their past from their future, as it were, and hollow out an abyss between what they had been and what they wished to become. To that end, they took any number of precautions to ensure that they would carry over nothing from the past into their new condition. They imposed all sorts of constraints on themselves so that, in fashioning the people they were to be in the future, they would not resemble their fathers. They spared no effort to make themselves unrecognizable.

In this singular enterprise I have always thought that they were far less successful than people outside France generally believe and than the French themselves believed initially. I was convinced that, unbeknownst to themselves, they had taken from the Ancien Régime most of the feelings, habits, and ideas that guided the Revolution which destroyed it, and that, without intending to, they had built the new society out of the debris of the old. Hence, in order to understand the Revolution and its achievements properly, we must temporarily avert our eyes from the France that exists today and begin our investigation at the tomb of the France that is no more. That is what I have tried to do here, but the task has proved more difficult than I could have imagined.

The early centuries of the monarchy, the Middle Ages, and the Renaissance have been extensively researched and have given rise to weighty tomes, from which we can learn not only what happened in these different periods of history but also what laws and customs prevailed and what spirit animated the government and nation. Until now, however, no one has delved as deeply into the eighteenth century. We think we know the French society of that era quite well because we are familiar with its glittering surface and, in minute detail, with the lives of its most famous personages, and because we have read clever and eloquent critiques of the works of its great writers. But as for the way in which public business was conducted, how institutions actually worked, how the various classes truly related to one another, the condition and feelings of those segments of the population that still could be neither seen nor heard, and the true basis of opinions and customs, we have only ideas that are at best confused and often misleading.

I have tried to strike to the heart of this Ancien Régime, so close to us in years yet hidden from us by the Revolution.

To that end, I have read more than just the celebrated works of the eighteenth century. I also sought to study many works that, while deservedly less well known, are perhaps more revealing of the true instincts of the age for the very reason that they were rather artlessly composed. I steeped myself in public records that reveal the opinions and tastes of the French as the Revolution approached. The minutes of meetings of the estates and, later, of provincial assemblies shed a great deal of light on these things. I made extensive use, moreover, of the *cahiers*, or grievance books, drawn up by the three orders in 1789. These grievance books, the original manuscripts of which are collected in a series of many volumes, will endure as the testament of the old French society, the supreme expression of its desires, the authentic manifestation of its last will. It is a document without historical parallel. But even that did not satisfy me.

In countries where the governmental apparatus is well developed, scarcely a thought, desire, or grievance can arise, scarcely an interest or passion come into being, without sooner or later coming under close scrutiny by the government. By visiting governmental archives, one acquires not only a very accurate idea of how the government works but also an overview of the country as a whole. A foreigner granted access today to all the confidential correspondence that fills the cartons of the Ministry of the Interior and the prefectures would soon know more about us than we know about ourselves. In the eighteenth century, as readers of this book will discover, the French governmental apparatus was already highly centralized, very powerful, and prodigiously active. We find it constantly offering assistance, raising obstacles, granting permission. It had much to promise and much to give. It already exerted its influence in a thousand ways, not only on the general conduct of affairs but also on the fate of individual families and the private lives of individual citizens. What is more, it operated in the shadows, so that people were not afraid to come before it to reveal the most private of infirmities. I spent a great deal of time studying its surviving records, both in Paris and in a number of provinces.*

There, as I expected, I found the Ancien Régime come to life, with all its ideas, passions, prejudices, and practices intact. Individuals spoke freely in their own idiom and gave voice to their most intimate thoughts. I was thus able to acquire many ideas about the French society of old that contemporaries did not have, because I had before my eyes evidence that they had never seen.

As I progressed in my study, I was astonished to find again and again in the France of that time any number of the features that would strike an observer of France today. I discovered a host of sentiments that I thought had been born with the Revolution, a host of ideas that I believed to have been revolutionary ideas, and a myriad of habits purportedly bequeathed to us by that great event alone. Everywhere I found the roots of today's society firmly implanted in the soil of the old. The closer I came to 1789, the more distinctly I perceived the inception, birth, and development of the spirit that made the Revolution. The entire physiognomy of that Revolution revealed itself to me little by little. Its temperament, its genius, could already be divined; it was already itself. I discovered not only the logic that would guide its first steps but, perhaps more important, early hints of its long-term aftereffects. For the Revolution went through two distinct phases: a first phase during which the French seemed to want to abolish everything from their past, and a second in which they would recover part of what they had left behind. Many of the laws and political traditions of the Ancien Régime suddenly disappeared in 1789 only to reappear a few years later, much as certain rivers plunge underground only to reemerge somewhat farther on, bringing the same waters to new shores.

The purpose of this book is to explain why this great Revolution, which was in gestation throughout most of Europe in this period, erupted in

---

* I made particularly heavy use of the archives of a few large intendances, especially Tours, which are very complete and pertain to a very large généralité located in the center of France and inhabited by more than a million people. I want to thank the young and able archivist in charge, M. Grandmaison. Other généralités, including those of Île-de-France, demonstrated to my satisfaction that things worked in the same way throughout much of the kingdom.

France rather than elsewhere, why it emerged fully formed from the society that it was to destroy, and, finally, how the old monarchy could have fallen so suddenly and completely.

As I conceive the work, however, there is more to be said. If time and energy permit, my intention is to follow, through the vicissitudes of the Revolution, the same Frenchmen with whom I lived on such familiar terms under the Ancien Régime that formed them and to observe how events changed and transformed them without altering their nature and how, despite certain modifications of their features, their faces remained recognizable.

I shall begin by exploring with them the Revolution's opening act, in 1789, when love of equality coexisted in their bosoms with love of liberty; when they hoped to establish institutions that were not only democratic but also free; when they sought not only to destroy privileges but to recognize and consecrate rights. This was a time of youth, enthusiasm, and pride, of generous and sincere passions, which will be eternally remembered despite its errors and which for many years to come will trouble the sleep of those who seek to corrupt and subjugate mankind.

In addition to briskly recounting the course of the Revolution, I will try to point out the events, errors, and miscalculations that led these same Frenchmen to abandon their original goal, liberty, and narrow their desires to but a single wish: to become equal servants of the master of the world. I will explain how a government more powerful, and far more absolute, than the one the Revolution overthrew then seized and concentrated all power, suppressed all the liberties for which such a high price had been paid, and put useless imitations in their place. I will show how this government applied the name "popular sovereignty" to the suffrage of voters who were unable to educate themselves, organize, or choose and how it applied the term "free vote" to the assent of silent or subjugated assemblies. And I will show how this government, even as it deprived the nation of the ability to govern itself, of the principal guarantees of law, and of the freedom to think, speak, and write – in other words, of the most precious and noble prizes won in 1789 – continued to invoke the august title "revolutionary."

I will end at the point where, in my view, the Revolution's work was all but finished and the new society had at last been born. I will then consider that society itself. I will try to identify the ways in which it resembled what preceded it and the ways in which it differed, and I will describe what we lost in this immense upheaval and what we gained. Finally, I will try to offer a glimpse of what lies in store for us.

Part of this second work has been sketched out, but it is still unworthy of being set before the public. Will I be granted the time to finish it? Who can say? The destiny of an individual is even more uncertain than that of a nation.

I hope to have written the present work without prejudice, but I do not claim to have written it without passion. It would hardly be possible for a Frenchman to write about his country or contemplate his times dispassionately. I confess that as I wrote about the various segments of the old society, I never entirely lost sight of the new. I sought not only to diagnose the illness to which the patient succumbed but also to ask how it might have been saved. I proceeded as doctors do when they examine defunct organs in the hope of discovering the laws of life. My goal was to paint a portrait that would be not only strictly accurate but also perhaps educational. Thus, each time I discovered in our forefathers one of those manly virtues that we so desperately need but no longer possess – a true spirit of independence, a yearning for greatness, faith in ourselves and in a cause – I tried to call attention to it. Similarly, when I found in the laws, ideas, and mores of that earlier period traces of the ills that, after devouring the old society, still eat away at the new, I took pains to point them out so that readers, apprised of the damage already done, might better understand the ravages that might yet lie ahead.

Because men are no longer tied to one another by bonds of caste, class, guild, or family, they are only too apt to attend solely to their private interests, only too inclined to think exclusively of themselves and to withdraw into a narrow individualism that stifles all public virtue. Despotism, far from combating this tendency, makes it irresistible, for it deprives citizens of all common passions, all mutual needs, all necessity to reach a common understanding, and all opportunity to act in concert. It immures them, as it were, in private life. They were already apt to hold one another at arm's length. Despotism isolated them. Relations between them had grown chilly; despotism froze them.

In this type of society, where nothing is fixed, everyone is racked constantly by the fear of falling lower in the social scale and by the ardor to rise. And since money, even as it has become the principal mark of class and distinction, has become unusually mobile, passing constantly from hand to hand, transforming the status of individuals, and raising or lowering families, virtually no one is exempt from the constant and desperate obligation to keep or acquire it. The most common passions are therefore the desire to acquire wealth in any way possible, a predilection for business, the love of gain, and the lust for material comforts and pleasures. These passions have spread readily to all classes, even those in which they were previously alien, and if nothing stops them they may soon enervate and degrade the entire nation. But it is of the very essence of despotism to encourage and spread such debilitating passions, which help it achieve its ends. They divert attention from public affairs, occupy the imagination of the people, and make them shudder at the very idea of revolution. Despotism alone has the power to create the secrecy and the shadows in which greed can thrive and dishonest profits can be amassed in defiance of dishonor. Without despotism these selfish passions would be strong; with it they rule.

Only freedom can effectively combat the flaws natural to societies of this type and keep them from sliding down a slippery slope. Only freedom can rescue citizens from the isolation in which the very independence of their condition has mired them. Only freedom can compel them to come together and warm each other's spirits through mutual exchange and persuasion and joint action in practical affairs. Only freedom can save them from the worship of Mammon and the petty vexations of their private business, enabling them to sense the constant presence of the nation above and alongside them. Only freedom can substitute higher, more powerful passions for the love of material comforts and supply ambition with goals more worthy than the acquisition of wealth. Only freedom, finally, can create the light by which it is possible to see and judge the vices and virtues of humankind.

Democratic societies that are not free may yet be rich, refined, ornate, and even magnificent, powerful by dint of their homogeneous mass. One may find in such societies many private virtues, good fathers, honest merchants, and worthy landowners. One may even come across good Christians, since the true Christian's homeland is not of this world and the glory of the Christian faith is to have produced good people in the midst of the worst corruption and under the vilest governments. The Roman Empire in its uttermost decadence was full of them. But what one will never find in such societies, I make bold to assert, is great citizens, much less a great people, and I maintain without fear of contradiction that the common level of hearts and minds will steadily diminish so long as equality and despotism remain conjoined.

I thought and said as much twenty years ago. Nothing has happened since then to make me think or say differently. Having expressed my high opinion of liberty at a time when it was in favor, I can hardly be blamed for standing firm at a time when others are abandoning it.

Mark well, moreover, that in this particular respect I am less different from most of my adversaries than they may assume. Is there any man of soul so base that he would rather be subject to the whim of a man no different from himself than obey laws that he himself helped to make, provided that he believed his nation to possess the virtues necessary to make wise use of its freedom? I think not. Not even despots deny that freedom is an excellent thing, only they wish to keep it all for themselves and insist on the utter unworthiness of everyone else. Thus, people differ not as to the opinion that one ought to have of liberty but as to the smaller or greater esteem in which one ought to hold one's fellow man. Hence, it is rigorously accurate to say that one's liking for absolute government is strictly proportional to one's contempt for one's own country. I ask to be allowed a little more time before accepting such a view of France.

Without boasting unduly, I think I may say that a great deal of labor has gone into this book. One brief chapter alone cost me more than a year's research. I might have cluttered my pages with notes, but it seemed better to keep relatively few in the text and place the rest at the end of the volume with references to the relevant pages. Examples and evidence may be found in these endnotes. I could provide more if anyone deems this book sufficiently valuable to ask.

Book I

I.1 – Contradictory Judgments of the Revolution at Its Inception

Nothing is more apt to remind philosophers and statesmen of the need for modesty than the history of the French Revolution, for no event was greater or longer in the making or more fully prepared yet so little anticipated.

Not even Frederick the Great, for all his genius, sensed what was coming. He was in contact with it yet failed to see it. Indeed, his actions were in accord with the spirit of the Revolution before the fact. He was its precursor and, in a manner of speaking, its agent. Yet he did not see it looming on the horizon, and when at last it did show its face, the remarkable new features that would set it apart from a host of other revolutions initially went unnoticed.

Outside of France the Revolution aroused universal curiosity. It made people everywhere think that new times were coming and stirred vague hopes of change and reform, but no one yet suspected what it was to become. Princes and their ministers lacked even the shadowy forebodings that agitated the masses. At first they regarded the Revolution as one of those periodic maladies to which the constitutions of all nations are liable, whose only effect is to afford new opportunities to the policy of their neighbors. If by chance they hit upon the truth about the Revolution, they did so unwittingly. To be sure, the sovereigns of the various German states, meeting in Pillnitz in 1791, proclaimed that the danger that imperiled the French monarchy was common to all the old powers of Europe and that all were just as vulnerable as France. At bottom, however, they did not believe it. Secret documents from the period reveal that they viewed such declarations as cunning pretexts with which they masked their real intentions or colored them for the sake of the crowd.

The princes and ministers themselves were convinced that the French Revolution was but a fleeting, local incident and that the only serious challenge it posed was how best to take advantage of it. To that end, they hatched plans, prepared for action, and entered into secret alliances. They vied over how to divide the prospective prey, fell out with one another, found common ground. There was virtually no contingency for which they did not prepare, except what actually happened.

The English, who, thanks to their own history and long practice of political freedom had a better understanding of what was happening, recognized as through a thick veil that a great revolution was under way. But they could not make out its form, and the influence that it would soon exert on their own fate and the fate of the world remained hidden from them. Arthur Young, who was traveling in France on the eve of the Revolution and recognized its imminence, had so little inkling of its significance that he wondered whether the result might not be to increase privilege. "As to the nobility and clergy," he said, "if a revolution added anything to their scale, I think it would do more mischief than good."[1]

Burke, whose mind was sharpened by the loathing that the Revolution inspired in him from its inception, was nevertheless hesitant at first about what to think. What he predicted initially was that France would be sapped of its strength by the Revolution and all but destroyed. "We may assume," he said, "that France's military might will be extinguished for some time to come, and that in the next generation men will echo the ancient dictum, *Gallos quoque in bellis floruisse audivimus*" [We have heard it said that the Gauls, too, once excelled in war].

Judgment close to an event is no better than judgment from afar. In France, on the eve of the Revolution's outbreak, no one yet had a clear idea of what was about to happen. Only two of the innumerable grievance books indicate any apprehensiveness in regard to the people. What did arouse fear was the likelihood that the royal government, or "court," as it was still called, would retain the preponderance of power. What worried contemporaries was that the Estates General were weak and short-lived. There was fear that they would be vulnerable to violent intimidation. The nobility was particularly alarmed by this possibility. Any number of

---

[1] The quotation can be found in Arthur Young, *Travels in France* (London: George Bell and Sons, 1906), p. 98.

grievance books expressed the view that "the Swiss troops should swear an oath never to turn their weapons against the citizenry, even in case of riot or revolt." Leave the Estates General free to do their work, and all the abuses would be easily eliminated. Vast reforms were needed, but reform would be easy.

The Revolution nevertheless pursued its own course. The monster reared its head, and its novel and terrifying features were revealed. After destroying political institutions, it abolished civil institutions. First it changed laws, then mores, customs, and even language. Having shredded the fabric of government, it undermined the foundations of society and ultimately went after God himself. Then the Revolution spilled across French borders, employing previously unknown means, new tactics, and murderous maxims – "opinions in arms," as Pitt called them. The ramparts of empires were swept away by an unprecedented force, which toppled thrones and rode roughshod over peoples, yet – wonder to behold! – simultaneously won them over to its cause. What the princes and statesmen of Europe had initially taken to be an unremarkable historical incident suddenly seemed a phenomenon so new and so different from anything that had ever happened before, yet so monstrous and incomprehensible, that the human mind could not grasp it. Some thought that this unknown force, which seemed neither to require nourishment nor to brook opposition, which no one could stop, and which could not stop itself, would lead to the complete and final dissolution of human society. Some regarded it as a visible sign of the devil's influence. "The French Revolution has a satanic character," M. de Maistre said in 1797. By contrast, others saw in it a beneficent plan of God, whose wish was to alter the face of the world as well as of France, indeed to create a new man. In any number of writers from this period, we find something of the religious terror that Salvianus experienced at the sight of the barbarians. Burke, making this idea his own, exclaimed:

> Deprived of the old Government, deprived in a manner of all Government, France, fallen as a Monarchy, to common speculators might have appeared more likely to be an object of pity or insult, according to the disposition of the circumjacent powers, than to be the scourge and terror of them all. But out of the tomb of the murdered Monarchy in France, has arisen a vast, tremendous, unformed spectre, in a far more terrific guise than any which ever yet have overpowered the imagination and subdued the fortitude of man. Going straight forward to its end, unappalled by peril, unchecked by

remorse, despising all common maxims and all common means, that hideous phantom overpowered those who could not believe it was possible she could at all exist.[2]

Was the event really as extraordinary as it seemed to contemporaries? Was it as unprecedented and as deeply disturbing as they imagined? What was its true meaning? What was its actual character? What were the enduring effects of this strange and terrifying Revolution? What precisely did it destroy? What did it create?

The time has come to investigate these questions and answer them. I believe that we stand today at the precise point from which this great event can best be perceived and judged. We are far enough from the Revolution that the passions that once clouded the view of those who made it have waned, yet close enough to empathize with them and understand the spirit that led them to it. This will soon become more difficult, because great revolutions that succeed erase the causes that produced them and become incomprehensible by dint of their very success.

---

[2] The quotation can be found in Edmund Burke, *Four Letters on the Proposals for Peace with the Regicide Directory of France*, ed. Edward John Payne (Oxford: Clarendon Press, 1892), pp. 7–8.

I.2 – That the Fundamental and Final Purpose of the Revolution Was Not, as Some Have Thought, to Destroy Religious Authority and Weaken Political Authority

One of the French Revolution's first acts was to attack the Church, and among the passions born of the event the first to be kindled and the last to be extinguished was the irreligious passion. Even after enthusiasm for liberty had vanished and the French were reduced to paying for tranquility with servitude, still they rebelled against religious authority. Napoleon, who had been able to vanquish the Revolution's liberal genius, tried in vain to tame its anti-Christian spirit. Even in our own time we find men who believe they can redeem their servility to the pettiest of officials by their insolence toward God and who, even as they have abandoned all that was freest, noblest, and proudest in the doctrines of the Revolution, still boast of remaining true to its spirit by rejecting religion.

Today, however, it is easy to see that the war on religion was merely an incidental aspect of the great Revolution, a salient yet transitory feature of its physiognomy, a temporary consequence of ideas, passions, and specific circumstances that preceded the Revolution and laid the groundwork for it, rather than of the revolutionary spirit itself.

Eighteenth-century philosophy is rightly regarded as one of the principal causes of the Revolution, and it is true that that philosophy was deeply irreligious. It is essential, however, to note that it consisted of two distinct and separable parts.

One part consisted of new or freshly revived opinions about social conditions and the principles of civil and political law, including, for example, the natural equality of human beings, the consequent abolition of all privileges of caste, class, and profession, popular sovereignty, the omnipotence of the social power, the uniformity of rules, and so on. All these doctrines were not merely causes of the Revolution but also constituted its substance, so to speak. Among its achievements these were the most fundamental, the most durable, and the most true in the eyes of posterity.

For the rest, the eighteenth-century *philosophes* attacked the Church with a kind of fury. They attacked its clergy, its hierarchy, its institutions, and its dogma, and, the better to demolish all these things, they sought to undermine the very foundations of Christianity itself. But this aspect of eighteenth-century philosophy, being rooted in circumstances that the Revolution eliminated, was destined to vanish as they did and be buried beneath the Revolution's triumph. I will add just a word to clarify my meaning for now, because I want to return to this important subject later: it was much less as religious doctrine than as political institution that Christianity aroused such fanatical hatred. It did so not because priests claimed to govern the other world but because they were landowners, feudal lords, tithe collectors, and administrators in this one; not because the Church had no place in the new society that the people were about to institute but because it occupied the most privileged and powerful place in the old society, which was to be dashed to pieces.

Consider the way in which the passage of time has brought this truth to the fore and kept it in the limelight. As the political achievements of the Revolution have been consolidated, its antireligious efforts have come to naught. As the ancient political institutions that the Revolution attacked were utterly destroyed; as the powers, influences, and classes that were particularly odious to it were progressively crushed; and – ultimate sign of their defeat – as even the hatreds they had once inspired withered and the clergy separated itself from everything that had fallen along with it, one began to see a gradual restoration of the power of the Church and a reaffirmation of its influence over the minds of men.

Do not assume, moreover, that this phenomenon is peculiar to France. There is scarcely a Christian church anywhere in Europe that has not undergone a revival since the French Revolution.

It is a serious error to believe that democratic societies are naturally hostile to religion. Nothing in Christianity or even in Catholicism is absolutely contrary to the democratic spirit, and a number of things are favorable to it. Indeed, the experience of centuries shows that the religious instinct has always struck its most tenacious roots in the heart of the people. Dying faiths have invariably found their last refuge there, and it would be strange indeed if institutions that tend to promote the ideas and passions of the people had the inevitable and enduring effect of encouraging impiety.

What I have just said about the religious power I would affirm even more strongly of the social power.

When people saw all the institutions and customs that had previously maintained the social hierarchy and defined the rules of human conduct succumb to the Revolution, they not unreasonably assumed that its ultimate result would be to destroy not just a particular social order but order in general, not just a particular government but social power itself, and inevitably they concluded that its nature was essentially anarchic. Nevertheless, I make bold to affirm that this, too, was a misleading appearance.

Less than a year after the Revolution began, Mirabeau wrote secretly to the king: "Compare the new state of affairs with the Ancien Régime, and you will find the first glimmerings of consolation and hope. Much of the most important legislation passed by the National Assembly is clearly favorable to monarchical government. Is it of no consequence to be rid of Parlement, *pays d'états*, the organized clergy, the privileged classes, and the nobility? The idea of a society composed of but a single class of citizens would have pleased Richelieu: a uniform surface facilitates the exercise of power. Several reigns of absolute government would not have done as much for royal authority as this single year of Revolution." Here was comprehension of the Revolution worthy of a man capable of leading it.

Since the French Revolution had as its objective not simply to change the existing government but to abolish the existing form of society, it was obliged simultaneously to attack all established powers, to undermine all acknowledged influences, to efface traditions, to renew mores and customs, and somehow to rid the human mind of all the ideas on which respect and obedience had previously been founded. This accounts for its singularly anarchical character.

But clear away all this debris and you will see an immense and unified central government, which has drawn in and devoured all the bits of authority and influence that were once parceled out among a host of secondary powers, orders, classes, professions, families, and individuals – scattered, as it were, throughout the social body. No comparable power has existed in the world since the fall of the Roman Empire. The Revolution created this new power, or, rather, it created the ruins from which the new power emerged on its own. The governments that it instituted are, to be sure, more fragile but a hundred times more powerful than those that it toppled – fragile and powerful for the same reasons, as we shall see in due course.

It was this simple, harmonious, stately structure that Mirabeau glimpsed through the dust of half-demolished old institutions. Despite its grandeur, it was still invisible to the multitude, but little by little the passage of time has laid it bare for all to see. Today it fascinates the princely eye above all. Monarchs view it with admiration and envy – not only those whom the Revolution engendered but even those most alien and hostile to it. All strive to eliminate immunities and abolish privileges within their states. All blur distinctions of rank, equalize conditions, replace the aristocracy with functionaries, substitute uniform rules for local privileges, and impose unified government where once there was a diversity of powers. They diligently devote themselves to this revolutionary labor, and should they encounter any obstacle, they will occasionally borrow the Revolution's own methods and maxims. They have been known, when the need arose, to rouse the poor against the rich, the commoner against the noble, the peasant against his lord. The French Revolution was both their scourge and their instructor.

I.3 – How the French Revolution Was a Political Revolution That Proceeded in the Manner of Religious Revolutions, and Why

All civil and political revolutions were once confined to the land in which they were born. The French Revolution had no territory of its own. More than that, its effect was in a sense to wipe the map clean of all existing borders. It united some men and divided others in spite of laws, traditions, characters, and language, at times turning compatriots into enemies and strangers into brothers. Or, rather, it transcended all particular nationalities to create a common intellectual fatherland, which could accommodate men of all nations as citizens.

Search all history's annals and you will not find a single political revolution possessing this character, which is found only in certain religious revolutions. If an analogy can help us understand the French Revolution, the term of comparison must therefore be with religious revolutions.

Schiller, in his history of the Thirty Years' War, justly remarks that the great Reformation of the sixteenth century suddenly diminished the distance between peoples that had previously barely known one another, spurring new sympathies and fostering close unity among them. Indeed, one saw Frenchmen stand shoulder to shoulder with Englishmen to do battle with other Frenchmen, while men born in the remotest regions of the Baltic raced to the heart of Germany to protect Germans of whom they had previously never heard. All foreign wars took on certain aspects of civil war, and in all civil wars foreigners took part. Nations forgot their old interests in favor of new ones. Territorial issues gave way to issues of principle. All the rules of diplomacy became jumbled and confused, to the great surprise and chagrin of politicians of the time. This is precisely what happened in Europe after 1789.

The French Revolution was therefore a political revolution that developed in the manner of a religious revolution and took on something of the character of one. What specific individual traits account for this resemblance? Like religious revolutions, the French Revolution spread far and wide and did so, as they did, by preaching and propaganda. Think how novel it was for a political revolution to inspire proselytism and to be preached as ardently abroad as it was zealously prosecuted at home. Of all the unprecedented things that the French Revolution introduced into the world, this was surely the most novel. But that is not all: let us delve a little deeper and ask whether this similarity of effects might stem from a hidden similarity of causes.

Religions typically consider man in himself, ignoring what the laws, customs, and traditions of a particular country may have added to the common fund of humankind. Their principal aim is to regulate man's relationship with God in general and to specify in general his rights and duties in relation to other men, independent of the form of society. The rules of conduct that religions lay down pertain not so much to man in a particular country or period as to the son, the father, the servant, the master, the neighbor. Because religions are thus rooted in human nature, they can be accepted equally by all men and applied everywhere. That is why religious revolutions have often enjoyed such vast theaters and, unlike political revolutions, have seldom been confined to the territory of a single people or even a single race. Looking at the subject still more closely, we find that the more abstract and general the religion, the more widely it has spread, despite differences of law, climate, and men.

The pagan religions of Antiquity were all more or less tied to the political constitution or social state of each people, and their dogma reflected certain national or even municipal traits, so that they were usually confined within territorial boundaries and seldom spread beyond them. They sometimes bred intolerance and persecution, but proselytism was virtually unknown. Hence, there were no great religious revolutions in the West before the advent of Christianity. Easily transcending all the obstacles that had halted the spread of pagan religions, Christianity quickly conquered a substantial portion of the human race. I do not think it is disrespectful to this holy faith to say that it owed its triumph in large part to its having gone further than any other religion in shedding specific ties to any people, form of government, social state, period, or race.

The French Revolution proceeded with respect to this world in precisely the same way that religious revolutions proceeded with respect to the other. It took an abstract view of the citizen, outside any particular society, just as religions treated man in general, independent of country and time. It did not seek to determine the particular rights of the French citizen but rather the general rights and duties of man in the political realm.

The French Revolution always sought out what was least particular and, so to speak, most *natural* in regard to social state and government. That is why it was able to make itself comprehensible to all, and why it could be imitated in a hundred places at once.

Since it appeared to aim at the regeneration of the human race even more than at the reform of France, it kindled a passion that not even the most violent political revolutions had ever aroused before. It inspired proselytism and propaganda and therefore came to resemble a religious revolution, which was what contemporaries found so frightening about it. Or, rather, it itself became a new kind of religion – an imperfect religion, to be sure, without God, cult, or afterlife – yet a religion that, like Islam, inundated the earth with its soldiers, apostles, and martyrs.

Make no mistake, moreover: the methods of the Revolution were not without precedent, nor were all the ideas it developed entirely new. There have always been agitators, even in the depths of the Middle Ages, who sought to alter local customs by invoking general laws of human society and by setting the natural rights of humanity in opposition to their country's constitution. But all such efforts failed. The torch that set Europe ablaze in the eighteenth century was easily extinguished in the fifteenth. In order for arguments of this type to provoke revolutions, the minds of men must be prepared to accept them by certain prior changes in social conditions, customs, and mores.

There are times when men are so different from one another that the idea of a single law applicable to all is almost incomprehensible. There are other times when it is enough to show them the vague and distant image of such a law for them to recognize it instantly and hasten after it.

The most extraordinary thing was not that the French Revolution employed the methods or conceived the ideas that it did. The great novelty was that so many nations had reached the point where such methods could be used effectively and such maxims could be readily accepted.

I.4 – How Almost All of Europe Had Exactly the Same Institutions, and How Those Institutions Were Crumbling Everywhere

The peoples that overthrew the Roman Empire and ultimately formed modern nations differed by race, country, and language; they resembled one another only in their barbarism. After settling on imperial territory, they clashed with one another for many years, and when the vast confusion at last gave way to stability, they found themselves separated by the very ruins with which they had littered the landscape. Because civilization had been virtually wiped out and public order destroyed, social relations became fraught and perilous, and European society fragmented into a myriad of distinct lesser societies, which lived in hostile isolation. Yet out of this incoherent mass uniform laws suddenly emerged.

The new institutions were not imitations of Roman ones. Indeed, they were so at odds with Roman institutions that Roman law was later used to transform and abolish them. Novel in form, the new laws stood apart from all other legal systems. There was a symmetry to them, and, taken together, they formed a legal system so taut that not even our modern legal codes are more rigorously uniform. Yet these sophisticated laws were intended for use by a semibarbarous society.

How could such legislation have been formulated, propagated, and ultimately established throughout Europe? I do not intend to pursue this question here. What is certain is that in the Middle Ages this system of law could be found in almost every corner of the continent, and in many countries it reigned to the exclusion of all others.

I had occasion to study medieval political institutions in France, England, and Germany, and the further I went in my research, the more astonished I was by the remarkable similarity of the laws in these various countries, and the more I marveled at the way in which such different peoples, who had so little to do with one another, had been able to equip themselves with such similar institutions. To be sure, there was constant and nearly endless variation in detail from one place to another, but the basis of the laws was everywhere the same. Whenever I found a political institution, rule, or power in old Germanic legislation, I knew in advance that if I searched diligently, I would find something substantially similar in France and England, and invariably I did find what I knew would be there. Each of these three peoples helped me to a better understanding of the other two.

Among all three peoples government followed the same precepts, and political assemblies were composed of the same elements and endowed with the same powers. Society was divided along similar lines, and the same hierarchy could be observed among the various classes. The position of nobles was identical. They had the same privileges, the same characteristics, the same attitudes: they were not different in different places but everywhere the same men.

Town constitutions were similar, and countrysides were governed in the same way. The condition of the peasantry showed little variation. Land was owned, occupied, and cultivated identically, and peasants were subject to identical burdens. From the Polish border to the Irish sea, the manor, the lord's court, the fief, ground rents, obligatory services, feudal dues, guilds – all were alike. Sometimes even the names were the same, and what is even more remarkable, a single spirit animated all of these analogous institutions. It is not unreasonable, I think, to assert that the social, political, administrative, judicial, economic, and literary institutions of Europe were perhaps even more alike in the fourteenth century than they are today, when civilization seems to have gone out of its way to open every conceivable avenue and clear away every possible obstacle.

It is not my purpose to explain how this ancient European constitution gradually broke down and collapsed. I merely note that by the eighteenth century it lay half in ruins everywhere. Broadly speaking, the breakdown was less pronounced in the eastern part of the continent, more so in the west, but the age and often the decrepitude of the system were visible everywhere.

The gradual decay of medieval institutions can be followed in the archives. Each manor kept registers known as *terriers*, in which were recorded, century after century, the boundaries of fiefs, lands subject to rent, rents due, services owed, and local customs. I have seen fourteenth-century *terriers* that were masterpieces of method, clarity, precision, and intelligence. They became progressively more obscure, jumbled, incomplete, and confused as time wore on, despite the general progress of education. It seems that political society lapsed into barbarism as civil society achieved enlightenment.

Even in Germany, where the original features of Europe's old constitution were better preserved than in France, some of the institutions to which it had given rise had already ceased to exist everywhere. But the best way to gauge the ravages of time is not to look for what is missing but to examine the state of what remains.

Municipal institutions, which had turned the leading German towns into small, rich, enlightened republics, still existed in the eighteenth century, but they had been reduced to mere hollow shells. Their laws were nominally still on the books. The offices they had established still bore the same names and seemed to discharge the same responsibilities. But the industry, energy, and communal patriotism they had inspired, the fecund male virtues they had fostered, had disappeared. The old institutions may have retained their original form, yet they seemed to have shrunk.

All the surviving powers of the Middle Ages were afflicted with the same disease. All exhibited the same weakness and listlessness. More than that, everything that was associated with the constitution of that time without exactly belonging to it, everything that bore its stamp, promptly lost its vitality. The aristocracy, for instance, contracted a senile dementia. Political liberty, which had filled the Middle Ages with its good works, seemingly fell sterile wherever it retained characteristically medieval traits. Provincial assemblies that failed to amend their ancient constitutions did not promote the progress of civilization but impeded it. They seemed hostile to the new spirit of the times, impervious to change. Thus, they lost their grip on the hearts of the people, who turned instead to princes. Antiquity did not make institutions venerable. On the contrary, age only discredited them further. Yet oddly, the more decadent they became and thus the less capable of doing harm, the more hatred they inspired. As one German contemporary friendly to the old regime put it, "the existing state of affairs seems to have become an affront to all and an object of contempt for some. It is striking to see how everything old is now judged negatively. The new ways of looking at things have insinuated themselves into our families and sown trouble in our homes. Even our housewives are unwilling to put up with their old furniture any longer." Yet in Germany, as in France at this time, society was on the move and prosperity was steadily on the rise. But mark the following point well, for it completes the picture: everything that was vital, active, and productive was new, and not simply new but in contradiction with the old.

The monarchy, for instance, no longer had anything in common with the monarchy of the Middle Ages. It wielded different powers, occupied a different place, exhibited a different spirit, and inspired different sentiments. The administrative apparatus of the state expanded everywhere, establishing itself on the ruins of local authorities. A hierarchy of state officials increasingly replaced the government of nobles. All these new powers employed methods and adhered to precepts of which the Middle Ages had either known nothing or else rejected, precepts associated with a state of society of which medieval men simply had no inkling.

In England, where one might be tempted at first glance to say that the old European constitution remained in force, things were no different. Once you look past the old names and set aside the archaic forms, you find that the feudal system had in substance been abolished in England by the seventeenth century. Classes mingled, the nobility faded, the aristocracy opened its gates, and wealth became power. Equality before the law existed, as did equality of taxation, freedom of the press, and public debate. All these new principles were unknown in the Middle Ages. Moreover, it was these innovations, introduced gradually and skillfully, that made it possible to revive the old body without risk to its integrity, giving it a new lease on life while preserving its ancient forms. The England of the seventeenth century was already a fully modern nation that merely preserved within it, embalmed as it were, a few relics of the Middle Ages.

This brief glance beyond the borders of France was necessary to lay the groundwork for understanding what follows, for I venture to say that he who has seen no other country and who studies only France will never understand the French Revolution.

I.5 – What Was the Essential Achievement of the French Revolution?

The aim of the preceding chapters was simply to illuminate the subject and lay the groundwork for an answer to the question that I posed at the outset: What was the true purpose of the Revolution? What, in the end, was its intrinsic character? Why exactly did it occur? What did it do?

The purpose of the Revolution was not, as some have thought, to break religion's grip on human beliefs. It was, in spite of appearances, essentially a social and political revolution. In contrast to other, similar institutions, its effect was not to perpetuate disorder, somehow to make it stable, or, to borrow a phrase from one of its principal adversaries, to "impose method" on anarchy. Rather, it tended to increase the power and prerogatives of public authority. It was not obliged, as others have supposed, to change the character of our civilization or halt its progress or even modify in any essential way any of the fundamental laws underlying our western societies. When we isolate the Revolution from all the contingencies that momentarily altered its aspect in various times and places and consider it only as it was in itself, we see clearly that its sole effect was to abolish the political institutions, usually called feudal, that had for centuries reigned unopposed in most of the nations of Europe, and to replace them with a simpler and more uniform social and political order based on equality of conditions.

That sufficed to constitute an immense revolution, for quite apart from the fact that these old institutions were still ingrained in, not to say intertwined with, all of Europe's religious and political laws, they had also given rise to a host of ideas, sentiments, habits, and mores from which they were all but inseparable. A terrible convulsion was required to destroy all of these and at one stroke extract from the body of society what was in this sense a constituent element of all its organs. This made the Revolution appear to be even greater than it was. It seemed to destroy everything, because what it did destroy was connected to, indeed part of, everything else.

However radical the Revolution may have been, it was nevertheless far less innovative than is generally assumed, as I will show later. What is true is that it completely destroyed, or is in the process of destroying (for it endures to this day), every aspect of the old society that derived from aristocratic and feudal institutions, everything that was in any way associated with those institutions or bore the *slightest* impression of them. Of the old world it preserved only what had always been alien to those institutions or could exist without them. What the Revolution was least of all was an accident. To be sure, it took the world by surprise, yet it was merely the culmination of a long labor, the sudden and violent end of an effort to which ten generations had contributed. Had it not taken place, the old social edifice would still have collapsed sooner or later everywhere, but it would have continued to crumble piece by piece rather than collapse all at once. The Revolution brought to a sudden conclusion, without transition, precaution, or regard, what would eventually have come about little by little on its own. That was its achievement.

It is surprising that what seems so easy to see today remained so muddled and veiled, even in the eyes of the most perspicacious observers.

"You wanted to correct the abuses of your government," said Burke to the French, "but why start from scratch? Why not cling to your ancient traditions? Why not limit yourselves to regaining your former liberties? Or, if it was impossible for you to make out the shape of your ancestral constitution, why not cast a glance in our direction? There you would have found the old common law of Europe." Burke failed to behold what was before his eyes, namely, that it was the Revolution that was in fact destined to abolish this old common law. He did not recognize that this and nothing else was what it was truly about.

But why did this Revolution break out in France rather than somewhere else, when the groundwork for it was laid and the threat loomed everywhere? Why did it take on certain characteristics in France that elsewhere emerged only partially, if at all? This further question surely deserves to be asked. Its examination will be the subject of the books that follow.

Book II

II.1 – Why Feudal Prerogatives Had Become More Odious to the People in France Than Anywhere Else

At first glance, it is surprising that the Revolution, whose essential object was to abolish what remained of medieval institutions everywhere, did not break out in countries where those institutions, being better preserved, made people more aware of their oppressiveness and rigor, but rather in countries where these things were felt the least. Thus their yoke seemed most unbearable where in fact its burden was lightest.

Throughout nearly all of Germany, serfdom had yet to be completely abolished by the end of the eighteenth century, and in most of the country the people were still attached to the soil, as in the Middle Ages. Almost all the soldiers in the armies of Frederick the Great and Maria Teresa were true serfs.

In most German states in 1788, a peasant could not leave his lord's domain, and if he did leave he could be pursued wherever he went and forcibly returned. He was subject to the jurisdiction of his lord, who kept an eye on his private life and punished his intemperance and laziness. He could not improve his position, change his profession, or marry without his master's approval. Much of his time was devoted to the service of his lord. Several years of his youth had to be spent in domestic service to the manor. The institution of compulsory labor service to the lord remained in full force and in some countries consumed as many as three days per week of a peasant's labor. It was the peasant who rebuilt and maintained the lord's buildings, hauled his produce to market, drove his carriage, and carried his messages. Although serfs could own land, their title was always far from perfect. They were obliged to cultivate their fields in a certain way, under the lord's supervision. They could not sell or mortgage their property at will. In some cases they were forced to sell what they produced, in others prevented from selling. For the serf, farming the land was obligatory. His estate did not even pass entirely to his children; a portion of it was usually retained by the lord.

To discover these regulations I did not have to scour obsolete law books. I found them in the code prepared by Frederick the Great and promulgated by his successor just as the French Revolution began.

Nothing like these things had existed in France for quite some time. Peasants came, went, bought, sold, negotiated, and worked just as they pleased. The last vestiges of serfdom had disappeared, except in one or two provinces of the east – conquered provinces. Serfdom had completely vanished everywhere else, and its abolition lay so far in the past that the date had been forgotten. Recent scholarship has proved that by the thirteenth century it was nowhere to be found in Normandy.

Another, very different revolution in the status of the people had also occurred in France, however: the peasant had not only ceased to be a serf; he had become a *landowner*. This fact is still so little known and, as we shall see, had such important consequences that I beg the reader's indulgence if I pause a moment to explore it further.

It was long believed that the division of landed property dated from the Revolution and was solely a consequence of it. In fact, all sorts of evidence shows that the contrary is true.

At least twenty years before the Revolution, agricultural societies were already deploring the excessive subdivision of the land. At about the same time, Turgot said, "inheritances are sliced up so much that a parcel big enough to support but a single family is divided among five or six children. Consequently, these children and their families can no longer live solely on the land." A few years later, Necker said that there was an *immense number* of small rural properties in France.

In a secret report submitted to an intendant a few years before the Revolution, I found the following: "Inheritances are alarmingly subdivided into equal shares, and since each heir wants a piece of every parcel, every plot is endlessly divided and subdivided." Might this not have been written today?

I went to great lengths to reconstruct as well as I could the cadaster of the Ancien Régime, and in this I was partially successful. Under the law of 1790, which established a tax on land, each parish was required to prepare a list of existing properties within its borders. Most of these lists have vanished. I was nevertheless able to locate the lists for a certain number of villages, and by comparing these with tax rolls from our own time, I was able to determine that the number of landowners in 1790 was as high as half or even two-thirds of the present number. This is quite remarkable, given that the total population of France has increased by more than a quarter since that time.

The peasant's love of his property in land was already as extreme as it is today, and all the passions kindled by land ownership were already aflame. "Land today sells for more than it is worth," wrote an excellent contemporary observer, "owing to the passion of all the inhabitants to become landowners. All the savings of the lower classes, which elsewhere are invested with private individuals or public funds, in France go to purchase land."

Among all the novel things that Arthur Young saw in this country when he visited us for the first time, none struck him more than the great division of land among the peasants. He states that they owned half the land in France. "I had no idea that anything like this existed," he said often, and indeed, nothing of the kind could be found anywhere except in France and immediately contiguous regions.

In England, some peasants owned land, but their numbers had already diminished. In Germany, as we have seen, in all periods and parts of the country there were some free peasants who enjoyed full ownership of tracts of land. The special and often bizarre laws that governed peasant property can be found in the oldest surviving records of German customary law. But this type of property was always the exception rather than the rule, and the number of these small landowners was quite limited.

The parts of Germany where peasants in the late eighteenth century owned their own land and were almost as free as in France were mostly situated along the Rhine. This was also where the revolutionary passions of the French spread most rapidly and have always been strongest. By contrast, the parts of Germany that were for a long time most impervious to those passions were those in which nothing similar had yet been seen. These points are worth noting.

To believe that the division of landed property in France dates from the Revolution is therefore to repeat a common error. In fact, it occurred much earlier. To be sure, the Revolution sold off all land belonging to the clergy and much of what had been owned by nobles. But if you consult the records of those sales, as I had the patience to do in a few cases, you will find that most of these properties were purchased by people who already owned others, so that even though property changed hands, the number of owners increased far less than one might imagine. To repeat Necker's histrionic but accurate phrase, their number was already "immense."

The effect of the Revolution was not to divide the land but to liberate it for a time. All these smallholders were in fact highly constrained in the exploitation of their land, which was subject to numerous obligations from which there was no escape.

These burdens were undoubtedly heavy, but what made them seem unbearable was precisely the circumstance that one might have thought would lighten the load. In France more than anywhere else in Europe, peasant landowners were exempt from seigniorial government. This was a revolution no less great than the one that had made them landowners.

Although the Ancien Régime is still quite close to us, since we daily encounter people born under its laws, it already seems to be receding into the night of time. The radical Revolution that stands between it and us had the same effect as the passage of centuries: what it did not destroy it plunged into obscurity. Hence, few people today can give a precise answer to this simple question: How was the countryside administered before 1789? Indeed, the question can be answered accurately and in detail only after studying not the books but the administrative archives of that time.

I have often heard people say that while the nobility had long since ceased to take part in governing the state, it continued to administer the countryside to the very end. The lord governed the peasants. This appears to be a mistaken view.

In the eighteenth century, all parish affairs were in the hands of officials who were no longer the lord's agents or appointees. Some were named by the provincial intendant, while others were elected by the peasants themselves. It was up to these officials to apportion taxes, repair churches, build schools, and convoke as well as preside over the parish assembly. They supervised and regulated the use of communal property and brought and prosecuted lawsuits in the name of the community. Not only was the lord no longer in charge of all these minor local affairs, but he did not even oversee their administration. All parish officials were supervised or controlled by the central government, as I will show in the next chapter. More than that, the lord seldom acted as the king's representative in the parish, as the intermediary between the king and its inhabitants. No longer was he the person in charge of enforcing the general laws of the state, mustering militias, levying taxes, publishing royal orders, or distributing assistance. All these duties and prerogatives belonged to others. The lord was in reality nothing more than a resident whose immunities and privileges separated and cut him off from everyone else. His status was different, not his power. As intendants were at pains to say in letters to their subordinates, *the lord is merely first among your constituents.*

Turning attention from the level of the parish to that of the canton, we find that the situation was identical. Nowhere did nobles administer cantonal affairs either individually or as a group. This was unique to France. Everywhere else the old feudal society remained partially intact: ownership of land was still associated with government of people.

England was administered as well as governed by the principal landowners. In the very parts of Germany, including Prussia and Austria, where princes were most successful in freeing themselves from noble oversight in general affairs of state, they allowed the nobles to retain much of their role as administrators of the countryside, and even though princes in some places went so far as to monitor the action of landlords, nowhere had they yet taken the lord's place.

In fact, French nobles had long impinged on public administration in only one area, the administration of justice. The leading nobles retained the right to have judges decide certain cases in their name, and from time to time they still issued police regulations applicable within the boundaries of their estates. But royal power had gradually truncated, limited, and subordinated seigniorial justice, to the point where those lords who still exercised it regarded it less as a power than as a source of revenue.

It was the same with all the specific prerogatives of the nobility. Their political aspect had disappeared; only the pecuniary portion remained, and in some cases its significance had greatly increased.

For now, I want to speak only of those revenue-producing privileges known specifically as feudal dues, because these weighed particularly heavily upon the people.

It is not easy to explain today what these dues still amounted to in 1789 because their number was immense and their variety great, and some had already disappeared or been transformed. Therefore, the meanings of the words that described them, which were already obscure to contemporaries, have become even more so for us. Nevertheless, if one consults the books of eighteenth-century specialists in feudal law and does diligent research into local customs, it becomes clear that all the dues that remained extant can be reduced to a small number of principal types. Many others remained, to be sure, but merely as isolated cases.

Vestiges of compulsory labor service to the lord survived in most places. Although most highway tolls had been reduced or eliminated, there were few provinces in which one did not encounter several instances of them. Landlords everywhere imposed fees on fairs and markets. Throughout France they enjoyed exclusive hunting rights. Generally speaking, only they were allowed to have dovecotes and keep pigeons. Nearly everywhere they compelled peasants to mill flour at the lord's mill and press grapes at the lord's press. A universal and very onerous charge went by the name of *lods et ventes*. This was a tax paid to the lord whenever land was bought or sold within the boundaries of his estate. Finally, land throughout France was subject to rent, charges, and fees in money or in kind payable to the lord by the owner, who could not redeem them. Despite this diversity, all of these dues shared the common feature of being, to one degree or another, attached to the land or its produce; all were borne by those who farmed the land.

Ecclesiastical lords enjoyed the same advantages, because the Church, which had a different origin, destination, and nature from feudalism, ultimately became intimately involved with it. Although the Church remained an alien body in the feudal system and was never fully incorporated into it, it penetrated so deeply that it remained encrusted within.

Thus, bishops, canons, and abbots owned fiefs and ground rents in virtue of their ecclesiastical functions. Convents usually had lordship over the village or region in which they were located. They had serfs in the only part of France where they still existed. They commanded compulsory labor services, collected fees from fairs and markets, operated ovens, mills, and presses, and kept stud bulls. In addition, the clergy enjoyed the right to collect the tithe, not only in France but throughout the Christian world.

What matters to me here, however, is the fact that these same feudal dues – *precisely the same ones* – existed throughout Europe at the time, and in most other countries of the continent they were much more oppressive than they were in France. I will mention only compulsory labor service to the lord. In France, it was rare and mild. In Germany, it was still universal and harsh.

What is more, any number of the dues of feudal origin that our ancestors found most repellent and regarded as inimical not only to justice but also to civilization also existed to one degree or another in England: the tithe, inalienable ground rents, perpetual charges, and taxes on the purchase and sale of land, which were referred to in the somewhat bombastic language of the eighteenth century as "the enslavement of the earth." Several of these charges can still be found in England. They do not prevent English agriculture from being the most advanced and productive in the world, and the English people are scarcely aware of their existence.

Why, then, did these same feudal dues arouse such hatred in the heart of the French people, hatred so powerful that it outlived its object and seemed ineradicable? The reason is, on the one hand, that the French peasant had become a landowner and, on the other hand, that he had been completely emancipated from the control of his lord. There are many other causes as well, but I think that these are the principal ones.

If the peasant had not owned land, he would have been impervious to any number of the burdens that the feudal system placed on landed property. Of what importance is the tithe to a man who is merely a farmer? He can simply deduct the tithe from what he pays in rent. Of what importance is ground rent to a man who does not own the property? Of what importance are restrictions on land use to the man who exploits the land on someone else's behalf?

Furthermore, if the French peasant had still been subject to the administration of his lord, feudal dues would have seemed far less unbearable to him because he would have seen them only as a natural consequence of the country's constitution.

When the nobility possesses not only privileges but also powers, when it governs and administers, its special prerogatives can be greater and yet at the same time less noticed. In feudal times, the nobility was seen in much the same way as we see the government today: people accepted the burdens it imposed in exchange for the guarantees it offered. Nobles possessed irksome privileges and onerous prerogatives, but they maintained public order, administered justice, enforced the law, came to the aid of the weak, and took charge of common affairs. To the extent that the nobility ceases to do these things, its privileges seem more burdensome, until ultimately it becomes impossible to understand why they even exist.

I ask you to imagine the French peasant of the eighteenth century, or even the peasant you know today, for he remains forever the same: his condition has changed, but not his state of mind. See him as he is depicted in the sources I have cited, so passionately in love with the land that he uses all his savings to purchase more, no matter what the price. To acquire this new land he must first pay a fee, not to the government but to other nearby landowners, who have as little influence over public affairs and are almost as powerless as he. When at last he gets the land he wants, he plants his heart in it along with his seed. This little corner of the earth that he can call his own fills him with pride and independence. Yet now the same neighbors arrive to take him away from his field and force him to work somewhere else for no pay. Should he try to protect his harvest from their wild game, these same neighbors stop him. They await him at the river crossing to demand that he pay a toll. He encounters them again at the market, where they sell him the right to sell his own produce. And when he returns home and wants to put the remainder of his grain to his own use – grain that he planted with his own hands and watched grow with his own eyes – he cannot do so unless he sends it to be milled in mills and baked in ovens owned by these same men. Part of the income of his small farm goes to paying them rent, and that rent is perpetual and irredeemable.

No matter what he does, he encounters these vexatious neighbors along his path, interfering with his pleasure, impeding his work, eating his produce. And when he has finished with them, others, clad in black, arrive and take the lion's share of his harvest. Imagine this man's condition, needs, character, and passions, and calculate if you can the wealth of hatred and envy that he has stored up in his heart.

Feudalism had remained the greatest of our civil institutions while ceasing to be a political institution. Thus diminished, it aroused far more hatred than before. It is therefore true to say that the partial destruction of the institutions of the Middle Ages made those that remained far more odious.

II.2 – Why Administrative Centralization Is an Institution of the Ancien Régime and Not, As Some Say, the Work of the Revolution or Empire

Back in the days when we had political assemblies in France, I once heard an orator refer to administrative centralization as "that admirable triumph of the Revolution, for which we are the envy of Europe." I am prepared to grant that centralization was an admirable triumph and that we are the envy of Europe for it, but I maintain that it was not a triumph of the Revolution. On the contrary, it was a product of the Ancien Régime, and, I would add, the only portion of the political constitution of the Ancien Régime that survived the Revolution because it was the only one that could adapt to the new social state that the Revolution created. The reader who has the patience to read this chapter attentively will perhaps find that I have proved my thesis with a superfluity of evidence.

First, I beg the reader's indulgence if I neglect for now the so-called *pays d'états*, that is, provinces that administered themselves, or, rather, still appeared to administer themselves, at least in part.

The *pays d'états*, occupying the far reaches of the kingdom, contained scarcely a quarter of the total population of France, and in only two of them was provincial liberty really still alive. I will show later the extent to which the central government had subjected them to the same rules as the rest of the country.

Here I will be concerned primarily with those provinces known in the administrative language of the time as *pays d'élection*, although elections were less common there than elsewhere. They completely surrounded

Paris. They formed a continuous region that constituted not just the heart but also the most prosperous part of France.

At first glance, the old administration of the kingdom strikes one as thoroughly diverse: diverse in its rules, diverse in authority, a true hodge-podge of powers. France was replete with administrative bodies and isolated officials, with none subordinate to any other and all participating in government by virtue of some right they had purchased, which could not be reclaimed. Often their functions overlapped or impinged on one another to such a degree that they dealt with very closely related matters, resulting in frequent friction and clashes.

Courts of justice wielded legislative power indirectly. They had the right to issue administrative regulations enforceable within the limits of their jurisdiction. At times they challenged the central administration, forthrightly denounced its policies, and arrested its agents. Local judges issued police regulations in the cities and towns in which they resided.

Towns had very diverse constitutions. Their magistrates bore a variety of names or derived their powers from different sources: here a mayor, there consuls, elsewhere aldermen. Some were chosen by the king, others by the old lord or the royal prince who held the region in appanage. Some were elected for a year by their fellow citizens, while others purchased the right to govern in perpetuity.

These were remnants of old powers. Gradually, however, there emerged or evolved in their midst something relatively new, which I must now describe.

At the center of the kingdom, close to the throne, a singularly powerful administrative body, the King's Council, took shape; within it power was concentrated in a novel way.

Its roots were ancient, but most of its functions were of recent date. It was many things at once: a supreme judicial court, because it had the right to overturn the decisions of all the regular courts, as well as a superior administrative tribunal, with appellate power over all lesser jurisdictions. As a government council, it also possessed, under the king's authority, legislative power; it proposed and debated most laws and set and apportioned taxes. As the superior administrative council, it had the power to establish the general rules that guided the government's agents. It decided all important matters and oversaw the work of all inferior authorities. All government business ultimately came before the council, and the impetus that set all the wheels of government in motion came from it. Yet it had no jurisdiction of its own. It was the king alone who decided, although it was the council from which the decision seemed to emanate. Even though it appeared to render justice on its own, it was composed, as Parlement said in one of its remonstrances, exclusively of *donneurs d'avis*, or advice givers.

Council members were not great lords but persons of middling-to-low birth, former intendants and others accomplished in practical affairs and serving at the king's discretion.

The council usually acted quietly and discreetly, always demonstrating not so much pretentions as power. By itself it made no great impression, or, rather, it paled before the splendor of the throne, to which it stood in close proximity. So powerful that it had a hand in everything, it was at the same time so obscure that history has scarcely taken note of it.

Just as the entire administration of the country was directed by a single body, all internal affairs were entrusted to a single agent, *the comptroller general*.

If you open a directory of the Ancien Régime, you will find that each province had its own special minister, but when you examine the records of the administration, you soon discover that the provincial minister's opportunities for action were rare and relatively unimportant. Regular business was conducted by the comptroller general, who little by little took charge of all matters involving money, which is to say nearly the entirety of the public administration. One finds him playing now the role of minister of finance, now that of minister of the interior or commerce or public works.

Just as the central administration had in truth only one agent in Paris, it also had but a single agent in each province. In the eighteenth century you still find great lords bearing the title *provincial governor*. They were the ancient and often hereditary representatives of feudal royalty. Though still granted honors, they no longer had any power. All the reality of government was vested in the *intendant*.

The latter was a man of common birth, always from outside the province, young, and yet to make his mark in the world. He did not wield power by virtue of election, birth, or purchased office. He was chosen by the government among the lower-ranking members of the State Council and could be removed at any time. Detached from that body, he became its representative, and for that reason he was referred to, in the administrative language of the time, as a "seconded commissioner." Nearly all the powers that the council itself possessed were placed in his hands, and he exercised them in the first instance. Like the council, he was both administrator and judge. The intendant was in correspondence with all the ministers. Within the province he was in every respect the sole agent of the government's will.

Below him, and appointed by him in each canton, was an official known as a *subdelegate*, who could be removed at any time. The intendant was usually a man who had recently been ennobled; the subdelegate was always a commoner. Yet he represented the entire government in the small district assigned to him, just as the intendant represented it in the larger district, or *généralité*. He was subordinate to the intendant, just as the intendant was subordinate to the minister.

The marquis d'Argenson recounts in his memoirs that John Law once said to him: "I never would have believed what I saw when I was comptroller of finance. The fact is that the kingdom of France is governed by thirty intendants. You have neither parlement nor estates nor governors. Thirty *maîtres des requêtes* are dispatched to the provinces, and it is on these thirty men that happiness or unhappiness, abundance or sterility, depend."

These very powerful officials were nevertheless eclipsed by the vestiges of the old feudal aristocracy and all but lost in its residual glow. That is why contemporaries barely noticed them, even though they already had a hand in everything. In society, nobles enjoyed over them the advantages of rank, wealth, and esteem that still attached to ancient things. In government, the nobility surrounded the prince and formed his court. It commanded fleets and led armies. In short, it did those things that struck contemporary eyes most forcefully and still, in all too many cases, captivate posterity's gaze. A great lord would have been insulted to learn that he was to be appointed to the post of intendant. The poorest gentleman of breeding would likely have disdained such an offer. In his eyes, the intendants were the representatives of an outside power, new men designated to govern the bourgeoisie and peasantry, and socially beneath notice. Yet these men governed France, as Law said and as we shall see.

Let us begin with the power to tax, which in a sense contains all the others.

As is well known, some taxes were collected by tax farmers. To that end, the King's Council negotiated with financial companies, set the terms of contracts, and regulated the manner of collection. All other taxes, such as the *taille, capitation*, and *vingtièmes*, were established and levied directly by agents of the central administration or under their all-powerful supervision.

Every year the council issued a secret decision setting the amount of the taille and its many subsidiary taxes, as well as its apportionment among the provinces. The taille thus grew from year to year without any advance warning.

Since the taille was an old tax, its assessment and collection had formerly been entrusted to local agents, who were all more or less independent of the government because they exercised their powers by right of birth or election, or because they had purchased their offices. Among these agents were the lord, the parish tax collector, the treasurers of France, and elected officials. These authorities still existed in the eighteenth century, but some had absolutely nothing to do with the taille by then, while others played only a very minor and entirely subordinate role. In every case, power was entirely in the hands of the intendant and his agents. In reality, he alone apportioned the taille among parishes, instructed and supervised the collectors, and granted deferrals or abatements.

Other taxes, such as the capitation, were of recent date, so that the government was no longer hampered by vestiges of old powers. It acted alone, without any intervention by the governed. The comptroller general, the intendant, and the council set the rates.

Let us turn now from money to men.

Some people find it surprising that the French bore the burden of military conscription so patiently at the time of the Revolution and afterward. Bear in mind, however, that they had long been accustomed to it. Before conscription there was the militia, which imposed a heavier burden even though the required contingents were not as large. Rural youth were periodically compelled to draw lots to determine which of them would serve six-year tours in regiments of the militia.

Since the militia was a comparatively modern institution, none of the old feudal powers took any interest in it. The entire operation was entrusted to agents of the central government exclusively. The council set the total size of the contingent and the share to be supplied by each province. The intendant determined the number of men to be recruited in each parish. His subdelegate presided over the drawing of lots, heard requests for exemption, chose which militiamen would be allowed to live at home and which would be required to depart, and, finally, delivered the latter to the military authorities. The only avenue of appeal was to the intendant and the King's Council.

Outside the *pays d'états*, moreover, all public works, even those whose purpose was purely local, were approved and managed by agents of the central government alone.

Independent local authorities, such as the lord, local finance bureaus, and surveyors of highways, did exist and could participate in this aspect of local administration, but in most places these old powers did little or nothing, as even a hasty perusal of contemporary administrative documents reveals. All major highways and even roads linking one town to another were built and maintained with the proceeds of general taxes. The King's Council decided routes and awarded contracts. The intendant supervised the work of the engineers, and the subdelegate conscripted the labor needed to implement the plan. Only the smallest roads were left to the discretion of the old local powers, and those roads consequently remained impassable.

Then as now, the principal agent of the central government in the management of public works was the Department of Bridges and Roads. Here, despite the passage of time, strikingly little has changed. The department has a council and a school. It has inspectors who annually travel throughout France. It has engineers who manage all construction work under orders from the intendant. Many more Ancien Régime institutions survived the advent of the new society than is commonly assumed, but most lost their names in the transition even if they retained their formal organization. This one kept both, however: a rare occurrence.

The central government, with the help of its agents, assumed responsibility for maintaining law and order in the provinces. Small police brigades existed throughout the kingdom, and these operated under the command of the intendants. With these policemen and, if need be, the army, the intendant responded to unforeseen dangers, arrested vagabonds, repressed begging, and put down the riots that erupted frequently in response to fluctuating grain prices. The government never called upon the governed, as it had done in the past, to aid it in this part of its task, except in the towns, where there was usually some sort of urban guard whose soldiers were selected and officers appointed by the intendant.

The judiciary retained, and often made use of, the right to issue police regulations, but these applied to only a portion of the country, indeed usually to a single place. The King's Council could always quash these regulations and did so repeatedly when they emanated from the lower courts. Meanwhile, it daily issued general regulations that applied to the entire kingdom, some of which dealt with matters other than those regulated by the courts, while others dealt with the same matters but in a different way. The number of these regulations, or council decrees, as they were called at the time, was enormous and increased steadily as the Revolution drew closer. Virtually no aspect of the social economy or political organization of France was left untouched by council decrees in the forty years prior to the Revolution.

In the old feudal society, if the lord possessed great rights, he also bore great burdens. It was his responsibility to aid the indigent within the limits of his domains. We find a last vestige of this old law of Europe in the Prussian code of 1795, which states that "the lord shall see to it that poor peasants receive an education. Insofar as possible he shall provide those of his vassals who have no land with the means of subsistence. Should any lapse into indigence, he shall come to their aid."

No comparable law had existed in France for quite some time. Because the lord had been deprived of his former powers, he shed his former obligations. No local authority, council, or provincial or parish association had taken his place. No one was any longer obliged by law to take care of the rural poor. The central government had rashly assumed sole responsibility for their needs.

Every year the King's Council assigned to each province a certain sum drawn from general tax revenues, which the intendant then distributed to the parishes for the purpose of poor relief. Needy farmers were obliged to turn to him for assistance. In times of famine, it was the intendant who ordered that wheat or rice be distributed to the people. The council annually designated certain places for the establishment of charity workhouses, where the poorest peasants could find work in return for a meager wage. It is easy to imagine how charity dispensed from such a distance must often have been blind or capricious and always quite inadequate.

The central government did not limit itself to aiding peasants in their misery. It sought to teach them the art of how to enrich themselves, as well as to help and, if necessary, force them to do so. To that end, it had its intendants and subdelegates distribute from time to time short pamphlets on the agricultural art. It founded agricultural societies, promised bonuses, and spent large sums on nurseries and on the distribution of their products. It might seem that it would have been more efficient to reduce the burdens under which agriculture labored or to diminish their inequality, but this thought appears never to have occurred to anyone.

In some instances the council sought to compel people to prosper regardless of what they thought about it. There were countless decrees ordering artisans to adopt certain methods and manufacture certain products. Moreover, since there were not enough intendants to enforce all these rules, inspectors general of industry were sent into the provinces to lend them a hand.

The council also issued decrees prohibiting the planting of certain crops on land deemed inappropriate for the purpose. One even finds orders to uproot vines planted in what the council deemed to be poor soil. This shows how far the government had already moved beyond the role of sovereign into that of guardian.

II.3 – How What Today Is Called Administrative Tutelage Is an Institution of the Ancien Régime

In France, municipal liberty survived feudalism. At a time when lords no longer administered the countryside, towns maintained the right to govern themselves. Until the end of the seventeenth century, towns still resembled small democratic republics, in which officials were freely elected by, and responsible to, all the people; municipal life was public and active; and citizens remained proud of their collective rights and quite jealous of their town's independence.

It was not until 1692 that elections were generally abolished for the first time. Municipal functions were then transformed into venal offices, meaning that in each town the king sold to a small number of residents the right to govern the rest in perpetuity.

This change sacrificed the prosperity of the towns along with their liberty. Although the transformation of public functions into venal offices often proved beneficial in regard to the courts, because the primary requisite of a good judicial system is that judges must be completely independent, it invariably did serious harm when it came to the administration proper, where the paramount requirements are responsibility, hierarchy, and zeal. The government of the old monarchy was under no illusion on this score: it was careful not to adopt for itself the regime that it imposed on the towns, and it refrained from transforming the functions of subdelegates and intendants into venal offices.

What deserves history's utmost scorn, moreover, is the fact that this truly revolutionary change was introduced with no political purpose in mind. Louis XI had curtailed municipal freedoms because he feared their democratic character. Louis XIV did not fear them but destroyed them nonetheless. Proof that this was the case can be seen in the fact that he was willing to sell these freedoms back to any town that could pay for them. In fact, his intention was not so much to abolish as to trade in them, and if he did abolish them, it was done as it were inadvertently, as a purely expedient financial policy. Strangely enough, this game continued for eighty years. During that time, towns were sold the right to elect their officials on seven different occasions, and no sooner had they savored the privilege anew than it was taken back to be sold yet again. The motive for this policy was always the same and in many cases avowed. The preamble to the edict of 1722 states that "our financial exigencies compel us to seek the surest means of alleviating them." The method was sure, but it was also ruinous for those who bore the burden of this peculiar tax. "I am stunned by the enormous sums that have been paid at various times to purchase municipal offices," one intendant wrote to the comptroller general in 1764. "Spent on useful projects, these funds would have yielded profits to the town, which instead has felt only the burden of the authority and privileges bestowed upon these offices." I see no feature of the Ancien Régime more shameful than this.

To describe precisely how towns were governed in the eighteenth century seems difficult today. Apart from the fact that the source of municipal powers changed constantly, as we have just seen, each town preserved vestiges of its former constitution and local customs. Perhaps no two cities in France were absolutely alike, but this diversity was deceptive and hid an underlying similarity.

In 1764, the government tried to impose a general law on town administration. From its intendants it solicited reports on the way in which things were done in each town. Having read portions of this survey, I find that municipal affairs were handled in much the same way everywhere. The differences were merely superficial, a matter of appearances; the reality was the same.

Town government was usually entrusted to two assemblies. This was the case with all the large towns and most of the small ones.

The first assembly was made up of municipal officials, whose number varied from place to place. This was the executive power of the town, called the *town council*. When the king permitted elections, or when the town was able to buy back its municipal offices, the members of this council exercised temporary power, subject to election. By contrast, when the king opted for venal offices and succeeded in selling them, they held their charges in perpetuity in exchange for cash. But offices did not always sell because the merchandise became more and more debased as municipal authority fell increasingly under central domination. In no case were municipal officers paid a salary, but they always enjoyed certain tax exemptions and privileges. There was no hierarchy among them: administration was collective. No single official was in charge and responsible for what happened. The mayor was the president of the town council, not the administrator of the city.

The second assembly, known as the *general assembly*, elected the town council where elections still existed and continued to have a hand in the principal town affairs everywhere.

In the fifteenth century, the general assembly often included everyone who lived in the town. According to one of the reports in the survey mentioned previously, this practice "was consistent with the popular spirit of our ancestors." The people as a whole elected the municipal officials. At times the people were consulted about other matters, and it was to the people that officials were responsible. At the end of the seventeenth century, this state of affairs still existed in some places.

In the eighteenth century, the general assembly no longer consisted of all the people acting as a body. It was almost always representative. What needs to be pondered carefully, however, is the fact that nowhere was the general assembly still elected by the mass of the people and imbued with its spirit. Everywhere it consisted of *notables*, some of whom owed their membership to a right that belonged to them personally, while others served as delegates of guilds or companies, which they represented under bound mandate.

As the century wore on, the number of notables possessing the right to be members of the assembly increased. Deputies representing trade guilds became less numerous or ceased to attend. Only delegates of constituted corporations (*corps*) were found. In other words, the assembly now contained only citizens of the urban elite[1] and almost no artisans. The people, who are less easily fooled by the mere semblance of freedom than one might imagine, everywhere lost interest in town affairs and lived as strangers within their own town walls. From time to time officials would try in vain to revive the municipal patriotism that had worked such wonders in the Middle Ages, but the people remained deaf

---

[1] *Bourgeois.* In order to avoid confusion with later uses of the term *bourgeois*, I have translated it here as "urban elite." Under the Ancien Régime, according to the *Dictionnaire Robert*, a *bourgeois* was a "person who did not belong to the clergy or nobility, did not work with his hands, and owned property."

to their appeals and seemed completely indifferent to the most important issues. In towns where officials felt they had to maintain the appearance of free elections, they tried to persuade the people to vote. The people stubbornly abstained. Nearly every ruler who sets out to destroy liberty attempts initially to preserve its forms. This has been true from the time of Augustus to the present. In this way they hope to combine the moral force inherent in public consent with the advantages peculiar to absolute power. Nearly all have failed in the attempt, however, for they soon discover that it is impossible to keep up such deceitful appearances for long when the reality has ceased to exist.

By the eighteenth century, therefore, municipal government had everywhere degenerated into a small oligarchy. A few families directed all public business for private ends, far from the public eye and not answerable to the people. This was a disease that afflicted the administration of towns throughout France. All the intendants reported it, but the only remedy they could think of was to subject local authorities to ever greater control by the central government.

It was difficult, however, to do this better than it had already been done. Apart from the edicts that from time to time altered the administration of all towns, laws peculiar to specific towns were often overturned by arbitrary regulations issued by the King's Council at the prompting of the intendants, and this was done without prior investigation and at times without the knowledge of the residents of the town themselves.

The residents of one town affected by such a decree observed that "this measure has stunned citizens of every order in the town, none of whom anticipated anything of the kind."

Towns could not establish a toll, levy a tax, mortgage or sell property, bring suit, lease or administer resources, or use surplus income without a council order based on a report of the intendant. All public works were based on plans and budgets approved by council decree. Contracts were awarded by the intendant or his subdelegates and usually supervised by a state engineer or architect. These facts may surprise those who believe that everything we see nowadays in France is new.

The central government had penetrated town administration even more deeply than this discussion might suggest. Its power was far more extensive than its rights.

Take the following memorandum, which the comptroller general sent to all the intendants around the middle of the century: "You will pay close attention to everything that takes place in the municipal assemblies.

You will prepare scrupulously detailed reports of all deliberations and send them to me, together with your recommendations, before any action is taken."

Indeed, the correspondence between the intendants and their subdelegates shows that the government had a hand in town business in all towns, from the smallest to the largest. It was consulted about everything and had firm opinions about everything. Its rules extended even to feast days. Indeed, at times it was the government itself that insisted on manifestations of public joy and ordered that fires be lit and homes illuminated. I found one intendant who imposed a fine of 20 livres on members of the local guard who failed to turn up for a *Te Deum*.

Town officials were consequently aware of their insignificance.

Some of them wrote to one intendant: "My Lord, we beg you most humbly to grant us your benevolence and protection. We will endeavor to be worthy of these boons by obedience to the orders of Your Excellency."

"We have never resisted your wishes, my lord," wrote others who still claimed for themselves the splendid title of "peers of the town."

This was how the bourgeois class prepared to govern and how the people prepared for liberty.

If only the strict submission of the towns had saved their finances! But it did not. Some argue that without centralization the towns would soon have ruined themselves. I do not know whether this is true, but there can be no doubt that in the eighteenth century, centralization did not prevent them from doing so. The administrative history of the age is filled with their chaotic affairs.

If we turn from the towns to the villages, we find different authorities and different political forms but the same dependency.

I am well aware of the evidence that in the Middle Ages, the inhabitants of each village formed a community independent of the lord. The lord made use of this community, kept an eye on its activities, and governed it, but it owned certain property in common, elected its own leaders, and administered itself democratically.

This old parish constitution existed in all feudal nations and in all countries to which feudal nations brought vestiges of their laws. We find traces of it all over England, and it continued to flourish in Germany as recently as sixty years ago, as the code of Frederick the Great makes clear. Even in France, traces still existed in the eighteenth century.

I recall that when I began my research on parishes in the Ancien Régime in the archives of one intendance, I was surprised to find in these poor, subjugated communities several of the features that had struck me so forcefully in the rural towns of North America, features that I wrongly thought at the time were peculiar to the New World. Neither had a permanent representative body, a town council in the strict sense of the term. Both were administered by officials who acted individually under the direction of the community as a whole. From time to time, both held general assemblies in which all residents came together to elect their officials and make important decisions. In short, the resemblance between the two was as close as that between a living individual and a corpse can be.

Indeed, despite the different destinies of these two types of community, both shared the same origin.

Transported at a stroke far from feudalism and granted absolute dominion over itself, the rural parish of the Middle Ages became the New England town. Separated from the lord but gripped in the powerful hand of the state, what it became in France I will now describe.

In the eighteenth century, the number and titles of parish officials varied from province to province. Old documents show that the number of local officials had been greatest when local life was most active. Their number decreased as local life lapsed into torpor. In most eighteenth-century parishes, only two officials remained: the collector and the syndic. These municipal officials were usually still elected, or were supposed to be, but everywhere they had become instruments of the state rather than representatives of the community. The collector levied the taille on direct orders from the intendant. The syndic, who was placed under the daily supervision of the intendant's subdelegate, represented him in all operations related to public order or government. He was the subdelegate's primary agent with respect to the militia, state public works, and enforcement of all general laws.

The lord, as we have already seen, remained aloof from all these details of government. He no longer even kept a watchful eye on them. He did nothing to assist in governing. More than that, the effort by which he formerly maintained his power now seemed unworthy of him, insofar as his power itself was increasingly ruined. In the end, his pride would have been wounded had he been invited to participate in local government. Although he no longer governed, his presence in the parish and his privileges prevented the establishment of a good parish government in his stead. An individual so different from the rest, so independent, and so favored destroys or weakens the power of all rules.

As I will show later, the lord's presence had driven nearly everyone with any wealth or education into the towns, so that, besides the lord himself, only a herd of crude and ignorant peasants remained in the countryside, and they were in no position to take charge of the administration of common affairs. As Turgot rightly said, "a parish is a collection of huts occupied by equally passive people."

Eighteenth-century administrative documents are filled with complaints born of the incompetence, laziness, and ignorance of parish collectors and syndics. Ministers, intendants, subdelegates, and even nobles all deplored this state of affairs endlessly, but none traced it back to its root causes.

Until the Revolution, the government of the French rural parish preserved aspects of democracy that it had possessed in the Middle Ages. When it came time to elect municipal officials or discuss some item of community business, the village bell called the peasants to the door of the church, where the poor as well as the rich had the right to participate. To be sure, when all had assembled, there was no deliberation as such, nor was a vote taken. But each person could express his opinion, and a notary summoned for the purpose kept written minutes of this open-air forum.

When we recognize that these empty semblances of liberty went hand in hand with the absence of any real power, we can already see on a small scale how the most absolute rule can be combined with some forms of the most extreme democracy, compounding oppression with the ridicule engendered by failing to notice it. The democratic parish assembly could indeed express its wishes but had no more right to do as it wished than did the town council. It could not even speak until allowed to open its mouth, for it was not free to meet until the express permission of the intendant had been sought and granted "at his pleasure," as the saying went. Even a unanimous assembly could not tax, buy, sell, rent, or sue without the permission of the King's Council. A decision of the council had to be obtained to repair wind damage to the roof of the church or to rebuild a crumbling presbytery wall. The rural parishes most remote from Paris were as bound by this rule as those closest to the capital. I came across cases in which parishes begged the council's permission to spend twenty-five livres.

To be sure, residents usually retained the right to elect their officials by universal suffrage. But it was often the case that the intendant designated a candidate who was then elected unanimously by this small body of voters. In other cases, he threw out the results of a spontaneously held election, appointed the collector and syndic himself, and indefinitely postponed any new election. I found innumerable examples of this type of behavior.

It is impossible to imagine a fate crueler than that of these local officials. The lowliest agent of the central government, the subdelegate, had them at his beck and call. He often imposed fines on them. Sometimes he put them in prison. The guarantees that still existed elsewhere to protect citizens against arbitrary power no longer existed here. In 1750 one intendant said: "I ordered the imprisonment of some leaders of the discontented communities and ordered them to bear the expense of sending in the mounted police. In this way they were easily subdued." Accordingly, parish offices were regarded less as honors than as burdens to be avoided by all sorts of subterfuges.

Nevertheless, the peasants still cherished these last remaining vestiges of the old parish government, and even today the only public liberty they really understand is parish liberty. This is the only sort of public business that really interests them. The same person who is quite willing to leave the government of the entire nation in the hands of an autocrat balks at the idea of not having a voice in the administration of his village – such is the residual weight of the hollowest of political forms.

What I have just said about towns and parishes must be extended to nearly all corporate bodies that stood on their own and owned property collectively.

Under the Ancien Régime the situation was just as it is today: no city, town, village, or hamlet however small, and no hospital, factory, convent, or school anywhere in France, was allowed to manage its private affairs independently or administer its property as it saw fit. Then as now, all French citizens labored under government tutelage, and if the insolence of the word had yet to manifest itself, the thing itself already existed.

II.4 – How Administrative Justice and the Immunity of Public Officials Were Institutions of the Ancien Régime

In no other country of Europe were the regular courts less subservient to the government than in France, but by the same token there were few other countries in which recourse to special courts was more common. These two things were more closely related than one might imagine. The king had virtually no influence on the fate of judges. He could not remove them, transfer them, or even, as a general rule, promote them. In short, he had no hold over them, whether through ambition or fear. He soon came to regard this independence as an impediment to his will. Hence, more than anywhere else, he was driven to deny them jurisdiction over cases directly impinging on royal power and to create alongside the regular courts, for his own private use, a more subservient type of tribunal, one that would offer a certain semblance of justice to his subjects without obliging him to fear the reality.

In countries, including certain parts of Germany, where the regular courts had never been as independent of the government as were the French tribunals of the time, no such precautions were taken, and administrative justice never existed. The prince already wielded enough power over judges that he had no need for *commissaires*, or commissioners, as French administrative judges were called.

If you take the trouble to read the royal edicts and declarations published in the last century of the monarchy, as well as the royal council decrees issued in the same period, you will find few instances in which the government, after taking a decision, failed to say that any challenges that might emerge or any litigation that might arise from it would be handled exclusively by the intendants and the King's Council: "Be it further ordered by His Majesty that any dispute that may arise pursuant to the execution of the present decree, and anything depending on or arising from it, shall be brought to the attention of the intendant to be judged by him, subject to appeal to the Council. We forbid our courts and tribunals to sit in judgment thereof." This was the usual formula.

In matters subject to ancient laws or customs, where this precaution had not been taken, the King's Council regularly intervened by way of a procedure known as *évocation*, whereby a case in which the government had an interest could be removed from the jurisdiction of regular judges and taken in hand by the council. The council's records are filled with decrees invoking this special procedure. Little by little, the exception became the rule, and fact was transformed into theory. It became an established tenet not of law but in the minds of those who applied the law, a maxim of statecraft, as it were, that any case that involved the public interest or arose out of the interpretation of an administrative act did not come under the jurisdiction of regular judges, whose only role was to decide cases in which one private interest was pitted against another. In this area we have done nothing but come up with a formula; it was the Ancien Régime that came up with the idea.

In those days, most disputes about taxes fell under the exclusive jurisdiction of the intendant and council. This was also true of all disputes relating to the regulation of traffic, public transportation, highways, river navigation, etc. Broadly speaking, any case in which the public authorities had an interest took place before an administrative tribunal.

The intendants were at great pains to expand this special jurisdiction endlessly. They alerted the comptroller general and prodded the King's Council. The reason given by one of these officials to obtain an *évocation* is worth preserving: "The regular judge," he said, "is subject to fixed rules, which oblige him to sanction an illegal action, but the Council can always bend the rules for a useful purpose."

In keeping with this principle, the intendants and council often took charge of cases that had only the most tenuous connection with public administration, or none at all. One nobleman, involved in a dispute with his neighbor and unhappy with his judges' rulings, asked the council to take jurisdiction in the case. The intendant, who was consulted in the matter, answered: "Although this case involves only private claims, jurisdiction over which belongs to the courts, His Majesty can if he so chooses assert jurisdiction in any case without being accountable for the grounds."

By way of *évocation*, any person of the lower orders who disturbed the peace by some act of violence was usually tried before the intendant or the provost of the constabulary. Most of the riots that so often erupted when grain prices rose too high resulted in *évocations* of this sort. The intendant then handpicked a certain number of graduates to sit as a sort of prefectural council in a criminal proceeding. I found judgments issued in this manner condemning men to the galleys or even to death. Criminal trials in which the intendant sat as judge were still common at the end of the seventeenth century.

Modern jurists assure us that there has been great progress in administrative law since the Revolution: "Previously," they say, "judicial and administrative powers were conflated. Distinctions have since been established, and each has been restored to its proper place." To appreciate properly the progress these authorities have in mind, one must never forget that although the judicial power in the Ancien Régime repeatedly reached beyond its natural sphere of authority, it never completely filled that sphere. Anyone who looks at only one aspect of this phenomenon without the other will have an incomplete and distorted view of the subject. At times the courts were permitted to issue administrative regulations, although this was clearly beyond their jurisdiction. At other times they were prohibited from trying what were truly private lawsuits, although this was to exclude them from their proper domain. It is true that we have banished the courts from the administrative sphere, to which they had been improperly admitted under the Ancien Régime, but at the same time, as we have seen, the government repeatedly trespassed on the natural sphere of the courts, and we have allowed it to remain there, as if the confusion of powers were not as dangerous from this side as from the other, and perhaps even more dangerous, because the intervention of the courts in administrative affairs merely harms efficiency, whereas administrative interference with the courts corrupts people and tends to make them at once revolutionary and servile.

Among the nine or ten constitutions that have been adopted in perpetuity in France over the past sixty years, there is one that states explicitly that no agent of the administration can be tried before the regular courts without prior authorization. This article was apparently so well crafted that when the constitution of which it was a part was overthrown, care was taken to extract it from the ruins, and ever since it has been strenuously protected from the consequences of revolution. Administrators still customarily refer to the privilege granted them under this article as one of the great conquests of 1789, but in this they are also mistaken, because the government of the old monarchy was scarcely less assiduous than today's government in protecting its officials from the unpleasantness of having to defend their actions in court like ordinary citizens. The only essential difference between the two periods is this: before the Revolution, the government could protect its agents only by recourse to inequitable and arbitrary measures, whereas since then it has had the legal power to allow them to violate the law.

Whenever the courts of the Ancien Régime attempted to prosecute a representative of the central government, the King's Council usually issued an order taking the accused out of the hands of his judges and sending him before commissioners appointed by the council, because, as one state councilor wrote at the time, an administrator subject to this sort of attack would have found the regular court judges prejudiced against him, and the king's authority would have been compromised. *Évocations* of this kind were not infrequent but daily occurrences, and they pertained not only to the most important agents of the government but also to the least important. It was enough to have only the most tenuous connection with the administration to have nothing to fear except from the administration itself. A foreman employed by the Department of Bridges and Roads to supervise compulsory labor details was accused by a peasant of mistreating him. The council assumed jurisdiction in the case, and the chief engineer sent a confidential memorandum to the intendant: "The fact is that the foreman's behavior was quite reprehensible, but that is no reason to let the case run its course, because it is of the utmost importance for the Department of Bridges and Roads that the ordinary courts should neither hear nor receive complaints against foremen from those subject to compulsory labor. If this precedent were allowed, public works would be hampered by the constant lawsuits to which the public's animosity toward the officials in question would give rise."

In another case, involving a state contractor who took construction materials from a neighbor's field, the intendant himself wrote to the comptroller general: "I cannot overstate the degree to which it would be prejudicial to the interests of the administration to abandon its contractors to the judgment of the regular courts, whose principles can never be reconciled with those of the administration."

These lines were written precisely a century ago, yet it seems that the administrators who wrote them might be our contemporaries.

II.5 – How Centralization Was Thus Able to Insinuate Itself among the Old Powers and Supplant Them Without Destroying Them

Let us now briefly recapitulate what was said in the three previous chapters: a single body at the center of the kingdom controlled the public administration throughout the country; the same minister was in charge of nearly all domestic affairs; in each province, a single agent managed all details; there was no subordinate administrative body or any other type of body that could act without prior authorization; special courts heard all cases in which the administration had an interest and protected all its agents. What is this if not the centralization with which we are familiar? Its formal institutions were less identifiable than they are today, its procedures were less regulated, its existence was more agitated, but it was the same being. In the interim, it was unnecessary to add or take away anything essential. It was enough to eliminate everything that had been built around it to reveal what we see today.

Most of the institutions that I have just described were subsequently imitated in a hundred different places, but at the time they were peculiar to France, and we shall soon see what a great influence they had on the French Revolution and its aftermath.

But how was it possible for institutions of such novel design to establish themselves in France amid the rubble of feudal society?

It was a task that required patience, skill, and time, rather than strength and unchecked power. At the time the Revolution broke out, almost none of the old administrative edifice had been destroyed in France. Another had been built beneath it, as it were.

59

There is nothing to indicate that the government of the Ancien Régime followed a deeply meditated plan in carrying out this difficult labor. It simply yielded to the instinct that drives all governments to attempt to take sole charge of everything, an instinct that never varied despite the diversity of the government's agents. It left the old powers with their ancient names and honors but little by little deprived them of their authority. It did not force them out of their respective seats of power but quietly ushered them out. It took advantage of this one's inertia and that one's selfishness to take their place. It availed itself of all their vices, never seeking to correct but only to supplant them, and in the end it had in fact replaced nearly all with a single agent, the intendant, a title that did not even exist when they were born.

In this great enterprise of the Ancien Régime, only the judicial power stood in the way, but here again the central government ultimately seized the substance of power while leaving only the shadow to its adversaries. It did not exclude the parlements from the administrative sphere but gradually expanded its own activity there until nearly no room remained for anything else. In certain exceptional and fleeting circumstances – in times of food scarcity, for example, when popular passions served as platforms for ambitious magistrates – the central government allowed the parlements to govern temporarily, to raise a fuss that history has not forgotten. Before long, however, it silently resumed its place and discreetly reasserted its control over everyone and everything.

When we look closely at the parlements' struggle against royal power, we find that the two almost always clashed on the terrain of politics rather than administration. Disputes ordinarily erupted over a new tax. In other words, the two adversaries quarreled not about administrative power but about legislative power, which the one had as little right to seize as the other.

These quarrels became increasingly common as the Revolution drew near. The more inflamed popular passions became, the more the Paris Parlement intervened in politics, and since, at the same time, the central power and its agents gained experience and skill, this same parlement played a smaller and smaller role in the administration proper; with each passing day it became less of an administrative organ and more of a tribune.

Time, moreover, regularly opened new fields of action to the central government, fields where the courts lacked the agility to follow because they involved new issues for which no precedents existed and which were alien to the courts' routine. Society, which was making rapid progress, constantly engendered new needs, each of which was a new source of power for a central government that was alone capable of satisfying them. While the administrative sphere of the tribunals remained fixed, that of the central government was mobile, and it steadily expanded along with civilization itself.

The impending Revolution had begun to agitate French minds everywhere, stirring a thousand new ideas to which only the government could respond. Before overthrowing the government, the Revolution fostered its development. It perfected itself along with everything else. This is particularly striking when one studies the archives. The comptroller general and the intendant of 1780 no longer bore any resemblance to the intendant and comptroller general of 1740. The administration had been transformed. Its agents remained the same, but the spirit that moved them had changed. As it became more meticulous and all-encompassing, it also became more systematic and better informed. As its assertion of total control neared its end, it oppressed less and led more.

The first efforts of the Revolution destroyed that great institution, the monarchy. It was restored in 1800. Despite what is often said, it was not the principles of 1789 in regard to public administration that triumphed then and after but quite the opposite: all the principles of the Ancien Régime were then reinvigorated and have remained in place.

If someone were to ask me how this portion of the Ancien Régime could have been carried over intact and incorporated into the new society, I would answer that the reason why centralization did not perish in the Revolution is that it was in itself the beginning of the Revolution as well as its sign. And I would add that when a people destroys the aristocracy in its midst, it propels itself toward centralization. It then takes far less effort to hasten its way further down this slope than to hold it back. There is a tendency for all the powers within it to become one, and it is only with a great deal of art that they can be kept apart.

The democratic revolution that destroyed so many institutions of the Ancien Régime was therefore bound to consolidate this one. So naturally did centralization find its place in the society forged by the Revolution that it was easy to mistake centralization for one of its achievements.

II.6 – On Administrative Mores under the Ancien Régime

It is impossible to read the correspondence of an intendant of the Ancien Régime with his superiors and subordinates without being astonished by the way in which the institutional similarity between then and now made the administrators of that time resemble the administrators of today. They seem to link hands across the abyss of the Revolution. I would say the same thing of the people subject to their administration. No better illustration exists of the power of legislation over the minds of men.

Ministers had already conceived the desire to scrutinize personally every detail of the government's action and to monitor everything from Paris. As time went by and the administration perfected its methods, this passion increased. By the end of the eighteenth century, it was impossible to set up a charity workshop in a remote corner of some distant province without attracting the notice of the comptroller general, who would seek personally to monitor all expenditure on the project, draft the regulations governing it, and select its location. If a poorhouse was built, he would want to be apprised of the names of the beggars who turned up and the precise dates at which they entered and left. Toward the middle of the century (1733), M. d'Argenson wrote: "The amount of detail with which ministers must deal is enormous. Nothing is done without them, nothing is done except by them, and if their knowledge is not as extensive as their power, they are compelled to leave everything to clerks, who become the real men in charge."

The comptroller general asked not only for reports on government affairs but also for insignificant details about individual citizens. The intendant would then turn to his subdelegates for answers, and he never failed to report what they told him word for word, as though he had personal knowledge of the situation.

In order to direct everything from Paris and have knowledge there of affairs throughout the country, a thousand new means of control had to be invented. The volume of written documents was already enormous, and administrative procedures were so slow that in no case did I find that it took less than a year for a parish to obtain authorization to rebuild a church steeple or repair a presbytery. Usually two or three years passed before the request was granted.

The council itself observed in one of its decrees (dated March 29, 1773) "that administrative formalities lead to endless delays and all too often to eminently justifiable complaints." It added that "however, all these formalities are necessary."

I used to think that the taste for statistics was peculiar to today's administrators, but I was wrong. Toward the end of the Ancien Régime, intendants often were sent short printed forms so that all they had to do was have these forms filled out by their subdelegates and parish syndics. The comptroller general solicited reports on the nature of the land, crops grown, type and quantity of produce, number of livestock, and local industry and mores. The information obtained in this way was scarcely less detailed or more reliable than that supplied in similar cases nowadays by prefects and mayors. On these occasions, subdelegates generally offered rather unflattering judgments of the character of the people subject to their administration. They frequently remarked that "the peasant is naturally lazy and would not work if he were not obliged to in order to survive." This economic doctrine appears to have been quite widespread among administrators.

Even in terms of administrative language, the two periods are strikingly similar. The style of both is equally colorless, facile, vague, and flaccid. Each writer's individuality is obliterated and subsumed in the common mediocrity. If you read a prefect of today, you have read the intendant of yesterday.

Toward the end of the century, however, when the distinctive styles of Diderot and Rousseau had had time to spread and tincture the common tongue, the affected sentimentality that abounds in the works of these two writers acquired influence among administrators and even financiers. The administrative style, ordinarily quite dry in tone, then became unctuous at times and almost tender. A subdelegate complained to the intendant of Paris "that in the performance of his duties he often suffers pangs that rend the heart of a sensitive soul."

The government distributed then, as it does today, certain charitable assistance to the parishes, on condition that the residents make a contribution of their own. When the sum they offered was sufficient, the comptroller general would write in the margin of the distribution slip, "Good, express satisfaction." But when it was more than adequate, he would write: "Good, express satisfaction and emotion."

Administrative officials, who were nearly all bourgeois, already formed a class with its own spirit, traditions, virtues, honor, and pride. It was the aristocracy of the new society, already fully formed and drawing breath. It was simply waiting for the Revolution to make a place for it.

What was already characteristic of the administration in France was its indiscriminate hatred of all, noble or bourgeois, who sought to play a role in public affairs outside its control. It was terrified of any independent body, no matter how insignificant, that showed signs of wanting to organize without its cooperation. Any free association, however minor and no matter what its purpose, was a source of vexation. Only those associations whose members it chose at will and over which it presided were allowed to subsist. Even the great industrial companies pleased it but little. In short, it had no intention of allowing citizens to intervene in any way in overseeing their own affairs. It preferred sterility to competition. But since the French must always be allowed a small degree of license as consolation for their servitude, the government allowed them to debate quite freely all sorts of general and abstract theories in religion, philosophy, ethics, and even politics. It rather readily tolerated attacks on the fundamental principles on which society then rested, and even discussion of God himself, provided that its least officials were immune from criticism. It reckoned that these things were none of its business.

Although eighteenth-century newspapers, or gazettes, as they were called at the time, contained more quatrains than polemics, the administration already looked upon this minor power with quite a jealous eye. Though indulgent toward books, it was already quite hard on newspapers. Unable to stamp them out altogether, it tried to make use of them for its own exclusive purposes. I found a circular dated 1761, addressed to all the intendants of the kingdom, which announced that the king (Louis XV) had decided that the *Gazette de France* would henceforth be put together under the government's watchful eye: "His Majesty wishes to make this paper interesting and assure its superiority over all others.

You will therefore send me a bulletin of everything that occurs in your district that might be of interest to the public, especially anything related to natural science or natural history, along with unusual and interesting facts." Accompanying this circular was a prospectus announcing that the new gazette would appear more often and include more content than the newspaper it was to replace, yet would cost subscribers much less.

Armed with these documents, the intendant wrote to his subdelegates and ordered them to go to work, but their initial response was that they had no information. A new letter then arrived from the minister, who complained bitterly about the torpor of the province: "His Majesty orders me to tell you that it is his intention that you should treat this matter with the utmost seriousness and issue the most explicit orders to your agents." This time the subdelegates did as they were told: one of them reported that a salt smuggler had been hanged and had shown great courage; another that a woman had given birth to triplet daughters; a third that there had been a terrible storm, although it caused no damage. One declared that despite his best efforts he had turned up nothing worthy of being reported but that he would personally subscribe to such a useful gazette and was going to invite all respectable people to do the same. All this effort seems to have yielded relatively little, however, for we learn from yet another letter that "the king, who," according to the minister, "has been good enough to delve personally into the details of measures pertaining to the improvement of the gazette, and who wants to give this newspaper all the superiority and celebrity it deserves, expressed considerable displeasure that his expectations were so sorely disappointed."

Clearly, history is a gallery of paintings in which there are few originals and many copies.

It must be recognized, moreover, that the central government in France never followed the example of those governments of southern Europe that took control of everything yet seemingly spread barrenness everywhere. The French government has often demonstrated great intelligence in its undertakings and has always been prodigiously active. But its activity has often been unproductive and even harmful because it tried to do things that were beyond its powers or beyond anyone's control.

It seldom tackled or soon gave up on the most necessary reforms, which require persistent energy if they are to succeed, yet it constantly tinkered with certain regulations and laws. Within its sphere, nothing ever remained at rest. New rules succeeded one another with such singular rapidity that the government's agents, by dint of being subjected to such frequent commands, often found it difficult to divine what sort of obedience was required. Municipal officials complained to the comptroller general himself about the extreme instability of secondary legislation: "The financial regulations alone change so often that even a town official with life tenure has no time for anything but to study new regulations as they appear, to the point where he is compelled to neglect his regular duties."

Even when the law did not change, the way in which it was implemented varied daily. If you have not seen the administration of the Ancien Régime at work in the secret documents it left behind, you cannot imagine the contempt for the law that eventually developed in the minds of those whose job was to enforce it, and this at a time when there were no longer political assemblies or newspapers to moderate capricious action or restrain the arbitrary and fickle humor of ministers and their bureaus.

One finds few council decrees that do not refer to previous laws, often of quite recent date, that were promulgated but not executed. Indeed, there was not a single edict, royal declaration, or solemnly registered letter-patent that did not suffer a thousand modifications in practice. Letters issued by the comptrollers general and intendants show that the government authorized countless exceptions to its own orders. The law, though rarely broken, was daily bent this way and that to accommodate special cases and ease the government's own task.

One intendant wrote to a minister about a toll charge from which a state contractor sought exemption: "There is no doubt that if the edicts and decrees I have just cited are interpreted strictly according to the letter, no one in the kingdom is exempt from these tolls. But those who are well versed in these matters know that these peremptory measures are of a piece with the penalties they announce, and even though they can be found in nearly all edicts, declarations, and decrees relating to the establishment of taxes, this has never stood in the way of granting exceptions."

Here we have the Ancien Régime in a nutshell: rigid rules, lax practice. Such was its character.

Anyone who would judge the government of that time by examining the body of its laws would stumble into the most foolish errors. I found a royal declaration dated 1757 imposing the death sentence on anyone who wrote or printed a text hostile to religion or the established order. A bookseller who sold such a text or dealer who hawked it among his wares was subject to the same penalty. Had we perhaps reverted to the age of Saint Dominic? No, it was in fact the age of Voltaire.

A commonly heard complaint is that the French have no respect for law. When, alas, might they have learned to respect it? It is fair to say that under the Ancien Régime, the place that the notion of law ought to occupy in the mind of man was vacant. Every petitioner asked that established rules be violated in his favor as insistently and confidently as if he were asking that the rules be respected, and the issue of the law was indeed never raised unless the authorities wished to deny the man's request. The people were still completely submissive to authority, but their obedience was a consequence of custom rather than will. If for some reason they became aroused, the smallest incitement would lead at once to violence, which would then almost always be put down by violence and arbitrary repression rather than law.

In the eighteenth century, the central government in France had yet to acquire the sound and vigorous constitution that it would acquire later. Yet it had already destroyed all intermediary powers, and nothing remained between it and private individuals but a vast empty space, so that each citizen looked upon it from afar as the mainspring of the social machine, the sole and necessary agent of public life.

The best evidence for this can be found in the writings of the regime's detractors. As symptoms of the lengthy malaise that preceded the Revolution began to appear, all sorts of new theories of society and government started to emerge. The goals of the reformers were varied, but their method was always the same. They sought to enlist the hand of the central government to sweep everything away and rebuild it according to a new plan of their own devising. Each felt that only the state was equal to such a task. The power of the state, they argued, ought to be as unlimited as its prerogatives. Their only purpose was to persuade the state to use its power appropriately. The elder Mirabeau, a nobleman so enamored of the prerogatives of the nobility that he bluntly described intendants as interlopers, and who declared that if the appointment of magistrates were left up to the government alone, the courts of justice would soon be reduced to "gangs of commissioners" – this very same Mirabeau placed all his confidence in the action of the central government to realize his delusory dreams.

These ideas did not remain confined within the pages of books. They filtered down into people's minds, mingled with their mores, influenced their habits, and penetrated everywhere, into each of life's daily activities.

No one could imagine succeeding in any important project unless the state became involved. Even farmers, people ordinarily refractory to instruction, came to believe that if there was no improvement in agriculture, the blame lay chiefly with the government, which failed to offer them adequate advice and assistance. One of them wrote to an intendant in a tone of irritation already redolent of the Revolution: "Why doesn't the government appoint inspectors, who would visit the provinces once a year to examine the condition of the crops, teach farmers how to improve them, explain how livestock should be used, how the animals should be fattened for market, how they should be bred and sold, and which markets are best? These inspectors should be well paid. The farmer who produces the best crop should be honored."

Inspectors and medals! No such idea would ever have occurred to a Suffolk farmer!

In the eyes of the majority, it was already the case that only the government could maintain public order. The people were afraid of nothing but the mounted police, and landlords trusted no one else. For both, the police were not only the principal defender of order but order itself. The provincial assembly of Guyenne put it this way: "No one can fail to have noticed how the sight of a mounted policeman suffices to subdue even those who revile obedience the most." Hence, everyone wanted a squadron of police at his gate. The archives of one intendance are full of demands of this sort. No one appears to have suspected that behind the protector might lurk the master.

What émigrés from France who arrived in England found most striking was the absence of this militia. This not only surprised them but in some cases made them contemptuous of the English. One of them, a worthy man but one whose education had not prepared him for what he was going to see, wrote: "It is perfectly true that an Englishman will boast of having been robbed by telling you that at least his country has no mounted police. Another, incensed by any disturbance of the peace, will nevertheless accept the release from custody of seditious rebels on the grounds that the letter of the law outweighs all other considerations." "These false ideas," he adds, "are certainly not shared by everyone. Some of the people are wise and hold opposite views, and in the long run it is wisdom that must prevail."

That these bizarre English ideas might have something to do with English liberties never occurs to him. He would rather explain his observations in more scientific terms: "In a country in which a damp climate and a lack of invigorating winds contribute to a somber temperament, people are disposed to prefer serious subjects. The English people are therefore naturally inclined to take an interest in matters of government. The French are put off by such matters."

The government thus having taken the place of Providence, it was natural for everyone to invoke its assistance in meeting their own individual needs. Thus, we find an enormous number of petitions still ostensibly based on the public interest but in fact dealing only with petty private interests. The cartons in which these petitions are stored are perhaps the only place in which all the classes of Ancien Régime society can be found mingled together. Reading these petitions is a melancholy affair: peasants ask to be indemnified for the loss of their livestock or home; wealthy landowners ask for help in exploiting their land more profitably; industrialists petition the intendant for privileges to protect them from bothersome competition. It is quite common to find manufacturers confiding in the intendant that business is bad and begging him to obtain assistance or a loan from the comptroller general. It appears, moreover, that an account existed for this purpose.

Noblemen themselves were sometimes major petitioners. Their noble status would barely have been evident were it not for the fact that they begged in such peremptory tones. For many of them, the *vingtième*, or 5 percent tax, was the principal link in their chain of dependence. Their share of this tax was set each year by the King's Council on the basis of a report by the intendant, and so it was ordinarily the intendant to whom they applied for deferrals and abatements. I read countless petitions of this kind from nobles, nearly all of whom were titled and quite a few of whom were great lords, who claimed that their income was insufficient or their affairs were not prospering. These noblemen generally addressed the intendant simply as "Monsieur," but in their petitions I noted that they always addressed him as "Monseigneur" (My Lord), just as the bourgeois did.

Sometimes poverty mingled with pride in these petitions in an amusing way. One nobleman wrote to an intendant thus: "Your kind heart would never allow a head of household of my estate to be taxed at the strict 5 percent rate, as a commoner head of household would be."

In times of scarcity, which were so common in the eighteenth century, the people of each district would turn as one to the intendant, as if they expected him and him alone to feed them all. True, everyone was already blaming the government for all their woes. It was responsible for even the most inevitable difficulties, including bad weather.

The marvelous ease with which centralization was restored in France at the beginning of the nineteenth century should no longer surprise us. The men of 1789 had toppled the edifice, but in the very soul of its destroyers its foundation had remained intact, and upon that foundation it was possible to rebuild it rapidly, and more solidly than before.

II.7 – How France, of All the Countries of Europe, Was Already the One in Which the Capital Had Achieved the Greatest Preponderance over the Provinces and Most Fully Subsumed the Entire Country

It is neither the location, the size, nor the wealth of a capital that is responsible for its political preponderance over the rest of the country, but rather the nature of the government.

London, whose population is as great as that of some kingdoms, has to date not exerted sovereign influence over the fate of Great Britain.

No citizen of the United States imagines that the people of New York can decide the fate of the American union. Indeed, no one even in the state of New York imagines that that city's wishes should be the sole determinant of policy. Yet there are as many people living in New York today as there were living in Paris at the outbreak of the Revolution.

Paris itself, during the Wars of Religion, was as populous compared to the rest of the kingdom as it would be in 1789. Yet it could decide nothing on its own. At the time of the Fronde, it was still only the largest city in France. By 1789 it had become France itself.

In 1740 Montesquieu wrote to a friend: "In France there is only Paris, together with the remote provinces, because Paris has not yet had time to devour them." In 1750, the marquis de Mirabeau, a man of bizarre but at times profound intelligence, spoke of Paris without mentioning it by name: "Capitals are necessary, but if the head grows too large, the body becomes apoplectic, and everything perishes. What will happen, then, if the provinces are reduced to a kind of direct dependency, and provincials are somehow regarded as mere second-class subjects, if they are left with no means to gain recognition and no careers open to ambition, so that all men of any talent are lured to the capital?" He described this as a silent revolution, which would drain the provinces of their leaders and businessmen and those commonly referred to as "men of intellect."

The reader who has attentively read the preceding chapters already knows the causes of this phenomenon, and so to repeat them here would be to try his patience.

The government was not unaware of this revolution, but it was chiefly concerned with its most material manifestation, the growth of the city. It saw Paris growing larger daily and was afraid that it might become difficult to administer such a large city properly. We find a good many royal ordinances, primarily from the seventeenth and eighteenth centuries, whose purpose was to halt this growth. The kings of that time increasingly centralized all public life in Paris or its environs, yet they wanted the capital to remain small. They forbade the building of new houses, or they insisted that new construction must rely on the most costly methods and be confined to the least attractive locations, which were specified in advance. To be sure, each of these ordinances noted that despite the previous one, Paris had not ceased to grow. Six times during the reign of Louis XIV that all-powerful monarch tried and failed to halt the growth of Paris; the city continued to spread without interruption despite his edicts. Its preponderance increased even faster than its walls expanded. What ensured this dominant position was not so much what happened within those walls as what happened outside.

At the same time, in fact, local liberties disappeared everywhere. Everywhere signs of independent life vanished. The distinguishing features of the various provinces grew faint. The last traces of the old public life were erased. This was not because the nation had sunk into torpor, however. On the contrary, movement was apparent everywhere, but now the only motor behind it all was to be found in Paris. I will give but one example among many. Ministerial reports on the state of the book trade show that in the sixteenth century and the beginning of the seventeenth, there had been substantial printing operations in provincial cities from which printers later either vanished or lapsed into inactivity. Yet there can be no doubt that the volume of printed matter of all sorts was far greater at the end of the eighteenth century than at the end of the seventeenth. Thought now emanated only from the center, however. Paris had completely devoured the provinces.

At the outbreak of the French Revolution, this first revolution was fully accomplished.

The celebrated traveler Arthur Young left Paris shortly after the meeting of the Estates General and not long before the storming of the Bastille. The contrast between what he had just seen in the city and what he found outside it astonished him. Paris was all bustle and noise. Each moment yielded a new political pamphlet: as many as ninety-two were published every week. Never, said Young, had he seen such a torrent of publication, not even in London. Outside of Paris, he found only inertia and silence. Few brochures were printed and no newspapers. Yet the provinces were aroused and ready for action, though for the moment still quiet. If citizens assembled, it was to hear news that they were expecting from Paris. In each town Young asked people what they were going to do. "The response was the same everywhere," he said. "We are a provincial town. We must wait to see what is done at Paris." "They dare not even have an opinion of their own," he added, "till they know what Paris thinks."[1]

It is astonishing to discover the surprising ease with which the Constituent Assembly was able to destroy at one fell swoop all the ancient provinces of France, several of which were older than the monarchy itself, and methodically divide the kingdom into eighty-three distinct parts, as if it were dealing with the virgin territory of the New World. Nothing surprised and even terrified the rest of Europe more; it was not prepared for such a spectacle. "I believe the present French power is the very first body of citizens who, having obtained full authority to do with their country what they pleased, have chosen to dissever it in this barbarous manner," Burke wrote. "It was the first time that people butchered their country in such a barbarous manner."[2] It seemed that bodies were being flayed alive, but in fact it was only corpses that were being dismembered.

Even as Paris finally gained omnipotence outside its walls, inside the city another change, no less worthy of the attention of history, was taking place. Paris ceased to be only a city of trade, commerce, consumption,

---

[1] Quoted from Arthur Young, *Travels in France*, p. 201.
[2] From Edmund Burke, *Reflections on the Revolution in France*, in *The Works of Edmund Burke* (New York: Harper, 1860), vol. 1, p. 537.

and pleasure and completed its transition to a city of industry and manufacturing. This second change lent new and greater importance to the first.

The origins of this second change lay in the remote past. It seems that by the Middle Ages, Paris was already the most industrial city in the kingdom, as well as the largest. This fact became more obvious as the modern era approached. As Paris became the focal point of all administrative affairs, industry hastened there as well. As Paris increasingly became the model and arbiter of taste, the sole center of power and of the arts, the principal focus of national activity, the industrial life of the nation withdrew within the city's walls and became more and more concentrated there.

Although the statistical records of the Ancien Régime generally deserve little credibility, I think that one can safely affirm that during the sixty years leading up to the French Revolution, the number of workers in Paris more than doubled, while in the same period the overall population of the city increased by barely a third.

Apart from the general causes discussed here, there were some very special causes that drew workers to Paris from all over France and gradually concentrated them in certain neighborhoods, which in the end they came to occupy almost exclusively. The fetters placed on industry by the fiscal legislation of the time had been rendered less onerous in Paris than anywhere else in France. Nowhere was it easier to escape the yoke of the guild masters. Certain suburbs, such as the Saint-Antoine and Temple Districts, enjoyed very substantial privileges in this respect. Louis XVI greatly increased the prerogatives of Saint-Antoine and did his utmost to settle a huge population of workers there, "wishing," as that unfortunate monarch said in one of his edicts, "to give the workers of the *faubourg* Saint-Antoine a new sign of our protection, and to free them from restraints that are prejudicial not only to their interests but also to the freedom of commerce."

The number of factories, workshops, and blast furnaces in Paris had increased so much in the period just before the Revolution that the government ultimately became alarmed. The sight of this progress provoked some quite imaginary fears. For example, a council decree of 1784 states that "the King, fearful that the rapid growth of factories might lead to a level of wood consumption that would interfere with the city's supply, henceforth forbids the creation of establishments of this kind within a radius of fifteen leagues." No one worried about the real danger to which such a concentration might give rise.

Thus, Paris became the master of France, and already the army was gathering that would make itself master of Paris.

There is fairly wide agreement today, I think, that administrative centralization and Parisian omnipotence played a large part in the fall of all the governments that we have seen succeed one another over the past forty years. It will not be difficult for me to show that the same conjunction of circumstances was largely responsible for the sudden and violent collapse of the old monarchy, and that it must be included among the principal causes of that first revolution of which all the others were offspring.

II.8 – That France Was the Country Where People Had Become Most Alike

Anyone who examines Ancien Régime France closely will come away with two quite different images.

At times it seems that everyone who lived there, particularly those who occupied the middle and upper regions of society – the only ones visible to us – was exactly like everyone else.

Yet within this uniform multitude there remained an astonishing variety of small barriers, which divided the multitude into many different parts, and within each of these enclaves there emerged something like a separate society, which was concerned only with its own interests and did not take part in the life of the whole.

When I think of this almost infinite division and reflect on the fact that nowhere else were citizens less prepared to act in common and help one another out in a time of crisis than in France, I can understand how a great revolution was able to turn such a society upside down in an instant. I can imagine all those little barriers overturned by the great upheaval itself. And when I do this, I immediately see a social body perhaps more compact and homogeneous than the world has ever known.

I have explained how the distinctive life of the various provinces throughout the kingdom had long since been snuffed out. This contributed greatly to making all the French quite similar to one another. Despite persistent diversities, the unity of the nation was already transparent. The uniformity of legislation makes this clear. As we proceed through the eighteenth century, we see a growing number of edicts, royal declarations, and council decrees that apply the same rules in the same way to all parts of the kingdom. It was not only the governors but also the governed who imagined legislation so general and uniform that it could be the same for everyone everywhere. The idea of such legislation can be found in all the reform projects that were proposed one after another during the thirty years leading up to the Revolution. Two centuries earlier, the material basis for such an idea, if I may put it that way, would have been lacking.

Not only were the provinces increasingly alike, but within each province people of different classes also became more and more similar despite the particularities of their condition, at least if we except the lower orders.

Nothing brings this out more clearly than reading the grievance books submitted by the various orders in 1789. It is apparent that the people who drafted these grievances differed profoundly in terms of their interests, yet in all other respects appear to have been similar.

If you study how things proceeded in earlier sessions of the Estates General, you will come away with an entirely different picture: bourgeois and noble then had more common interests and joint concerns. They exhibited far less reciprocal animosity but still seemed to belong to two distinct races.

Time, which had maintained and in many respects aggravated the privileges that separated them, had done a remarkable job of making them similar in every other way.

French nobles had been growing steadily poorer for several centuries. "Despite its privileges, the nobility is daily falling deeper into ruin and annihilation, and the Third Estate is snapping up fortunes," one nobleman sadly observed in 1755. Yet the laws that protected the property of nobles remained the same as always. Nothing in their economic condition seemed to have changed. Nevertheless, they grew poorer everywhere in precise proportion to their loss of power.

One might say that human institutions resemble man himself in that, quite apart from the organs that fulfill the various vital functions, there is an invisible central force, which is the very principle of life. When that life-giving flame is extinguished, the organs may appear to function as before, yet in vain, for everything withers at once and dies. French nobles still had entailments. Indeed, Burke remarks that in his time entailments were more common and obligatory in France than in England, along with primogeniture, perpetual ground rents, and the various things collected under the head of "usage rights." French nobles had been relieved of the very onerous obligation to make war at their own expense, yet their immunity from taxation had been maintained and in fact expanded considerably.

In other words, they retained the indemnity while shedding the burden. In addition, they enjoyed several other pecuniary advantages that their fathers had never possessed. Yet they gradually grew poorer as they lost the habit and spirit of government. Indeed, this gradual impoverishment must bear part of the blame for the great division in landed property that we remarked on previously. The nobleman had ceded his land to the peasants plot by plot, retaining only the seigniorial rents for himself, thereby preserving the appearance rather than the reality of his former estate. Several French provinces, including Limousin, of which Turgot wrote, had only a small, impoverished nobility, which owned almost no land and lived almost exclusively on seigniorial dues and ground rents.

"In this district," said one intendant as early as the beginning of the century, "there are still several thousand noble families, yet not fifteen of them have an income of twenty thousand livres." In 1750, another intendant (for Franche-Comté) sent his successor a briefing of sorts, in which he said: "The nobility of this region is reasonably decent but quite poor, and as proud as it is poor. Its humiliation is proportionate to what it was in the past. It would not be bad policy to maintain it in this impoverished state so as to oblige it to serve us and leave it in need of our assistance." He added: "It is a fraternity that accepts only those who can prove four quarters of nobility. It is not licensed but merely tolerated, and it meets only once a year, in the presence of the intendant. After dining and attending mass together, these nobles return home, some on their Rosinantes, others on foot. The comical aspect of this gathering is something you cannot miss."

This gradual impoverishment of the nobility was more or less visible not only in France but also throughout the continent, where the feudal system was nearing its end, as in France, but had not yet been replaced by a new form of aristocracy. In the German nations along the Rhine, this decadence was especially obvious and quite widely noted. The opposite was true only in England, where the old noble families that had survived had not only preserved but greatly increased their wealth. They remained first in wealth as well as power. The new families that had risen alongside them had merely imitated their opulence without surpassing it.

In France, it seemed that all the property that nobles lost ended in the hands of commoners. It was almost as if the whole of what they gained came at the nobles' expense. Yet no law prevented the bourgeois from ruining himself or helped him to grow rich; he steadily enriched himself nevertheless. Many commoners became as wealthy as the nobleman, and some even wealthier. What is more, the bourgeois's wealth was of the same kind as the noble's: although he usually lived in a town, he often owned fields and sometimes even acquired a seigneury.

Education and lifestyle had already created a thousand other resemblances between the bourgeois and the noble. The former was as well educated as the latter, and – mark this well – his education drew on precisely the same sources. Both were illuminated by the same sun. The education of both had been equally theoretical and literary. Paris, which increasingly became France's sole tutor, ultimately imposed a common mold and style on all intellect.

At the end of the eighteenth century, it was probably still possible to perceive a difference between the manners of the nobility and those of the bourgeoisie, for nothing is slower to achieve equality than that superficial aspect of mores known as manners. At bottom, however, all who stood above the common people resembled one another. They had the same ideas and habits, shared the same tastes, indulged in the same pleasures, read the same books, and spoke the same language. The only remaining difference between them was a matter of rights.

I doubt that this convergence had taken place to the same degree anywhere else, even in England, where the different classes, though solidly attached to one another by common interests, often still differed in regard to intellect and mores because political liberty, which has the admirable power to foster necessary relations and mutual ties of dependence among citizens of all classes, does not always make them similar in doing so. In the long run, it is government by a single individual that always has the inevitable effect of making people both similar to one another and mutually indifferent to the fate of their fellows.

II.9 – How Men So Similar Were More Separate Than Ever, Divided into Small Groups Alien and Indifferent to One Another

Let us now consider the other side of the picture and see how these same Frenchmen, who were alike in so many ways, were nevertheless more isolated from one another than people perhaps anywhere else, and more even than they had ever been previously in France.

It seems quite clear that at the time the feudal system established itself in Europe, what has since come to be called the nobility did not immediately constitute a *caste;* rather, it originally comprised the foremost men and women in the nation and was thus initially merely an aristocracy. This is not an issue I want to discuss here. Suffice it to say that by the Middle Ages, the nobility had become a caste, by which I mean that birth was its distinguishing characteristic.

The nobility did retain one essential characteristic of an aristocracy, that of being a body of citizens who govern, but birth alone decided those who would stand at the head of this body. Anyone who was not born noble was excluded from this closed and separate class and occupied a position in the state that could be high or low but always remained subordinate.

Wherever the feudal system became established on the European continent, it ended in caste. Only in England did it return to aristocracy.

I have always found it astonishing that a fact that sets England apart from all other modern nations, and which alone can explain the peculiarities of its laws, its spirit, and its history, has not drawn even more attention from philosophers and statesmen than it has, and I am surprised that habit has ultimately made it all but invisible to the English themselves. It has been half-noticed and half-described yet, to my mind, never fully and clearly perceived. To be sure, Montesquieu, visiting Great Britain in 1729, wrote: "Here I am in a country that bears little resemblance to the rest of Europe." But to that he adds nothing else.

What made the England of that time so different from the rest of Europe was less its Parliament, its freedom, the public nature of its political debate, and its jury system than something even more specific and influential. England was the only country where the caste system had been not altered but effectively destroyed. Nobles and commoners there jointly followed the same affairs, entered the same professions, and, what is even more significant, intermarried. The daughter of the greatest English lord could already marry a new man without hanging her head in shame.

If you want to know whether caste, together with the ideas, habits, and barriers that it invariably creates, has been definitively eliminated in any nation, look to marriage. There alone will you find the decisive evidence you need. In France, even today, after sixty years of democracy, you would often search in vain. Old and new families that may seem indistinguishable in every respect still avoid mixing in marriage as much as they possibly can.

It has often been said that the English nobility was more cautious, shrewd, and open than any other. What should have been said instead was that, strictly speaking, there has been no nobility in England for quite some time, if one takes the word in the ancient, circumscribed sense that it has retained everywhere else.

This remarkable revolution has vanished into the night of time, but a living token remains: in language. Centuries ago, the word *gentleman* took on an entirely new meaning in England, and the word *commoner* ceased to exist. It would already have been impossible to translate the following line from *Tartuffe* literally into English when Molière wrote it in 1664:

> Et, tel que l'on le voit, il est bon gentilhomme. ("And as you can see, he is a fine gentleman.")

Let us once again apply the science of language to the science of history: trace through space and time the fate of the word *gentleman*, which derives from the French word *gentilhomme*, and you will find that in England its meaning broadened as the gap between the two classes narrowed and noble and commoner began to mingle. As the centuries passed, the word began to be applied to men somewhat lower down the social scale. Ultimately it traveled with the English to America, and there it would be applied indiscriminately to all citizens. Its history coincides with the history of democracy.

In France, the word *gentilhomme* has always remained narrowly circumscribed by its original meaning. Since the Revolution, it has virtually disappeared from common usage, but its meaning never changed. The word, which served to denote the members of the noble caste, was preserved intact because the caste itself had been preserved, as isolated as ever from everyone else.

I am going to press this point much further, however: I contend that the noble caste had become much more isolated than it had been at the time of the word's inception, and that what took place in France was a change in the opposite direction from that which occurred in England.

Although bourgeois and noble became more similar in France, they had also increasingly isolated themselves from each other. We must take great care not to confuse these two phenomena. It is especially important to maintain this distinction because the two changes, instead of attenuating each other's effects, often reinforce them.

In the Middle Ages, and as long as feudalism persisted, anyone who held land of the lord (and who was therefore called his *vassal*, in feudal terminology) regularly joined the lord in governing the manor, even though the vassal was often not a noble. Indeed, participation in the government of the manor was the principal condition of his tenure. Not only was the vassal obliged to follow the lord in battle; he was also required, by virtue of the title to his property, to spend a certain part of the year at the lord's court, that is, to assist in the work of dispensing justice and administering the estate. The lord's court was the main cog in the machinery of feudal government. It figures in all the old laws of Europe. In our own day, I have found what are quite obviously vestiges of those laws in several parts of Germany. Edme de Fréminville, the learned scholar of feudal law who, thirty years before the French Revolution, wrote a thick book on feudal dues and the revision of the *terriers*, or land registers, tells us that he found in "the titles of any number of estates that the vassals were obliged to appear every two weeks at the lord's court, where they sat together with the lord or his regular judge and heard accusations and complaints that had arisen among the residents." He added that he found "in some cases eighty, in others a hundred and fifty, and in still others as many as two hundred of these vassals on one estate. A great many of them were commoners." I cite this here not as proof – there are countless others – but as an example of the way in which originally, and for a long time thereafter, the upper echelon of rural commoners approached the class of *gentilshommes* and regularly mingled with them in the conduct of joint business. What the lord's court did for small rural landowners, the provincial estates and later the Estates General did for the bourgeois of the towns.

It is impossible to study the surviving records of the Estates General of the fourteenth century without being astonished by the place that the Third Estate occupied and the power it exercised in those assemblies.

As an individual, the bourgeois of the fourteenth century was no doubt quite inferior to the bourgeois of the eighteenth, but the bourgeoisie as a body occupied a higher and more secure place in the political society of that earlier time. Its right to participate in government was uncontested. It always played an important and often a preponderant role in political assemblies. The other classes constantly felt the need to take its wishes into account.

What is most striking, however, is that the nobility and Third Estate then found it easier to administer affairs jointly, and to mount joint resistance to the central government, than they would later on. This can be seen not only in the Estates General of the fourteenth century, several of which assumed, because of the misfortunes of that era, an irregular and revolutionary character, but also in the provincial estates of the same period, which show no sign of having proceeded in anything other than the usual and regular fashion. Thus, for example, in Auvergne we see the three orders taking the most important decisions in common and choosing commissioners from the ranks of all three to oversee the execution of those decisions. We find the same thing happening in this period in Champagne. Everyone is familiar with the celebrated declaration whereby the nobles and bourgeois of many towns joined together at the beginning of the fourteenth century to defend the freedoms granted to the nation and the privileges awarded to their provinces against the encroachments of royal power. One finds in this period of our history any number of such episodes, which read like pages taken from the history of England. Nothing of the kind can be seen in subsequent centuries.

Indeed, as the government of the manor broke down, as meetings of the Estates General became increasingly infrequent or ceased altogether, and as general liberties finally succumbed, taking local liberties down with them, the bourgeois and the noble ceased to make contact in the conduct of public affairs. They no longer felt any need to come together or to reach an understanding. As they became steadily more independent, they also became more alienated from each other. By the eighteenth century this revolution was complete: bourgeois and noble no longer met at all, except by chance in private life. No longer were the two classes merely rivals; they had become enemies.

What seems quite peculiar to France, moreover, is the fact that even as the nobility as an order was thus losing its political powers, the noble as individual was acquiring a number of privileges that he had never before possessed, or increasing those which were already his. One might say that the limbs gained at the expense of the body. The nobility less and less enjoyed the right to command, but nobles more and more claimed the exclusive prerogative of being the principal servants of the master. It had been easier for a commoner to become an officer under Louis XIV than it was under Louis XVI. This type of promotion was common in Prussia when it was almost unheard of in France. Every privilege, once obtained, adhered to the blood; blood and privilege became inseparable. The more the nobility ceased to be an aristocracy, the more it seemed to become a caste.

Let us take the most odious of all these privileges, exemption from taxation. It is easy to see that tax exemptions grew steadily in France from the fifteenth century to the time of the French Revolution. The value of an exemption increased because public expenditure grew rapidly. When the taille yielded 1,200,000 livres under Charles VII, exemption was a minor privilege. When it yielded 80 million under Louis XVI, it was major. When the taille was the only tax on commoners, the noble exemption was not particularly glaring, but when taxes of this type proliferated under a thousand different names and in a thousand different forms, when four other taxes were assimilated to the basic charge, and when exactions unknown in the Middle Ages, such as the compulsory labor on public works, militia service, and other requirements were added to the mix, the noble exemption seemed immense. The inequality, though great, was, to be sure, more apparent than real, for the noble was often affected indirectly, through his tenants, by the tax from which he was himself exempt. But in such matters, the inequality one sees is more painful than the inequality one feels.

Louis XIV, pressed by the financial necessities that overwhelmed him at the end of his reign, had established two common taxes, the capitation and the *vingtièmes*. Nevertheless, as if tax exemption were in itself a privilege so worthy of respect that it had to be honored even in the breach, care was taken to ensure that even though the tax was common to all, the manner of collection would differ. For some it remained degrading and harsh, for others indulgent and honorable.

Although inequality with respect to taxes was established throughout the European continent, there were few countries in which it had become as visible and persistently painful as it was in France. Throughout much of Germany, most taxes were indirect. Even when taxes were direct, the privilege of the noble often consisted in paying a smaller share of the common charge. There were, moreover, certain taxes that fell exclusively on the nobility and were intended as a substitute for unremunerated military service, which was no longer required.

Of all the ways of distinguishing men and marking class divisions, unequal taxation is the most pernicious and the most apt to add isolation to inequality, rendering both incurable. Consider its effects: when the bourgeois and the noble are no longer subject to the same tax, the annual assessment and collection of taxes will reaffirm the clear, sharp class boundary that divides them. Year after year, each beneficiary of privilege will feel an immediate and urgent need to differentiate himself from the masses and renew his effort to set himself apart.

Since nearly every matter of public interest either arises from a tax or culminates in one, once the two classes are not subject to equal taxation they have virtually no reason to deliberate together and no occasion to experience common needs or sentiments. It is no longer necessary to keep them apart since the opportunity and desire to act together have in a sense been eliminated.

Burke, in the flattering portrait he paints of our ancient constitution, counts in favor of the institution of nobility in France the ease with which the bourgeois could obtain ennoblement by acquiring some office. This seemed to him in some ways analogous to England's open aristocracy. Louis XI did in fact increase the number of ennoblements. He did so in order to debase the nobility. His successors offered an even greater number of ennoblements in order to raise money. Necker tells us that in his day, the number of offices that conferred nobility was as high as four thousand. Nothing like this existed anywhere else in Europe, but the analogy that Burke sought to establish between France and England is all the more inaccurate because of it.

If the English middle classes, far from making war on aristocracy, have remained so intimately tied to it, the reason is not primarily that this aristocracy was open but, rather, as has been noted, that its shape was ill-defined and its boundary unknown. It was not so much because it was possible to join the aristocracy as because one never knew when one had succeeded in doing so. Hence, anyone who approached it could believe that he was part of it, join it in governing, and derive some luster or profit from its power.

In France, however, the barrier that separated the nobility from the other classes, though quite permeable, was always fixed and visible, and always recognizable by signs that were unmistakable and odious to those who remained outside. Once that barrier was breached, a person was set apart from everyone who remained in the milieu from which he had sprung by privileges that they found onerous and humiliating.

The system of ennoblements, far from diminishing the commoner's hatred of the nobleman, increased it beyond all measure. It was a hatred embittered by all the envy that the new noble inspired in his erstwhile equals. That is why the grievance books of the Third Estate invariably show greater animosity toward the ennobled than toward the old nobility, and why, far from demanding that the gateway out of common status be widened, they continually demanded that it be narrowed.

In no other period of French history was it so easy to acquire a title of nobility as in 1789, and yet the gap between bourgeois and noble had never been so great. Not only did nobles refuse to tolerate in their electoral assemblies anything that smacked of the bourgeoisie, but the bourgeois were equally firm in rejecting anyone who had the appearance of a nobleman. In some provinces, the newly ennobled were rejected on one side because they were not noble enough and on the other because they were already too noble. This is said to have been the case with the celebrated Lavoisier.

When we turn from the nobility to the bourgeoisie, we are confronted with a similar spectacle, as the bourgeois was almost as distant from the people as the noble was from the bourgeois.

Nearly all of the middle class lived in the towns under the Ancien Régime. There were two main reasons for this: noble privileges and the taille. The lord who lived on his estate usually displayed a certain familiar bonhomie toward his peasants, but his insolence toward the bourgeois, his neighbors, was almost without limit. That insolence did not stop growing as the noble's political power decreased, and, indeed, because it decreased, for, on the one hand, having ceased to govern, the noble no longer had any interest in indulging those who might help him with that task, while, on the other hand, as has often been noted, he liked to make immoderate use of his apparent rights in order to console himself for the loss of his real power. His very absence from his estate, rather than relieve his neighbors discomfited them even more. Absenteeism failed to alleviate the burden, because privileges exercised by proxy were all the more intolerable.

Still, I am not sure that the taille and other related taxes were not even more effective causes of discontent.

I could explain, I think, and in rather few words, why the taille and its associated levies weighed far more heavily on the countryside than on the towns, but to do so might strike the reader as pointless. Suffice it to say, therefore, that the bourgeoisie gathered in the towns had a thousand ways of alleviating the burden of the taille and often of evading it altogether, yet none of these means of evasion would have been available to them individually had they remained on their estates. More important still, they thus avoided the obligation to collect the tax, which they feared even more than the obligation to pay it, and rightly so, for there was never a worse position to be in under the Ancien Régime, or, I think, under any regime, than that of parish collector of the taille. I will have occasion to demonstrate this later on. Yet no one in the village, other than nobles, could evade this burden. Rather than accept it, the wealthy commoner rented out his land and withdrew to the closest town. Turgot corroborates the many secret documents I was able to consult when he tells us that "the collection of the taille transformed nearly all non-noble rural landholders into bourgeois living in the towns." In passing, it is worth noting that this is one reason why France had more towns, and especially more small towns, than most other European countries.

Thus ensconced inside town walls, the wealthy commoner soon forgot the flavor and spirit of rural life. He altogether lost touch with the travails and concerns of those of his peers who continued to live in the countryside. His life now had but one goal, as it were: he aspired to become a public official in his adoptive town.

It is a very serious error to believe that the passion that nearly all Frenchmen, and especially middle-class Frenchmen, feel today for public positions did not emerge until after the Revolution. It originated several centuries earlier, and since then it has grown steadily, feeding on a thousand carefully nurtured sources.

Public offices under the Ancien Régime were not always like ours, but there were, I believe, even more of them. The number of minor posts was virtually unlimited. It has been calculated that some forty thousand were created between 1693 and 1709 alone, and nearly all were within reach of the lowliest bourgeois. I found that in one rather small provincial town in 1750, there were as many as 109 individuals involved with dispensing justice and 126 others charged with carrying out their orders, all town residents. The ardor of the bourgeois to fill these posts was truly unrivaled. As soon as a bourgeois found himself in possession of a small capital, instead of investing it in trade he immediately sought to purchase a position. This squalid ambition did more to prevent progress in French agriculture and commerce than guild regulations or even the taille. When there were no positions to be had, job seekers put their imaginations to work and soon invented new ones. One Sieur Lamberville published a memoir proving that it was entirely compatible with the public interest to create inspectors for a certain industry, and he concluded by proposing himself for the job. Who among us has not known this Lamberville? Anyone who had some education and a modest fortune did not feel it proper to die without having served as a public official. As one contemporary put it, "Each man, according to his situation, wishes to be something by royal appointment."

In this respect, the greatest difference between the time I am describing here and our own is that the government then sold positions, whereas the government today gives them away. To acquire a post today, a man does not put up a sum of cash; he goes even farther and offers himself.

The bourgeois was separated from the peasant not only by place of residence and, even more, way of life but also, quite often, by interest. People complained with a good deal of justice about the noble privilege of exemption from taxation, but what about the privileges of the bourgeois? Thousands of offices exempted them, in whole or in part, from such public charges as serving in the militia or in compulsory labor details or paying the taille. One contemporary writer asked if there was any parish that did not count among its inhabitants several individuals other than nobles and ecclesiastics who had obtained some sort of tax exemption by way of an official post or commission. One of the reasons why a certain number of offices intended for the bourgeoisie were abolished from time to time was that the exemption of so many people from the taille resulted in smaller tax revenues. I have no doubt that the number of exemptions granted to the bourgeoisie was as large as the number granted to the nobility, and often larger.

These wretched privileges aroused the envy of those who did not enjoy them, as well as the most selfish pride of those who did. Throughout the eighteenth century, the hostility of the town bourgeois toward the peasants of the surrounding countryside was unmistakable, as was the country neighbors' jealousy of the town. "Each town," Turgot wrote, "being occupied with its own particular interest, is prepared to sacrifice the surrounding countryside and villages to it." Elsewhere, speaking to his subdelegates, he says: "You have often been compelled to counter the tendency of the towns to behave in a presumptuous and invasive manner toward the country and villages in their district."

The lower classes who lived alongside the bourgeois inside town walls became alienated from them as well, and almost enemies. Most of the local charges that the bourgeois established were designed to weigh particularly heavily on the lower classes. On more than one occasion, I was able to corroborate what Turgot says in another place in his work, that the bourgeois of the towns had found a way to levy duties on goods entering the town without having to bear the cost themselves.

What one sees above all in the actions of this bourgeoisie, however, is the fear that they might be conflated with the lower orders, as well as a passionate desire to evade any check that those lower orders might wish to place on their actions.

In a memorandum to the comptroller general, the bourgeois of one town said: "If it please the king to allow the office of mayor to become elective once again, it would be appropriate to require the electors to restrict their choice to the leading men of the town, and even to members of the presidial."

We have already seen how our kings made it their policy to deprive the people of the towns of the use of their political rights, one after another. From Louis XI to Louis XV, this intention is evident in all royal legislation. In many cases, the bourgeois of the town associated themselves with this policy, and sometimes they suggested it.

At the time of the municipal reform of 1764, one intendant consulted the municipal officials of a small town about whether artisans and "other commoners" should retain the right to vote for magistrates. The officials replied that, in fact, "the people have never abused this right, and it would no doubt be a kindness if the consolation they derive from choosing those who are to have command over them were maintained, but for the sake of good order and public tranquility it would be better still to rely on the assembly of notables." Meanwhile, the subdelegate reported that he had convened a secret meeting of "the six best citizens of the town." These six best citizens unanimously agreed that the best course of action would be to entrust the election not even to the assembly of notables, as the municipal officials had proposed, but to a certain number of deputies chosen from the various corporations of which that assembly was composed. The subdelegate, who was more tolerant of the people's liberties than these bourgeois, passed along their view but added "that it is nevertheless quite hard for these artisans to pay the sums imposed on them by their fellow citizens without being able to control how this money is used, especially when the fellow citizens in question, being exempt from taxation themselves, are perhaps the least interested in the question."

To complete the portrait, let us now consider the bourgeoisie in itself, apart from the common people, just as we considered the nobility apart from the bourgeois. In this tiny portion of the nation, set apart from the rest, we find endless divisions. It seems that the French people are like those supposedly elementary substances in which modern chemistry, as it studies them more closely, finds new particles that can be separated one from another. I found no fewer than thirty-six different bodies among the notables of one small town. These various bodies, though quite tiny, strove endlessly to make themselves still smaller. They daily endeavored to purge themselves of any heterogeneous parts they might contain so as to leave only the purest elements. With admirable effort, some of these bodies succeeded in reducing themselves to three or four members. Their character only became more acerbic as a result, and their disposition more quarrelsome. Each of these bodies was distinguished by certain petty privileges, of which even the least honest were taken to be signs of honor.

Eternal battles raged about which among them was to enjoy priority. The intendant and the courts grew tired of their raucous quarrels: "It has finally been decided that the holy water shall be given to the presidial before being given to the town corporation. The Parlement hesitated, but the king's council assumed jurisdiction in the case and decided on its own. It was high time; the case had the entire town in turmoil." If one corporation was granted priority over another in the general assembly of notables, the losing group would refuse to attend. It would rather turn its back on public affairs altogether than suffer what it regarded as an affront to its dignity. The wigmakers' guild in the town of La Flèche decided "to express by these means its justified pain at the award of priority to the bakers." Some notables in one town stubbornly refused to do their duty, the intendant reported, "because certain artisans had gained admission to the assembly, and the leading bourgeois found it humiliating to be associated with them." In another province, the intendant said that "if the post of alderman is given to a notary, it will disgust the other notables because notaries here are people of low birth who do not belong to notable families and all began as clerks." The six "best citizens" whom I mentioned earlier, who so readily decided that the people were to be deprived of their political rights, found themselves strangely perplexed when it came to deciding who should count as notables and what order of precedence should be established among them. In this matter they were gripped with modesty and filled with doubt. They were afraid, they said, "of inflicting too sharp a pain on some of our fellow citizens."

The natural vanity of the French was strengthened and sharpened by the constant friction among these self-obsessed little groups, and the legitimate pride of citizenship fell into oblivion. In the sixteenth century, most of the corporate bodies I have been discussing already existed, but their members, after dispatching the affairs of their particular association among themselves, regularly joined with all the other inhabitants to consider the town's general interests. In the eighteenth century, such groups were almost entirely turned inward because transactions involving town business had become rare and were always handled by delegates. Hence, each of these little societies lived for itself alone, was concerned only with itself, and transacted no business that did not affect it directly.

Our fathers did not have the word *individualism*, which we have forged for our own use, because in their day there was no such thing as an individual who did not belong to a group and could see himself as standing absolutely alone; yet each of the thousand small groups of which French society was composed thought only of itself. It was, if I may put it this way, a sort of collective individualism, which prepared souls for the true individualism that we have come to know.

What is stranger still, moreover, was that all these men who remained so aloof from one another had become so similar that had they been forced to change places, they would have been unrecognizable. More than that, anyone capable of sounding the depths of their minds would have discovered that all the petty barriers that divided these very similar people from one another struck them as both inimical to the public interest and hostile to common sense; in theory they already adored unity. Each of them clung to his own particular status only because others distinguished themselves by theirs, but all were ready to meld into a single mass, provided that no one else could claim any advantage for himself or rise above the common level.

II.10 – How the Destruction of Political Liberty and the Separation of Classes Caused Nearly All the Maladies That Proved Fatal to the Ancien Régime

Of all the maladies that afflicted the constitution of the Ancien Régime and condemned it to perish, I have just described the most mortal. I want now to take another look at the source of this most strange and dangerous malady and show how many other ills stemmed from it as well.

If, beginning in the Middle Ages, the English had lost all of their political liberty and all the local freedoms that cannot survive for long without it, the various classes that make up their aristocracy would more than likely have split apart from one another, as happened not only in France but also, to one degree or another, on the rest of the continent, while at the same time they would have separated themselves as a group from the people. But liberty forced all classes to maintain contact with one another so that when necessary they could find common ground.

It is interesting to observe how the English nobility, driven by ambition, was able to mingle with its inferiors and treat them as equals whenever it saw the need to do so. Arthur Young, whom I quoted earlier, and whose book is one of the most instructive works about old France that exists, tells how one day he happened to find himself at the country home of the duc de Liancourt, to whom he mentioned his wish to question some of the cleverer and wealthier farmers of the region. The duke then ordered his steward to bring the farmers to his guest, prompting this observation by the Englishman: "At an English nobleman's, there would have been three or four farmers asked to meet me, who would have dined with the family amongst the ladies of the first rank. I have had this at least an hundred times in the first houses of our islands. It is, however, a thing that in the present state of manners in France would not be met with from Calais to Bayonne."[1]

To be sure, the English aristocracy was by nature haughtier than the French and less inclined to mingle with people of inferior rank, but the necessities of its condition compelled it to do so. It was prepared to do anything to remain in command. For centuries, the only inequalities in English taxes have been those introduced from time to time for the benefit of the needy classes. I beg you to consider where different political principles can lead such similar peoples. In the eighteenth century in England, it was the poor man who enjoyed the tax privilege; in France it was the rich man. There, the aristocracy took the heaviest public responsibilities on itself so that it would be allowed to govern; here it retained the tax exemption to the end to console itself for having lost the government.

In the fourteenth century, the maxim "no taxation without consent" seemed as firmly established in France as in England. It was often cited: to go against it always seemed an act of tyranny, to abide by it to accept the rule of law. In this period we find, as I mentioned previously, many similarities between our political institutions and those of the English. Subsequently, however, the destinies of the two nations diverged and became increasingly dissimilar as time went by. Their fates were like two lines that start from adjacent points but at slightly different slopes and, therefore, grow ever farther apart the longer they extend.

I dare to affirm that on the day the nation, tired of the interminable disorders that had accompanied the captivity of King John and the dementia of Charles VI, allowed kings to levy a general tax without its consent, and when the nobility was cowardly enough to allow the Third Estate to be taxed provided that it remained exempt – on that day the seed was sown of practically all the vices and abuses that ravaged the Ancien Régime for the remainder of its existence and ultimately led to its violent death. I admire, moreover, the singular sagacity of Commynes when he said: "Charles VII, who won the argument over imposing the taille as he wished, without the consent of the estates, laid a heavy burden on his soul

---

[1] Arthur Young, *Travels in France*, p. 146. Young here refers to his host as the duc de La Rochefoucauld.

and the souls of his successors and inflicted on his kingdom a wound that would bleed for a long time thereafter."

Indeed, think how that wound has gaped wider over the years. Follow its consequences step by step.

As Forbonnais rightly says in his learned *Recherches sur les finances de la France*, in the Middle Ages kings generally lived on the income from their estates. "And," he adds, "since extraordinary needs were provided for by extraordinary contributions, they fell equally on the clergy, the nobility, and the people."

Most of the general taxes approved by vote of the three orders in the fourteenth century are in fact of this type. Nearly all the taxes established in this period were *indirect*, which is to say, they were paid by all consumers, without distinction. Sometimes the tax was direct; it then fell not on property but on income. Nobles, ecclesiastics, and bourgeois were required, for example, to sacrifice to the king a tenth of their income for one year. What I say here about taxes approved by a vote of the Estates General applies as well to those established in the same period by the various provincial estates within their territories.

It is true that the direct tax known as the taille already spared the noble. The obligation to provide unpaid military service dispensed him from that obligation. But the taille, as a general tax, was at that time sparingly used and applicable more to the manor than to the kingdom as a whole.

When the king attempted to levy taxes on his own authority for the first time, he realized that it would be necessary initially to choose one that did not appear to fall directly on nobles, because in those days they constituted a class that stood as a dangerous rival to the monarchy and would never have tolerated an innovation so prejudicial to themselves. He therefore chose a tax from which they were exempt: the taille.

Thus, to all the particular inequalities that already existed was added a more general inequality, which aggravated and perpetuated all the others. From that point on, as the needs of the Public Treasury grew apace with the prerogatives of the central government, the taille was extended and diversified. Soon it was multiplied tenfold, and all new taxes became tailles. Every year, inequality of taxation therefore separated classes and isolated individuals to a greater degree than ever before. From the moment the purpose of taxation became not to tax those most capable of paying but to tap those least capable of defending themselves, there was no escaping this monstrous consequence: spare the rich and burden the poor. It is said on good authority that Mazarin, in need of cash, thought of levying a tax on the leading Parisian houses, but when he encountered resistance on the part of those who would have been affected, he limited himself to adding the 5 million he needed to the general levy of the taille. He had wanted to tax the most opulent citizens but ended up taxing the poorest. The treasury, however, lost nothing as a result.

The yield of such ill-distributed taxes had limits, while the needs of princes no longer did. Nevertheless, they did not wish to convoke the estates to obtain subsidies from them, nor did they wish to tax the nobility and thus provoke it into calling for such a convocation.

The result was the prodigious and noxious fecundity of the financial mind, which was so strikingly characteristic a feature of the administration of public funds during the final three centuries of the monarchy.

One must study the administrative and financial history of the Ancien Régime in detail in order to understand the violent and dishonest practices to which the need for money can reduce a government that is benevolent but lacking in public oversight or control, once time has consecrated its power and delivered it from the fear of revolution – that ultimate safeguard of the people.

On every page of the monarchy's annals one finds royal property being sold and then confiscated on the grounds that it was inalienable. One comes across broken contracts and settled rights ignored. With each new crisis, the state's creditors are sacrificed, and the public trust is endlessly deceived.

Privileges granted in perpetuity were perpetually revoked. Were it possible to sympathize with the discomfiture born of foolish vanity, one might pity the fate of those ennobled unfortunates who, throughout the seventeenth and eighteenth centuries, were required from time to time to buy back the futile honors and unjust privileges for which they had already paid several times. For instance, Louis XIV annulled all titles of nobility granted during the previous ninety-two years, most of which had been granted by himself. They could be kept only if an additional sum was forthcoming, "all these titles having been obtained without our knowledge," according to the edict. The precedent was one that Louis XV did not fail to follow eighty years later.

The militiaman was forbidden to pay someone else to replace him, for fear, it was said, that this would drive up the cost to the state of new recruits.

Towns, communities, and hospitals were forced to renege on their commitments so that they would have the wherewithal to lend to the king. Parishes were prevented from undertaking useful projects for fear that if they dispersed their resources in this way, they would be less scrupulous in paying the taille.

The story is told that M. Orry and M. Trudaine, respectively comptroller general and director general of the Department of Bridges and Roads, came up with the idea of replacing compulsory road work with a cash payment to be made by the residents of each canton for the purpose of repairing their roads. The reason why these clever administrators were obliged to give up on their plan is instructive: they were afraid, it was said, that if such funds were collected, nothing could prevent the Public Treasury from diverting them for its own use, so that before long the taxpayers would have been forced to bear the burden of both the new tax and the compulsory road work. I do not hesitate to say that no private individual could have avoided running afoul of the courts had he managed his own wealth as the great king, in all his glory, managed the public's wealth.

Wherever you find either an ancient medieval establishment that defied the spirit of the age, continuing to exist while its flaws grew worse, or some pernicious innovation, delve down to the root of the evil: there you will find a financial expedient that was transformed into an institution. To pay the day's debts, new powers were instituted, which would endure for centuries.

In the very distant past, a special tax called the *droit de franc-fief* was levied on commoners who owned noble lands. This tax established a division between plots of land identical to that which existed between individuals, and these distinctions systematically reinforced each other. I am not sure that the *droit de franc-fief* did not do more than all the rest to keep the commoner and noble apart, because it prevented them from losing their identities through the one thing that most quickly and effectively eliminates distinctions among men, namely, the ownership of land. Thus, at intervals the gap was widened between the property of the noble and the property of his neighbor, the commoner. By contrast, nothing did more to hasten the cohesion of these two classes in England than the abolition in the seventeenth century of all signs distinguishing the fief from common land tenure.

In the fourteenth century, the feudal due of *franc-fief* was light and infrequently collected, but in the eighteenth century, when feudalism was almost destroyed, it was levied without fail every twenty years and represented a full year's income. A son paid it upon inheriting from his father. In 1761, the Agricultural Society of Tours said that "this tax does untold damage to progress in the agricultural art. Of all the taxes levied on the king's subjects, there is surely none whose sting is as onerous to rural France."

Another contemporary voice says that "this tax, which at first was collected only once in a lifetime, has since then become a very cruel burden." The nobility itself would have liked to see the tax abolished because it prevented commoners from buying noble land, but the needs of the treasury required that it be maintained and increased.

The Middle Ages are wrongly blamed for all the ills due to industrial guilds. All the evidence suggests that guild masters and juries were merely devices for establishing ties among people practicing the same trade and for setting up a small free government in each industry, whose mission was both to assist workers and to contain them. Saint Louis appears not to have wanted anything more.

It was not until the beginning of the sixteenth century, in the midst of the Renaissance, that for the first time the right to work was conceived of as a privilege, which the king could sell. Only then did each trade group become a small, closed aristocracy, until ultimately we witness the establishment of the monopolies that did so much to impede progress in the arts and so much to arouse our fathers' ire. From Henry III, who generalized the evil if he did not create it, to Louis XVI, who eliminated it, it is fair to say that the abuses of the guild system never for a moment ceased to grow and spread, even as social progress made them more unbearable and public reason focused more attention on their existence. Every year new trades ceased to be free; every year the privileges of the old ones were increased. Never was the malady more extensive than it became in what are usually called the golden years of the reign of Louis XIV, because the need for money was never greater and the determination not to appeal to the nation never firmer.

Letrosne was right to say in 1775 that "the state established industrial communities only to draw upon their resources, at times by selling licenses, at other times by creating new offices, which the communities were forced to buy. The edict of 1673 drew the ultimate consequences of the principles laid down by Henri III, by compelling all the communities to purchase letters of confirmation. Furthermore, all craftsmen who did not yet belong to a community were forced to join. This squalid affair yielded 300,000 livres."

We have seen how the constitutions of the towns were entirely over-turned, not for any political purpose but in the hope of obtaining resources with which to fill the treasury.

The same need for money, coupled with the desire not to request it of the estates, gave rise to the practice of selling offices, which gradually turned into something so peculiar that nothing like it had ever been seen anywhere in the world. Thanks to this institution, a product of the fiscal spirit, the vanity of the Third Estate had been held rapt for three centuries and directed exclusively toward the acquisition of public office, and the universal passion for position was instilled into the entrails of the nation, where it became the common source of both revolutions and servitude.

As financial difficulties grew, new charges were created, all rewarded with tax exemptions and privileges. And since it was the needs of the treasury rather than of the administration that mattered, an almost incredible number of totally useless or even harmful positions were established. In 1664, a survey instigated by Colbert found that the amount of capital invested in this miserable form of property totaled nearly 500 million livres. Richelieu is said to have destroyed a hundred thousand offices. They were immediately reborn under different names. In exchange for a small sum of money, the government deprived itself of the right to direct, control, and constrain its own agents. In this way, it gradually constructed an administrative machine so vast, complicated, cumbersome, and unproductive that it had to be allowed to turn to no purpose, as it were, while a simpler and more manageable instrument of government was built alongside it in order to carry out the functions that all those officials merely seemed to perform.

Surely none of these detestable institutions would have lasted twenty years had discussion of them been allowed. None would have been established or exacerbated had the estates been consulted, or had their complaints been listened to when they were still convened from time to time. The rare Estates General of the last centuries inveighed endlessly against these institutions. On several occasions we find the estates pointing to the power that the king arrogated to himself to raise taxes arbitrarily as the origin of all the abuses. Or, to put it in the energetic language of the fifteenth century, they blamed "the power of the king to batten on the flesh of the people without the consent and deliberation of the three estates." They were not concerned solely with their own rights.

They forcefully insisted upon, and often obtained, respect for the rights of provinces and towns as well. With each new session, voices were raised in the estates against inequality of taxation. The estates repeatedly called for elimination of the guild system. They attacked, more and more forcefully from one century to the next, the sale of offices. "Whoever sells an office sells justice," they said, "which is an infamous thing." After the venality of offices was established, they continued to complain about the abuse of office. They spoke out against useless posts and dangerous privileges, but always to no avail. Indeed, these institutions were directed at none other than themselves. They arose out of a desire not to convene the estates and from a need to disguise from the French people a tax that could not be shown in its true guise.

Note that the best kings resorted to these practices as well as the worst. It was Louis XII who finally established the sale of offices, while it was Henri IV who made the sold offices hereditary: the vices of the system were so much stronger than the virtue of the men who availed themselves of it.

The same desire to escape the tutelage of the estates led to the attribution to the parlements of most of their political prerogatives. This hobbled the judicial power in government in a way that was highly prejudicial to the orderly conduct of public business. There was a need to appear to provide new guarantees in place of those that had been eliminated because the French, who will put up rather patiently with absolute power as long as it is not oppressive, never like the sight of it, and it is always wise to raise some apparent barriers in front of it, barriers that cannot stop it but nevertheless hide it a little.

Finally, it was this desire, when asking the nation for money, to prevent it from asking to have its liberty restored that made it necessary to keep a constant eye on the classes, in order to prevent them from coming together in common resistance and to make sure that the government would never have to deal at any one time with more than a few individuals separated from all the rest. Throughout this long history, which witnessed the emergence of so many remarkable princes – some remarkable for their wit, others for their genius, and nearly all for their courage – we find not one who made the effort to bring the classes together and unify them, unless it was to make them all equally dependent. But wait, I am wrong: one and only one did want this and devoted himself to it with all his heart. And – who can fathom the judgments of God! – that one was Louis XVI.

The division of the classes was the crime of the old monarchy and later became its excuse, for when the wealthiest and best-educated segments of the nation can no longer find common ground and cooperate in government, it becomes all but impossible for the country to administer itself, and a master must intervene.

"The nation," Turgot sadly reported to the king, "is a society made up of various orders, which are poorly unified, and of a people comprising individuals with very few bonds between them, so that each one is concerned only with his own particular interest. Nowhere is an obvious common interest to be found. Villages and towns have no more mutual relations than the districts to which they are assigned. They cannot even agree among themselves to undertake necessary public works. In this perpetual war of claims and projects, Your Majesty is obliged to decide every case either by himself or through his delegates. Your specific orders are awaited before anyone will contribute to the public good, respect the rights of others, or, in some cases, exercise his own rights."

It is no small undertaking to bring together citizens who have lived for centuries as strangers or enemies and teach them to take joint responsibility for their own affairs. It was easier to divide them than it is to unite them. We have provided the world with a memorable example of this. When the various classes that made up the society of old France resumed contact with one another some sixty years ago after having been isolated by so many barriers for so long, they at first rubbed each other's sorest spots and renewed acquaintances, only to tear each other apart. Indeed, their jealousies and hatreds survive to this day.

II.11 – On the Kind of Liberty to Be Found under the Ancien Régime and Its Influence on the Revolution

If the reader were to stop reading this book now, he would come away with a highly imperfect image of the government of the Ancien Régime and a poor understanding of the society that made the Revolution.

Having seen citizens so divided and withdrawn into themselves and a monarchical government so extensive and powerful, he might think that the spirit of independence had disappeared along with all public liberties and that all the French were equally acquiescent in their subjection. This was not the case at all, however. The government had already achieved sole and absolute control of all common affairs, but it was still a long way from being the master of every individual.

In the midst of many institutions already prepared for absolute power, liberty lived, but it was a singular sort of liberty, which is difficult to grasp today and which must be examined closely if we wish to understand the good and evil it may have done to us.

While the central government supplanted all local powers and increasingly filled the entire sphere of public authority, certain institutions that it had either allowed to survive or itself created, along with old customs, ancient mores, and even abuses, impeded its movements, sustained a spirit of resistance in the minds of many, and left intact the resolve and firmness in the character of countless individuals.

Centralization already had the same nature, the same procedures, and the same goals as it has today, but not yet the same power. The government, in its desire to turn everything into money, had put most public offices up for sale and thus deprived itself of the ability to grant and revoke them at will. One of its passions had therefore seriously undermined the other, greed thwarting ambition. In order to act, it was thus repeatedly forced to rely on instruments it did not make and could not break. Hence, it often saw its most absolute will sapped in execution. This bizarre and flawed constitution of public functions served as a substitute for any kind of political guarantee against the omnipotence of the central government. It was an irregular and badly constructed dike that dispersed the government's force and blunted its impact.

Furthermore, the government did not yet have at its disposal the infinite variety of favors, assistance, honors, and cash to distribute that it has today. It thus had fewer ways either to induce or to compel.

What is more, the government itself had only imperfect knowledge of the precise limits of its power. None of its prerogatives were acknowledged as legitimate or firmly established. Its sphere of action was already immense, but it still proceeded warily, as if on obscure and unfamiliar ground. The terrifying shadows that hid the limits of power and shrouded all rights encouraged princes in their attacks on the liberty of their subjects but also served frequently to defend that same liberty.

The administration, aware of its recent origins and low birth, was timid in its approach to every obstacle. When one reads the correspondence of eighteenth-century ministers and intendants, it is striking to see how the government, which could be so overbearing and absolute as long as obedience was unquestioned, could be struck dumb by the sight of the least resistance. The slightest criticism disturbed it; the most minor protest terrified it. And then it would stop, hesitate, deliberate, take temperate steps, and often remain well within the natural limits of its power. The compliant egotism of Louis XV and the kindness of his successor lent themselves to such behavior. What is more, neither of these princes ever imagined that anyone might dream of dethroning them. They had none of the anxious, harsh temperament that fear often imparted to those who governed after them. They trampled only on people they did not see.

Any number of the privileges, prejudices, and false ideas that did the most to impede the establishment of lawful and beneficial liberty maintained a spirit of independence in many subjects and led them to resist abuses of authority.

Nobles deeply despised the administration (in the strict sense of the word), although they did on occasion petition it for favors. Even after relinquishing their former power, they retained something of the pride of their ancestors, a pride that was as hostile to servitude as it was to regulation. They showed little concern for the liberty of citizens in general and readily tolerated the heavier hand of government all around them. But they would not allow it to weigh on themselves, and to that end they were prepared if need be to run great risks. At the outbreak of the Revolution, the nobility, which ultimately would fall with the throne, still took an infinitely haughtier attitude toward the king and especially his agents, and spoke to them in much freer language, than did the Third Estate, which would soon overthrow the monarchy. It loudly demanded nearly all the guarantees against abuses of power that we have enjoyed during thirty-seven years of representative government. When we read the grievance books of the aristocracy, we sense, along with its prejudices and errors, its spirit as well as some of its noble qualities. We must always regret that rather than subject this nobility to the rule of law, the monarchy cut it down and uprooted it. This course of action deprived the nation of a necessary portion of its substance and inflicted a wound on liberty that will never heal. A class that for centuries marched at the head of the procession had acquired through such long and uncontested intimacy with grandeur a certain hearty pride, a natural confidence in its own strength, and a habit of regard that made it the most resistant part of the social body. Not only were its mores virile but it also increased, through its own example, the virility of the other classes. Eradicating it weakened even its enemies. Nothing could completely replace it. It can never regenerate itself. It may recover its ancestors' titles and property but not their soul.

The priests, who since that time have often been so slavishly submissive in civil matters to the temporal sovereign, whoever that sovereign might be, as well as his most outspoken flatterers so long as the appearance of favoring the Church was maintained, were formerly one of the most independent bodies in the nation and the only one whose special liberties the sovereign was obliged to respect.

The provinces had lost their privileges, and the towns retained only the shadow of what their former privileges had been. Without express permission from the king, ten nobles were not allowed to meet to deliberate on any matter whatsoever. The Church of France continued to hold periodic assemblies until the very end. Within the Church, limits on ecclesiastical power were respected. The lower clergy enjoyed genuine guarantees against the tyranny of its superiors; the bishop did not exercise unlimited power in a way that might have prepared his subordinates for passive obedience to the prince. I do not venture to judge the former constitution of the Church. I contend only that it did not prepare the priestly soul for political servility.

Many ecclesiastics were of noble blood, moreover, and brought with them into the Church the pride and fierce independence of their kind. In addition, all enjoyed elevated rank in the state along with certain privileges. The same feudal rights that proved so fatal to the moral authority of the Church endowed those individual clergymen who used them with a spirit of independence vis-à-vis the civil power.

What contributed most to giving priests the ideas, needs, sentiments, and often the passions of the citizen, however, was landed property. I have had the patience to read most of the reports and debates that have come down to us from the old provincial estates, and in particular those of Languedoc, where the clergy was even more involved than elsewhere in the details of public administration, together with the minutes of the provincial assemblies that met in 1779 and 1787. Reading these documents with ideas imported from my own time, I was astonished to find bishops and abbots, several of whom were as eminent for their holiness as for their learning, reporting on the construction of a road or a canal, dealing with the subject in a deeply informed way, discussing with an abundance of knowledge and art the best way to increase agricultural yields and secure the well-being of citizens and the prosperity of industry, and doing so at least as well as and often better than the laymen who dealt with the same matters alongside them.

Contrary to a widely held and firmly established opinion, I make so bold as to believe that nations that deprive the Catholic clergy of any participation in ownership of the land and transform all ecclesiastical revenues into stipends serve the interests of the Holy See and secular princes exclusively and deprive themselves of a very important component of liberty.

A man who devotes the best part of himself to a foreign authority and who can have no family in the country he inhabits is bound to the soil in one way only, through landed property. Sever that tie and he no longer belongs to any particular place. In the land in which he happens by accident to have been born, he lives as a stranger in the midst of civil society, almost none of whose interests can affect him directly. For his conscience he depends only on the pope, for his subsistence only on the prince. His only fatherland is the Church. In every political event he sees little but what serves or harms the interests of the Church. So long as it remains free and prosperous, what does the rest matter? His most natural political position is indifference. An excellent member of the Christian city, he is a mediocre citizen elsewhere. Such sentiments and ideas in a body that is the teacher of the young and moral guide of the entire nation cannot fail to sap the nation's soul with respect to public life.

If one wants to acquire an accurate idea of the revolutions that can be induced in the minds of men by a change in their condition, one must read the grievance books of the clerical order from 1789.

In them, the clergy showed itself to be frequently intolerant and at times stubbornly attached to any number of its former privileges but also as hostile to despotism, as approving of civil liberty, and as enamored of political liberty as the Third Estate or the nobility. It proclaimed that individual liberty must be guaranteed not by promises but by a procedure analogous to habeas corpus. It called for the destruction of political prisons, the abolition of special courts and transfers of jurisdiction, a public setting for all debates, life tenure for all judges, and eligibility of all citizens for state employment, which must be open to talent alone. It also called for military recruitment that was less oppressive and less humiliating to the people, and from which no one should be exempt; redemption of seigniorial dues, a product of the feudal regime that it held to be contrary to liberty; unlimited freedom to work; elimination of internal customs; expansion of private schools, of which there should be one in every parish, free of charge to pupils; lay charitable organizations such as almshouses and charity workshops in all rural areas; and a wide variety of encouragements to agriculture.

In politics proper, the clergy proclaimed more forcefully than anyone else that the nation has the absolute and inalienable right to assemble in order to make laws and vote on taxes without coercion. It insisted that no Frenchman could be forced to pay a tax on which he had not voted either personally or through a representative. It also called for annual meetings of the Estates General, whose members, it said, should be freely elected and should debate all issues openly before the nation. The laws passed by this body should be general laws, against which no custom or special privilege could apply. The estates should also prepare the budget and even supervise the expenditures of the royal household. Deputies should enjoy immunity from arrest, and ministers must at all times be responsible to them. The clergy also called for similar assemblies to be established in every province and for municipal councils in every town. Not a word was said about divine right.

All things considered, and despite the glaring flaws of certain of its number, I am not sure that there was ever, anywhere in the world, a more remarkable group of clerics than the Catholic clergy of France on the eve of the Revolution. It was more enlightened, more wedded to the nation, less barricaded behind its merely private virtues, and richer in both public virtues and faith, as persecution would quite clearly demonstrate. I began my study of the old society full of prejudices against it but ended full of respect. Indeed, its faults were simply those inherent in any tightly knit and well-organized corporate body, whether political or religious, namely, an invasive tendency, a somewhat intolerant spirit, and an instinctive, at times blind, attachment to special rights for the group.

The bourgeoisie of the Ancien Régime was also far better prepared than the bourgeoisie of today to demonstrate an independent spirit. Indeed, even some of the flaws of its organization contributed to this independence. As we have seen, it filled even more administrative offices then than it does today, and the middle classes demonstrated just as much ardor for official posts. But mark well the difference between then and now. Since most positions then were neither granted nor rescinded by the government, they enhanced the importance of the occupant without leaving him at the mercy of the powerful. In other words, what today consummates the subjection of so many people was precisely what most powerfully commanded respect in that earlier time.

The immunities of all sorts that so regrettably separated the bourgeoisie from the common people tended to make the former into a false aristocracy that often exhibited the pride and recalcitrance of the true one. In each of the many small associations into which it was divided, one readily forgot the general good but was constantly preoccupied with its interests and rights as a body. The members of this body had a common dignity and common privileges to defend. No one could seek refuge in the crowd or try to conceal unseemly bargains. The stage on which each man played his part was small but brightly lit, and he always faced the same audience, ever ready to applaud or hiss.

The art of stifling all sounds of resistance was far less perfected then than it is today. France had not yet become a place that muffles every echo, as it is now. On the contrary, it resounded with them, and, even though there was no sign of political liberty, it was enough to raise one's voice for it to carry far.

What ensured that the oppressed would have a way to make themselves heard in those days was the constitution of the courts. We had become a country of absolute government in our political and administrative institutions, but we remained a free people in our judicial institutions. The judicial system of the Ancien Régime was complex, cumbersome, slow, and costly. These were serious flaws, to be sure, but there was no servility to the government in the judicial system, servility being one of the forms of venality, and indeed the worst. This most serious vice, which not only corrupts the judge but soon infects the whole body of the people, was entirely unknown. The magistrate enjoyed life tenure and did not seek promotion, both necessary factors for ensuring his independence, for what does it matter if one cannot compel a judge to do a thing if one has a thousand ways of winning his assent?

It is true that the royal government had also succeeded in depriving the regular courts of jurisdiction in nearly all cases in which the public authorities had an interest, but it still feared the courts, even as it stripped them of power. Although it prevented them from deciding cases, it still did not dare to prevent them from receiving complaints and stating their opinion. Since, moreover, judicial language retained some of the style of old French, which liked to call things by their proper names, magistrates often found themselves bluntly describing the government's methods as despotic and arbitrary. The irregular intervention of the courts in government, which often disrupted the orderly dispatch of the public's affairs, thus served at times to safeguard liberty. It was a great evil that limited a still greater one.

Within and around the judiciary, ancient mores remained vigorous amid new ideas. The parlements were no doubt more preoccupied with themselves than with the public interest, yet there is no denying that in defending their independence and honor, they always proved to be intrepid and infused their spirit into everything they touched.

When the Paris Parlement was crushed in 1770, the magistrates associated with that body suffered the loss of their status and power, yet not one of them bowed to the king's will. What is more, courts of a very different kind, such as the Cour des Aides, which were neither attacked nor threatened, voluntarily exposed themselves to the same harsh treatment, even though punishment had by then become a certainty. Even more impressive, the leading attorneys who argued before the parlement chose to share its fate of their own free will. They gave up the basis of their fame and fortune and condemned themselves to silence rather than appear before dishonorable magistrates. In all the history of free peoples, I know of nothing greater than what took place on that occasion, and yet this happened in the eighteenth century, in proximity to the court of Louis XV.

Judicial habits had in many respects become national habits. The idea that every issue is subject to debate and every decision to appeal was taken from the courts, as were the practice of public discussion and the insistence on formal procedures, both impediments to servitude – only in this one respect did the Ancien Régime contribute to the education of a free people. The administration itself borrowed a great deal from judicial language and custom. The king believed himself to be under an obligation to state grounds for all his edicts and set forth his reasons before stating his conclusions. Lengthy preambles preceded many council decrees. Intendants dispatched bailiffs to promulgate their ordinances. In all administrative bodies with ancient roots, such as the Treasurers of France or municipal councils, issues were discussed publicly, and decisions were issued after opposing arguments were heard. All these habits and formalities were so many obstacles to arbitrary monarchical rule.

Only the people, especially in the countryside, found themselves nearly always unprepared to resist oppression by other than violent means.

Most of the means of defense enumerated here were in fact beyond the reach of the common man. To avail oneself of such weapons, one had to occupy a place in society from which it was possible to be seen and to make one's voice heard. Common people aside, however, there was no one in France who, if he had the courage, could not haggle over his obedience and resist while seeming to bow and scrape.

The king spoke to the nation as a chief rather than a master. In the preamble to an edict issued at the beginning of his reign, Louis XVI said, "We glory in the idea of commanding a free and generous nation." One of his forebears had already expressed the same idea in older language. Thanking the Estates General for the boldness of their remonstrances, he said, "We would rather speak to free men than to serfs."

The men of the eighteenth century were scarcely familiar with the kind of passion for well-being that is in a sense the mother of servitude, an irresolute yet tenacious and unalterable passion, which mixes readily and, as it were, intertwines with any number of private virtues, such as love of family, regular morals, respect for religious beliefs, and even lukewarm, if diligent, observance of established religious practices, and which allows for honesty, precludes heroism, and excels in making well-behaved but craven citizens. The men of the eighteenth century were both better and worse.

The French in those days loved joy and adored pleasure. They may have been more undisciplined in their habits and more chaotic in their passions and ideas than Frenchmen today, but they knew nothing of the temperate and decent sensualism that we see today. In the upper classes, more time was spent in embellishing life rather than in making it comfortable, and in seeking distinction rather than acquiring wealth. Even in the middle classes, no one allowed himself to become completely absorbed in the pursuit of prosperity. Many people abandoned that pursuit in favor of loftier and more refined pleasures. Everyone invested in some good beyond money. As one contemporary wrote in a style that, though bizarre, still showed pride, "I know my nation: though it is skilled in coining and squandering precious metals, to worship them is not in its nature, and it would be quite ready to hark back to its ancient idols – valor, glory, and I dare say magnanimity."

We must be careful, moreover, not to measure a man's baseness by the degree of his submission to the sovereign power; this would prove to be a misleading gauge. However subject the men of the Ancien Régime were to the will of the king, they were strangers to one kind of obedience: they did not know what it was to bow to an illegitimate or contested power, to a government that one barely honored and frequently scorned but to which one nevertheless submitted freely because of its power to help or harm. That degraded form of servitude was always alien to them. The king inspired sentiments that not even the most absolute rulers who have arisen in the world since then have been able to evoke – sentiments that have become all but incomprehensible to us because of the degree to which the Revolution plucked their roots from our hearts. Toward him they felt both the tender affection that one feels for a father and the respect that one owes only to God. In obeying his most arbitrary commands, they surrendered less to compulsion than to love, and often they maintained a very free spirit even in conditions of the utmost dependence. For them, the greatest evil in obedience was that it should be coerced; for us it is the least. The worst part of obedience is the servile sentiment from which it stems. Let us not despise our fathers; we have no right to do so. May it please God that we may recover, along with their prejudices and faults, a little of their grandeur!

It would therefore be quite wrong to believe that the Ancien Régime was a time of servility and dependence. Liberty was far more prevalent then than it is today, but it was a kind of irregular and intermittent liberty, always limited by class distinctions, always bound up with the idea of exception and privilege, which allowed people to defy the law almost as much as the exercise of arbitrary power and seldom went so far as to guarantee to all citizens the most natural and necessary rights. Though limited and twisted in this way, liberty remained fruitful. At a time when centralization tried more and more to reduce everything to equality, to bend and besmirch every distinctive character, liberty preserved the innate originality of many individuals; it brought out their color and relief, fed their pride, and in many cases made the desire for glory paramount among their desires. It shaped those vigorous souls, those proud and audacious geniuses, whose appearance on the scene we are about to witness and who would make the French Revolution an object of admiration as well as terror to succeeding generations. It would be strange indeed if such virtues had been able to grow on soil from which liberty had been banished.

But if liberty of this disorderly and unwholesome sort prepared the French to overthrow despotism, it made them perhaps less apt than any other people to establish in its place the peaceful and unfettered rule of law.

II.12 – How, Despite the Progress of Civilization, the Condition of the French Peasant Was Sometimes Worse in the Eighteenth Century Than It Had Been in the Thirteenth

In the eighteenth century, the French peasant may no longer have been prey to petty feudal despots; he was only rarely the target of violence by the government. He enjoyed civil liberty and owned a portion of land. But all the other classes had drawn apart from him, and he lived more isolated, perhaps, than had ever been the case anywhere else in the world. His oppression was of a new and singular sort, and the effects of this deserve close and particular attention.

Early in the seventeenth century, Henri IV complained, according to Péréfixe, that nobles were abandoning the countryside. By the middle of the eighteenth century, this desertion had become almost general. All contemporary sources mention this fact and deplore it: economists in their books, intendants in their correspondence, and agricultural societies in their reports. Incontrovertible proof can be found in the records of the capitation, which was collected at the actual place of residence. Receipts from all of the upper nobility and a portion of the middling nobility were collected in Paris.

Scarcely any nobles remained in the countryside except those with fortunes too small to enable them to leave. These found themselves, relative to their peasant neighbors, in a position in which I do not believe any wealthy landowner had ever found himself before. Since the noble was no longer the peasants' leader, he did not have the interest he once had in getting on with them, helping them out, and showing them the way forward. Since he was not subject to the same taxes they were, he could not feel warm sympathy for their plight, which he did not share, nor could he join them in their grievances, which were alien to him. These people were no longer his subjects, but he was not yet their fellow citizen: a historically unique situation.

This led to what might be called absenteeism of the heart – a more common and more devastating phenomenon than absenteeism in the usual sense. As a result, the noble who lived on his estate often expressed views and sentiments that his steward might have expressed in his absence. Like the steward, he saw his tenants only as debtors and insisted on receiving everything he was due by law or custom, so that in some cases the collection of what remained of feudal dues imposed more of a hardship than in feudal times proper.

Often weighed down by debt and always in need, he usually lived in quite straitened circumstances in his chateau, his every thought devoted to amassing the money that he would spend in town during the winter. Common folk, whose words often point directly to the essence of a thing, referred to lesser nobles of this sort as *hobereaux*, or hobby-hawks, these being the smallest of the birds of prey.

One could no doubt find individuals who did not fit this description, but I am speaking here of classes, which ought to be the sole object of the historian's interest. Who would deny that there were in those days many wealthy landowners who were concerned with the well-being of the peasants even though they were not obliged to be and shared no common interest with them? But those individuals, I am glad to say, successfully rebelled against the law of their new status, which impelled them in spite of themselves toward indifference, as it drove their former vassals toward hatred.

The nobility's abandonment of the countryside has often been attributed to the specific influence of certain kings and ministers, notably Louis XIV and Richelieu. Indeed, during the last three centuries of the monarchy, princes nearly always embraced the idea of separating the nobles from the people and enticing them to the court and public employment. This was especially apparent in the seventeenth century, when the monarchy still feared the nobility. Among the questions addressed to the intendants we still find this: "Do the nobles in your province wish to remain in their residences or leave?"

The letter of one intendant who responded to this query has survived. He complains that the nobles of his province are pleased to remain with their peasants rather than fulfill their obligations at court. It is worth noting that the province in question was Anjou, later known as the Vendée. The nobles who are said to have refused to do their duty toward the king were the only ones in France who would later take up arms in defense of the monarchy, some of whom would die in combat on its behalf. Moreover, they owed this glorious distinction to one thing only: the fact that they were able to retain the loyalty of those peasants among whom they were criticized for preferring to live.

We must nevertheless beware of attributing the desertion of the countryside by what was then the leading class of the nation to the direct influence of certain kings. The primary and persistent cause of this desertion was not the will of certain individuals but the slow and steady operation of certain institutions. Proof of this can be seen in the fact that when the government wanted to counter the evil in the eighteenth century, it could not even slow its progress. As nobles lost their political rights without acquiring others in their place, and as local liberties disappeared, the emigration of nobles increased. There was no longer any need to lure them from their homes because they no longer wished to stay in them. Country life had become insipid for them.

What I say here about nobles should be extended to wealthy landowners in all countries: centralization empties the countryside of wealthy and educated inhabitants. Indeed, I might add that centralization leads to agricultural inefficiency and lack of innovation – an observation that could be developed into a gloss on Montesquieu's very profound remark: "What makes land productive is not so much its fertility as the liberty of those who live on it." But I do not wish to wander from my subject.

We saw earlier how the bourgeois everywhere abandoned the countryside and sought refuge in the towns. On no other point are the records of the Ancien Régime quite so unanimous: in the countryside we almost never find more than one generation of rich peasants. No sooner did an industrious farmer manage to amass a little wealth than he ordered his son to abandon his plow, sent him to town, and purchased a minor office for him. It is to this period that we can trace the origin of what remains a common sentiment even today: the singular horror that the French farmer often feels toward the profession that made him rich. The effect has outlived the cause.

In fact, the only well-bred individual – the only "gentleman," as the English say – who continued to live among the peasants and remained in close touch with them was the priest. Thus, the priest would have been at the head of the rural population, Voltaire notwithstanding, had he not been so closely and visibly associated with the political hierarchy. Because he shared any number of the privileges of the hierarchy, he inspired some of the hatred to which it gave rise.

Hence, the peasant was almost entirely cut off from the upper classes. He was even estranged from those of his own class who might have been able to help and guide him. As the latter acquired education or wealth, they shunned him. He was winnowed from the nation and set apart.

This did not occur to the same degree in any of the other great civilized nations of Europe, and even in France it was of recent date. The peasant of the fourteenth century was at once more oppressed and better assisted. The aristocracy sometimes tyrannized him but never abandoned him.

In the eighteenth century a village was a community, all of whose members were poor, ignorant, and crude. Its magistrates were as uncultivated and contemptible as the rest. Its syndics did not know how to read. Its tax collector could not by himself keep the accounts on which his own fortune and the fortunes of his neighbors depended. Not only had the former lord of the village lost the right to govern it, but he had also reached the point of regarding any involvement in its government as degrading. Apportioning the taille, recruiting militiamen, and organizing labor details were servile chores, fit for an alderman. Only the central government concerned itself with the village, and since it was far away and had as yet nothing to fear from the people who lived there, it took little interest in them other than to draw from the place what profit it could.

Consider now what becomes of a neglected class, which no one wants to tyrannize but no one seeks to educate or help.

The heaviest burdens that the feudal system had placed on the rural population were no doubt alleviated or removed, but we know too little about the new burdens that replaced them, which may have been heavier still. The peasant did not suffer from all the ills that had afflicted his forebears, but he endured many miseries they never knew.

We do know that the tenfold increase in the taille over two centuries was borne almost entirely by the peasant. A word must be said here about the way in which this tax was levied, so as to show what barbarous laws can be established or maintained in civilized societies when the most enlightened men in the nation have no personal interest in changing them.

In a confidential letter from the comptroller general to the intendants, written in 1772, I find the following description of the taille, a small masterpiece of precision and brevity: "The taille, arbitrary in its apportionment, is a tax for which those on whom it is levied are jointly responsible. It is assessed on individuals, not land. In most of France it is subject to constant variation, owing to annual changes in the taxpayers' fortunes." Everything is summed up in these three sentences. It would be difficult to give a more artful description of the evil from which one profited.

The total sum that each parish owed was set annually. As the minister notes in his letter, it varied constantly, so that no farmer could predict what he would have to pay from year to year. Within the parish, one peasant was chosen at random each year to serve as collector and divide the tax burden among the rest.

I promised to describe the situation of this tax collector. To that end, let us turn our attention to the provincial assembly of Berry in 1779. Its word cannot be doubted since it was made up entirely of privileged individuals who were chosen by the king and did not pay the taille. "Because everyone wishes to avoid the collector's duty, each man must take his turn. Hence, the collection of the taille is entrusted to a new collector every year, without regard to his ability or honesty. Accordingly, the composition of the annual tax roll reflects the character of the man who draws it up. The collector leaves his mark in terms of fears, weaknesses, and vices. How, moreover, could he possibly succeed? He works in the dark, for who knows exactly how wealthy his neighbor is or how one man's wealth compares with another's? Yet the decision is left solely to the discretion of the collector, and he must answer for the entire sum, with his own property and even his person as surety. Ordinarily he must spend half of every day for two years running to the various taxpayers. Those who cannot read are obliged to find someone in the vicinity who can do the job for them."

Somewhat earlier, Turgot had said this about another province: "This task leaves those who take it on in despair and almost always in ruin. Thus, we reduce all the well-to-do families in a village to misery, one after another."

Yet this unfortunate individual was armed with immense arbitrary power. He was almost as much a tyrant as a martyr. While engaged in this exercise, in which he ruined himself, he held in his hands the power to ruin everyone else. Again quoting the assembly: "Preference for his kin and for his friends and neighbors, enmity and vengeance for his enemies, need for a protector, fear of displeasing a wealthy citizen with work to offer – these feelings contended in his heart with sentiments of justice."

Terror often made the collector merciless: in some parishes he never went out unless accompanied by sheriffs and bailiffs. "When he comes without bailiffs," one intendant told the minister in 1764, "the taxpayers are unwilling to pay." The provincial assembly of Guyenne remarked that "in the Villefranche district alone, 106 process servers and other sheriff's deputies are constantly on the road."

To escape this violent and arbitrary taxation, the French peasant, in the middle of the eighteenth century, acted like the Jew in the Middle Ages. He put on a show of being miserable even if by chance he was not. His affluence frightened him, for good reason. I find tangible proof of this in a document, which I take in this instance not from Vienne but from a hundred leagues away. The Agricultural Society of Maine announced in its 1761 report that it had conceived the idea of awarding prizes and incentives in the form of livestock. "The idea has been dropped," the report continued, "because of the risks to which the winners were exposed owing to the base jealousy of others, who could subsequently take advantage of the arbitrary way in which taxes were assessed in order to harass the winners."

In this system of taxation, each taxpayer had a direct and permanent interest in spying on his neighbors and informing the tax collector of any increase in their wealth. They were all trained to outdo one another in slander and hatred. Might one not be tempted to describe such goings-on as appropriate to the domain of some rajah of Hindustan?

Yet there were in France in this same period provinces where taxes were levied in a regular and uncoerced manner, namely, certain of the *pays d'états*. To be sure, these provinces had been granted the right to levy the tax themselves. In Languedoc, for example, the taille was levied only on real estate and did not vary with the wealth of the landowner. Its basis was fixed and visible: a carefully compiled cadaster, which was revised every thirty years and which assigned every plot of land to one of three classes, depending on its fertility. Each taxpayer knew in advance the share of the tax that he would be required to pay. If he did not pay, he alone, or, rather, his field alone, was responsible. If he believed that the assessment was unfair, he had the right to insist that his rate be compared with that of another inhabitant of the parish, whom he could choose himself. The procedure was thus what we would today call proportional equality.

Clearly, all these rules are precisely the ones we follow now. Little was done to improve them in the interim; they were merely generalized. It is worth noting that although we based the very form of our public administration on the government of the Ancien Régime, we refrained from imitating it in other respects. We borrowed our best administrative methods not from the government but from the provincial assemblies. Having adopted the machine, we rejected its product.

The habitual poverty of country people had given rise to maxims that were unlikely to put an end to it. "If the people were well off," Richelieu wrote in his political testament, "they would find it difficult to toe the line." In the eighteenth century it was no longer common to speak so bluntly, but many people continued to believe that the peasant would not work if he were not constantly spurred on by necessity: poverty was apparently the only guarantee against laziness. I have heard precisely the same theory in regard to Negroes in our colonies. This opinion is so widespread among people in government that nearly all economists feel compelled to refute it.

The original purpose of the taille was to enable the king to buy soldiers who would relieve nobles and their vassals of the need to perform military service. In the seventeenth century, however, the obligation to do military service was restored, as we have seen, in the form of the militia, and now it fell entirely on common people and mainly on the peasantry.

It suffices to consider the abundance of police reports that fill the intendants' archives, all having to do with the pursuit of shirkers and deserters, to see that recruitment of the militia was no easy task. There was apparently no public burden that peasants found more oppressive than this. To avoid the draft, they frequently fled into the woods and had to be pursued by armed men. This is surprising in light of the ease with which conscription proceeds today.

The extreme reluctance of Ancien Régime peasants to serve in the militia was due not so much to the principle of the law as to the way in which it was applied. Consider above all the lengthy period of uncertainty to which it subjected potential recruits (who could be called up until they were forty, unless they married); the arbitrariness of the exemptions, which nearly nullified the advantage of drawing a lucky number; the prohibition against procuring a replacement; distaste for a harsh and perilous profession offering no prospect of advancement; but above all the feeling that this burden fell on them alone, and indeed on the poorest of them, so that the rigors of the soldier's lot were compounded by the ignominy of his position.

I have held in my hands many transcripts of the draft lottery of 1769 from a large number of parishes. These indicate the names of those exempted from the draft: they include the servant of a nobleman, the guardian of an abbey, and the valet of someone identified as a bourgeois, to be sure, but a bourgeois *living nobly*. Wealth alone could confer an exemption: a farmer who numbered among those paying the largest amount in taxes year after year gained the privilege of having his sons exempted from service in the militia; this privilege went by the name of "encouragement to agriculture." The Physiocrats, who in all other respects greatly approved of equality, did not find this privilege shocking. They merely insisted that it be extended to other cases. In other words, they wanted the burden on the poorest and least protected peasants to become even heavier. As one of them put, "the soldier's poor pay, the quality of his room, board, and clothing, and his position of total dependence would make it too cruel to take anyone not from the dregs of the populace."

Until the end of Louis XIV's reign, highways were not maintained, or else they were kept up at the expense of those who used them, which is to say the state and abutting landowners. At about this time, however, repairs began to be made solely by forced labor, that is, at the expense of the peasants alone. This expedient, which made it possible to have good highways without paying for them, seemed so inspired that in 1737, Orry, the comptroller general, issued a circular ordering its adoption throughout France. Intendants were granted the power to imprison anyone who refused to work or to send the sheriff's men after them.

From then on, as trade increased and the need and desire for good roads spread more widely, forced labor was used on new roads and became more oppressive than ever. A report to the provincial assembly of Berry in 1779 found that the forced labor used in that poor province would have been valued at 700,000 livres. In Lower Normandy in 1787, a similar figure was reported. There is no more telling sign of the sad fate of the rural population: social progress made all the other classes of society rich but left country people desperate. Civilization turned against them alone.

In the correspondence of intendants from about the same time, I find that it was deemed appropriate to deny the use of compulsory labor details for private village roads because such labor was reserved exclusively for major highways – "the king's highways," as they were called at the time. The peculiar idea that it was appropriate to impose the cost of road building on the poorest of the king's subjects and those who were most unlikely to travel was a new one, yet it took root so naturally in the minds of those who profited from it that before long they could no longer imagine things being done any other way. In 1776 an attempt was made to transform compulsory labor service into a local tax. Inequality immediately followed suit and was incorporated into the new tax.

Compulsory labor, once a seigniorial prerogative, became a royal one and was little by little extended to all kinds of public works. In 1719 it was used to build barracks. "Parishes must send their best workers," the order read, "and all other projects must be subordinated to this one." Compulsory labor transported convicts to the galleys and beggars to workhouses. It carted military gear whenever troops changed locations – a considerable burden at a time when every regiment traveled with heavy baggage. Large numbers of carts and oxen had to be requisitioned to move the load. As the size of standing armies grew, labor required for this purpose, insignificant initially, became one of the heaviest burdens. I found state contractors who loudly insisted on compulsory labor details to transport lumber from the forests to naval arsenals. Peasants summoned for such work were usually paid a wage, but it was arbitrarily set and low. This ill-apportioned burden became so substantial at times that it worried the tax collectors. "The expenses for road repairs demanded of the peasants will soon make it impossible for them to pay the taille," one of them wrote in 1751.

Would all these new forms of oppression have become established if the peasant had had at his side wealthy and enlightened men with the taste and power, if not to defend him, then at least to intercede on his behalf with the common master who already controlled the fortunes of both pauper and rich man?

I came across the letter of one large landowner who in 1774 wrote to the intendant of his province asking him to build a new road. In his view, the new road would bring prosperity to a certain village, and he explained why before moving on to discuss the establishment of a fair, which he said would double the price of farm products. This good citizen added that with a small amount of assistance it might be possible to establish a school, which would provide the king with more industrious subjects. He had not previously given any thought to these necessary improvements and had become aware of them only because a *lettre de cachet* had kept him confined to his chateau for the previous two years: "The past two years in exile on my estate have convinced me that all of these things are extremely useful," he said ingenuously.

It was above all in times of scarcity, however, that the bonds of patronage and dependence that had once tied the great rural landowner to the peasants were loosened or broken. In these periods of crisis, the central government took fright at its isolation and weakness. It would have liked to revive for the occasion the individual influences and political associations it had destroyed. It called on them for help, but no one answered the call, and the government was regularly astonished to find dead those whom its own actions had deprived of life.

In such extremities, there were intendants in the poorest provinces, Turgot for example, who issued illegal orders to force wealthy landowners to feed their tenants until the next harvest. I found letters dated 1770 from several parish priests who proposed to the intendant that he ought to tax the large landowners in their parishes, including both ecclesiastic and lay lords "who own vast properties that they do not inhabit and from which they receive large incomes which they consume elsewhere."

Even in normal times, villages were infested with beggars. As Letrosne says, the poor were assisted in the towns, but in the countryside during the winter begging was a matter of absolute necessity.

These unfortunate paupers were periodically subjected to quite violent treatment. In 1767, the duc de Choiseul wanted to wipe out begging in France at a single stroke. One can see in his correspondence with intendants how ruthlessly he went about doing so. The police were ordered to arrest all beggars throughout the kingdom, and we are told that more than fifty thousand were seized. Able-bodied vagabonds were to be sent to the galleys. More than forty workhouses were built to receive the rest. It would have been better to ask the rich to open their hearts as in the past.

This Ancien Régime government, which as I have said was so mild and at times so timid and so enamored of formalities, leisurely procedures, and deferential treatment whenever gentlemen of high station were involved, was often brusque and always prompt in going after the lower classes, especially the peasants. Among the documents I examined, I did not see any order by an intendant for the arrest of a bourgeois, but peasants were constantly being arrested in connection with compulsory labor, military service, begging, disorderly conduct, and a thousand other things. For some there were independent courts, lengthy debates, and public hearings. For others there was the provost, who issued summary judgments that could not be appealed.

In 1785 Necker wrote: "The immense distance that separates the people from all other classes helps to divert attention from the way in which authority can be wielded against all who are lost in the crowd. Were it not for the mildness and humanity that are characteristic of the French and of the spirit of the age, this would be a source of constant distress for those capable of feeling the weight of a yoke from which they themselves are exempt."

What truly revealed oppression, however, was not so much the harm that was done to those unfortunates as the good that they were prevented from doing for themselves. They were free and owned land, yet they remained as ignorant as their ancestors, the serfs, and often more wretched. They remained unindustrious in the midst of prodigious technical progress, and uncivilized in a world of enlightened brilliance. Although they retained the distinctive intelligence and perspicacity of their kind, they did not learn how to make use of these qualities. They were unable to succeed even in the cultivation of the land, which was their only business. "I behold before my eyes the agriculture of the tenth century," said one celebrated English agronomist. They excelled only in the profession of arms. There, at least, they naturally and inevitably came into contact with the other classes of society.

It was in this abyss of isolation and misery that the peasant lived. There he dwelt, cut off and inaccessible. I was surprised and almost terrified to discover that less than twenty years before the Catholic religion was abolished without resistance and the churches profaned, the administration sometimes resorted to the following method when it wished to learn more about the population of a canton: parish priests recorded the number of people who came to church to take Easter communion; to that number one added the presumed number of very young children and the ill, and in this way one arrived at the total population. Nevertheless, contemporary ideas were already finding their way from many sources into these crude minds. These ideas followed roundabout and subterranean paths and, in narrow-minded and obscure places, assumed some peculiar forms. Yet outwardly nothing seemed to change. The peasant's mores, habits, and beliefs seemed the same as always. He was submissive. He was even joyous.

One should be wary of the gaiety that a Frenchman will often exhibit in the face of the greatest woes. This proves not that he does not feel his woes but only that, because he believes his misfortune to be inevitable, he will try to distract himself by not thinking about it. Show him a way out of the misery that seems to occasion so little suffering and he will hasten after relief so abruptly that he may run you down without seeing you if you happen to be in his way.

We can see these things clearly from where we now stand, but contemporaries did not see them. It is only with the utmost difficulty that the upper classes can ever perceive clearly what is going on in the soul of the people, and in particular in the soul of the peasants. The peasants' upbringing and way of life give them a unique perspective on human affairs, a perspective that remains closed to everyone else. But when the poor man and the rich man share virtually nothing in common, neither common interests nor common complaints nor common affairs, the darkness that hides the mind of one from the mind of the other becomes unfathomable, and the two could live forever side by side without ever penetrating each other's thoughts. It is strange to see the odd state of security in which those who occupied the middle and upper levels of the social edifice lived on the eve of the Revolution, and to hear them cleverly discussing among themselves the virtues, gentleness, devotion, and innocent pleasures of the people, when 1793 was already opening the ground beneath their feet. The spectacle is at once absurd and terrifying.

Let us pause here before moving on and consider for a moment, in the light of all the small facts I have just described, one of the greatest of God's laws governing the conduct of societies.

The French nobility stubbornly insisted on setting itself apart from the other classes of society. Nobles ultimately allowed themselves to be exempted from most of the public charges to which they were subject. They imagined that they would retain their eminence while avoiding these burdens, and at first this appeared to be the case. But soon an invisible internal malady seemed to become associated with their position, and their status diminished little by little, though no one did anything to make this happen; they grew poorer as their immunities grew more extensive. The bourgeoisie, with which the nobility had been so afraid of being confused, meanwhile gained in wealth and education, without the help of the nobility and in opposition to it. Nobles who had not wanted bourgeois as partners or fellow citizens now had to face them as rivals, before long as enemies, and ultimately as masters. An alien power had freed them from the obligation to lead, protect, and assist their vassals, but since it had left them their pecuniary rights and honorific privileges, they judged that nothing had been lost. Since they continued to march at the head of every procession, they believed that they were still leaders, and indeed they continued to be surrounded by men to whom they referred in official documents as their *subjects*. Others were referred to as their vassals, their tenants, and their farmers. In reality, they had no followers. They were alone, and when people at last rose up against them, they had no choice but to flee.

Although the trajectories of the nobility and bourgeoisie were quite different, they were alike in one respect: ultimately the bourgeois lived as separately from the common people as the nobleman himself. Instead of seeking proximity to the peasantry, he shunned the peasant's misery. Instead of allying himself closely with the peasant to contest a common inequality, he sought only to create new injustices that served his own purposes. The bourgeois was as ardent in procuring his exceptions as the nobleman was in maintaining his privileges. The peasants from whose ranks he sprang had become not only strangers to him but, in a sense, complete unknowns, and it was only after he had put arms in their hands that he realized he had aroused passions of which he had no inkling, which he was as powerless to restrain as to lead, and of which he was to become the victim after having been the promoter.

Astonishment will forever greet the ruins of the great House of France, which had once seemed destined to rule all Europe, but those who study its history carefully will have no difficulty understanding its fall. Nearly all the unfortunate defects, errors, and prejudices I have just described owe either their origin, duration, or development to the skill that most of our kings have had in dividing men in order to govern them more absolutely.

But when the bourgeois had thus been isolated from the noble, and the peasant from the noble and bourgeois, and when, by a similar process within each class, there emerged distinct small groups almost as isolated from one another as the classes were, it became clear that the whole society had been reduced to a homogeneous mass with nothing to hold its parts together. Nothing was left that could obstruct the government, nor anything that could shore it up. Thus, the princely magnificence of the whole edifice could collapse all at once, in the blink of an eye, the moment the society that served as its foundation began to tremble.

And finally, the people, who alone seemed to have profited from the blunders and errors of all their masters – although they did, in fact, manage to escape the dominion of their rulers, they were unable to shake off the yoke of false ideas, corrupt habits, and wicked inclinations that those rulers had imparted to them or allowed them to acquire. At times we find the people bringing the tastes of slaves with them into the very exercise of freedom, as incapable of governing themselves as they were unforgiving of their teachers.

Book III

III.1 – How, Toward the Middle of the Eighteenth Century, Men of Letters Became the Country's Leading Politicians, and the Effects That Followed from This

I will now set aside the persistent and general facts that prepared the way for the great revolution that it is my purpose to describe and turn to the particular and more recent facts that determined its place, birth, and character.

Of all the nations of Europe, France had long been the most literary. Yet men of letters had never before exhibited a spirit of the sort that emerged around the middle of the eighteenth century, nor had they previously occupied the place in society that they assumed at that time. Nothing like this had ever been seen in France or, I believe, anywhere else.

In France, men of letters did not regularly participate in affairs, as they did in England. Indeed, they had never been so far removed from the world of affairs. They were not invested with authority of any kind and fulfilled no public function in a society already replete with functionaries.

Yet unlike most of their German counterparts, they did not avoid politics entirely or confine themselves to pure philosophy or belles lettres. They took a persistent interest in subjects related to government. In truth, this was their defining occupation. They could be heard, whenever one wished, expounding the origins of society and primitive social forms, the fundamental rights of citizens and prerogatives of authority, the natural and artificial relations among men, the mistakenness or legitimacy of custom, and the essential principles of law. Delving daily into the foundations of society as it was then constituted, they studied its structure intently and criticized its overall plan. To be sure, not all of them pondered these great problems in a thorough or profound manner. Indeed, most touched on them only superficially, almost playfully. But all considered them. Abstract and literary politics of this sort was to be found in all the works of the period, though not to the same degree. None was entirely exempt, from the weightiest treatise to the most frivolous song.

The political systems of these writers varied so widely that it would be impossible to combine them all into a single theory of government.

Nevertheless, if we ignore details and look for fundamental ideas, we soon find that the authors of these various systems agreed on at least one very general notion, which each of them seems to have conceived on his own – a general notion that seems to have preexisted, and to be the common source of, all the other, more specific ideas. However much the authors of the time eventually diverged from one another, all started from the same place: all believed that it was proper to replace the complex traditional customs that governed the society in which they lived with certain simple, elementary rules, which could be deduced from reason and natural law.

Careful study reveals that what one might call the political philosophy of the eighteenth century consists, strictly speaking, in this single notion.

Such a thought was not new: for three thousand years it had periodically gripped the human imagination, though never for long. How was it that it now seized the minds of so many writers? Why, instead of remaining confined within a few philosophical heads, as had always been the case before, did it filter down to the masses and take on the substance and warmth of a political passion, to the point where we find general and abstract theories about the nature of society becoming the subject of daily conversation among those with nothing else to occupy them and inflaming the imaginations of even women and peasants? How did men of letters without rank, honor, wealth, responsibility, or power become, in fact, the leading politicians of the age – nay, the only politicians, since, while others engaged in government, they alone wielded authority? I would like to explain this briefly and show what extraordinarily powerful influence these facts, which seem to belong to the history of our literature, had on the Revolution and continued to have down to the present time.

It was no accident that the philosophers of the eighteenth century all conceived of notions so incompatible with those that still served as the basis of their society. The new ideas were prompted, in a natural way, by the sight of that very society, which lay before their eyes. The sight of so many abusive and ridiculous privileges, whose oppressiveness was increasingly felt yet whose grounds were less and less apparent, induced, or, rather, compelled, many thinkers to embrace the idea of a natural equality of conditions. Confronted with so many bizarre and haphazard institutions – relics of another era that no one attempted to reconcile with one another or accommodate to new needs, and which, despite having lost their virtue, seemed bound nevertheless to endure – these philosophers quickly became disgusted with ancient things and traditions and naturally wanted to rebuild society according to an entirely new plan, which each of them elaborated by the light of reason alone.

The situation of these writers fostered in them a taste for abstract, general theories of government, theories in which they trusted blindly. Living as they did almost totally removed from practical life, they had no experience that might have tempered their natural passions. Nothing warned them of the obstacles that existing realities might pose to even the most desirable reforms. They had no idea of the perils that invariably accompany even the most necessary revolutions. Indeed, they had no premonition of them because the complete absence of political liberty ensured that they not only failed to grasp the world of affairs but actually failed to see it. They had nothing to do with that world and were incapable of recognizing what others did within it. Hence, they lacked even that superficial instruction that the sight of a free society and word of what is said by free men impart to those least involved in government. They therefore grew bolder in their innovations, much more enamored of general ideas and systems, much more contemptuous of ancient wisdom, and much more confident of individual reason than one commonly sees in authors who write speculative works about politics.

A similar ignorance led the crowd to lend them their ear and surrender their heart to them. If the French had still participated in government through the Estates General, as they had in the past, if they had even still participated in the daily administration of the country through their provincial assemblies, it is safe to say that they would not have been inflamed by the ideas of these writers, as they were now. They would still have possessed a certain familiarity with government, and this would have alerted them to the dangers of pure theory.

If, like the English, they had been able, without destroying their ancient institutions, to change their spirit gradually, they might not have been quite so ready to imagine entirely new ones. But each of them felt hindered daily in his fortune, person, well-being, or pride by some old law, some ancient political custom, some relic of the old powers, and he saw no remedy ready to hand that he might apply to his particular woe. It seemed that the constitution of the country had to be either tolerated in its entirety or else entirely destroyed.

We had, however, preserved one liberty from the ruin of all the others. We were able to philosophize almost without restraint about the origins of society, the essential nature of government, and the primordial rights of the human race.

All who were hindered by the daily practice of legislation soon became enamored of literary politics. The taste for this sort of thing spread even to people whose nature or situation would normally have kept them aloof from abstract speculation. There was scarcely a taxpayer disadvantaged by the unequal apportionment of the taille who did not warm to the idea that all men should be equal. There was scarcely a small landowner whose property had been devastated by the rabbits of his neighbor, the nobleman, who was not pleased to hear that reason condemned all privileges without exception. Thus, every public passion disguised itself as philosophy. Political life was forcibly channeled into literature, and writers, taking it upon themselves to direct public opinion, for a while took the place that party leaders ordinarily occupy in free countries.

By this time, no one was in a position to challenge the writers' role.

An aristocracy, when it is vigorous, does not merely take the lead in public affairs. It also shapes opinions, sets the tone for writers, and imparts authority to ideas. By the eighteenth century, the French nobility had lost this portion of its dominion entirely. Its credibility had suffered the same fate as its power. The place it had once occupied in the government of the mind was vacant, and writers were free to assume this role to the exclusion of all others.

What is more, the very aristocracy whose place the writers took encouraged their enterprise. It had so completely forgotten how general theories, once accepted, are inevitably transformed into political passions and actions that it treated as mere ingenious intellectual games the doctrines most hostile to its privileges and even its existence as a class. To pass the time, it took part in these games itself, tranquilly enjoying its immunities and privileges while serenely discussing the absurdity of all established customs.

Many people have expressed astonishment at the peculiar blindness of the upper classes of the Ancien Régime, when they thus assisted in their own destruction. But who could have taught them otherwise? Free institutions are just as essential to the leading citizens of a country, in order to instruct them about the perils they face, as they are to the lowest of citizens, in order to secure their rights. For more than a century after the last traces of public life had disappeared in France, the people with the most direct interest in maintaining the old constitution received no warning, felt no jolt, heard no creak, that might have indicated that the ancient edifice was on the verge of collapse. In the absence of any outward change, they imagined that everything remained precisely the same. They continued to see things as their fathers had seen them. In the grievance books of 1789, the nobility seems to have been as preoccupied with the encroachments of royal power as it had been in the fifteenth century. Meanwhile, as Burke rightly notes, the unfortunate Louis XVI still saw the aristocracy as the principal rival of royal power right up to the moment he died in the eruption of democracy. He remained as wary of the aristocracy as if he had still been living in the time of the Fronde. And like his forebears, he saw the bourgeoisie and the people as the staunchest supporters of the monarchy.

To us, who have before our eyes the debris of so many revolutions, what may seem even stranger, however, is that the very notion of a violent revolution was absent from our ancestors' minds. It was not discussed; it had not been conceived. The small tremors that political liberty constantly imparts to the most firmly established societies serve as a daily reminder of the possibility of upheaval, which fosters a state of watchful public prudence. But in France in the eighteenth century, as society teetered on the brink of an abyss, there was still no warning of the precariousness of the situation.

I carefully read the grievance books prepared by the three orders before they met in 1789. When I say the three orders, I mean the nobility and the clergy as well as the Third Estate. Here I found that someone asked that a law be changed, there a custom, and I took note. When I came to the end of this vast collection of texts and put all these specific requests together, I was horrified to realize that what they were asking for was the simultaneous and systematic abolition of all the laws and customs in force throughout the country. I saw at once that this would lead to one of the most extensive and dangerous revolutions that had ever occurred anywhere in the world. But those who would become the victims of that revolution were totally unaware of this. They believed that the total and sudden transformation of such an old and complex society could be achieved without disruption, with the aid of reason and by its force alone. Poor fools! They even forgot the maxim that their forefathers had expressed four hundred years earlier in the simple, vigorous French of the time: "Ask for an excess of freedom and liberty and what you get is an excess of slavery."

It is not surprising that the nobility and bourgeoisie, which had been excluded from public life for so long, displayed such striking inexperience. What is more astonishing, however, is that the very men in charge of affairs – ministers, magistrates, and intendants – exhibited little more foresight. Yet any number of them were very able practitioners of their professions. They possessed thorough knowledge of the details of public administration. But when it came to the great science of government, which teaches one to understand the general direction of society, to judge what is going on in the minds of the masses, and to anticipate what will come of it, they were quite as untutored as the people themselves. Indeed, statesmen can learn that aspect of their art – the principal part – only from the operation of free institutions.

This can be seen quite clearly in a report that Turgot submitted to the king in 1775, in which, among other things, he advised the monarch to allow the nation as a whole to elect a representative assembly, which would then meet in the king's presence for six weeks every year, but not to grant that assembly any real power. It would concern itself solely with administration and never with government, and offer its opinions rather than express its will. In fact, its sole mission would be to discuss laws rather than make them. "In this way, royal power would be enlightened but not hobbled," Turgot said, "and public opinion would be satisfied without danger because these assemblies would have no authority to oppose essential operations, and if by some remote chance they were reluctant to comply, Your Majesty would still have the upper hand." It would be impossible to be more mistaken about the implications of a measure or the spirit of one's time. To be sure, it has often been possible to act with impunity in the way Turgot suggested, to grant the shadow of liberty without the substance. Augustus tried it and succeeded. A nation tired of endless debate may willingly consent to be duped, as long as it is granted calm, and history teaches that in such cases it is enough to recruit a certain number of obscure or subservient men from across the country and pay them to play the role of a political assembly before the nation. Several examples of this can be cited. But at the beginning of a revolution such measures always fail and merely inflame the people without satisfying them. The least citizen of a free country knows as much; Turgot, though a great administrator, did not.

Remember now that the same French nation that was so alienated from its own affairs and so deprived of experience, so hobbled by its institutions and so powerless to change them, was also the most literate of all nations as well as the most enamored of wit, and you will readily understand how writers became a political force in the country and ended up the most important political force of all.

In England, those who wrote about government mingled with those who governed, so that the latter introduced new ideas in practice while the former revised and pared down theories with the help of facts, but in France, the political world remained divided, as it were, into two separate provinces with no commerce between them. One administered while the other established the abstract principles that should have formed the basis of all administration. One took specific measures, as routine required; the other proclaimed general laws without ever thinking about the means to apply them. One took charge of public affairs, the other of people's minds.

On top of the real society, whose constitution remained traditional, confused, and haphazard, and in which laws were still diverse and contradictory, ranks clearly defined, conditions fixed, and tax burdens unequal, an imaginary society was constructed piece by piece, in which everything seemed simple and coherent, uniform, equitable, and shaped by reason.

Gradually, the imagination of the multitude deserted the former and retreated into the latter. People lost interest in what was in order to dream about what might be, and in their minds they lived in the ideal city that the writers had constructed.

Many have attributed our Revolution to the American one. The latter did in fact exert great influence on the French Revolution, but the Revolution in France owed less to what was done in the United States than to what people thought at the time in France. Whereas in the rest of Europe the American Revolution was still merely a novel and singular occurrence, in France it only made what people thought they already knew more palpable and striking. Elsewhere it astonished; here it persuaded.

The Americans seemed merely to have carried out what our writers had envisioned. They gave the substance of reality to what we were already dreaming. It was as if Fénelon were suddenly to have found himself in Salentum.

This most unusual historical situation – in which the entire political education of a great nation was carried out by men of letters – may have contributed more than anything else to the distinctive character of the French Revolution and to what we see today as its result.

Writers not only supplied the people who made the Revolution with ideas but also imparted something of their own temperament and disposition. Under their lengthy discipline, in the absence of other leaders, and given the profound ignorance of practice from which all suffered, the nation read their works and acquired the instincts, the cast of mind, the tastes, and even the peculiarities of those who wrote. So that when the nation finally had to act, it carried over into politics all the habits of literature.

When one studies the history of our Revolution, one finds that the spirit that guided it was precisely the same spirit that gave rise to so many abstract books on government: The same fondness for general theories, complete systems of legislation, and exact symmetry in the law; the same contempt for existing facts; the same confidence in theory; the same taste for the original, ingenious, and novel in institutions; the same urge to remake the entire constitution in accordance with the rules of logic and a coherent plan, rather than seek to amend its faulty parts. A terrifying spectacle! For what is meritorious in a writer is sometimes a flaw in a statesman, and the same qualities that have often issued in great literature can also give rise to great revolutions.

The language of politics itself took on some of the character of the language spoken by authors, replete with general expressions, abstract terms, pretentious words, and literary turns of phrase. This style, abetted by the political passions that employed it, penetrated all classes of society, filtering down with remarkable ease to the lowest among them. Well before the Revolution, the edicts of Louis XVI frequently spoke of natural law and the rights of man. I found peasants who, in their petitions, referred to their neighbors as fellow citizens, to the intendant as a respectable magistrate, to the parish priest as minister of the altars, and to God as the Supreme Being. All they needed to become rather mediocre writers was a knowledge of spelling.

So fully were these new qualities incorporated into the ancient well-spring of the French character that many observers ascribe to our nature what is merely a product of this peculiar education. I have heard it said that the taste, or, rather, the passion that for the past sixty years we have exhibited for general ideas, systems, and big words in political matters stems from I know not what peculiarity of our race, or from what is somewhat bombastically referred to as "the French spirit," as if the alleged trait had somehow suddenly burst forth at the end of the eighteenth century after remaining hidden throughout our previous history.

What is remarkable is that we have clung to habits we acquired from literature while losing our former love of letters almost entirely. In the course of my public life, I have often been astonished to see people who read few works of the eighteenth century, or any other century, for that matter, and who are quite contemptuous of writers, yet who quite faithfully preserve some of the principal defects that the literary spirit nurtured long before they were born.

III.2 – How Irreligion Was Able to Become a General and Dominant Passion in Eighteenth-Century France, and How It Influenced the Character of the Revolution

In the wake of the great revolution of the sixteenth century, when the critical spirit had applied itself to the task of distinguishing false from true among the various Christian traditions, bolder and more curious minds had repeatedly dared to contest or reject all of them. The same spirit that had led millions of Catholics to abandon Catholicism in Luther's time impelled a few individual Christians every year to abandon Christianity itself: unbelief followed heresy.

In general terms it is safe to say that by the eighteenth century, Christianity had lost much of its power throughout Europe. In most countries, however, it was neglected rather than violently combated. Even those countries that abandoned religion did so almost regretfully. Irreligion was widespread among princes and clever wits but had yet to penetrate deeply into the middle and lower classes. It was still an intellectual caprice, not a common opinion. In 1787, Mirabeau said that "it is widely believed in Germany that the Prussian provinces are full of atheists. The truth is that although some freethinkers can be found there, the common people are as devoted to religion as in the most devout countries, and indeed there is no shortage of fanatics."[1] It was deeply to be regretted, moreover, that

---

[1] The quotation is somewhat inaccurate. Mirabeau actually wrote that "it is a widespread prejudice in Germany that the Prussian provinces, and Berlin in particular, are populated exclusively by atheists." The second part of the quotation, which follows some intervening

Frederick II had not authorized the marriage of Catholic priests and, even more, that he had refused to allow those who did marry to keep the income from their benefices, "a measure, I daresay, that would have been worthy of that great man." Nowhere had irreligion yet become a general, ardent, intolerant, and oppressive passion, except in France.

There, something totally unprecedented occurred. Established religions had come under violent attack before, but the ardor directed against them had always stemmed from the zeal inspired by some new religion. Even the false and detestable religions of Antiquity did not arouse passionate adversaries in large numbers until Christianity offered itself as a replacement. Until then, the old religions had been dwindling quietly and steadily amid doubt and indifference: dying of old age, as it were. In France, Christianity was attacked with a kind of frenzy, yet no one even tried to replace it with another religion. Opponents of religion sought zealously and tirelessly to drain souls of their faith, then left them empty. A host of enthusiasts took this thankless task upon themselves. Absolute disbelief – a state contrary to man's natural instincts and most painful to the soul – somehow appealed to the multitude. What had previously produced only morbid enervation now gave rise to fanaticism and a proselytizing spirit.

The simultaneous appearance of a number of major writers disposed to deny the truths of the Christian religion seems insufficient to account for such an extraordinary occurrence. Why did all these writers, without exception, turn in this direction rather than some other? Why did none think of defending the opposite thesis? And why did they, more than any of their predecessors, find the masses so eager to give them a hearing and believe what they said? Only causes quite specific to their time and place can explain what they tried to do and, even more, why they succeeded. The Voltairian spirit had long since found its place in the world, but Voltaire himself could hardly have triumphed anywhere but in France in the eighteenth century.

Grant first that the Church was no more vulnerable to attack in France than anywhere else. Indeed, the vices and abuses that had become mixed up with religion were less serious in France than in most Catholic countries. The Church was infinitely more tolerant than it had been previously in France and elsewhere still was. Hence, the specific causes of this

text, refers to "those fanatics known in Germany as *Pietists.*" See *De la monarchie prussienne sous Frédéric le Grand*, vol. 5 (London, 1788), p. 22.

phenomenon are to be sought not so much in the state of religion as in the state of society.

To understand this, one must never lose sight of what I said in the previous chapter: that because the spirit of political opposition to which the deficiencies of the government gave rise could not manifest itself in public life, it sought refuge in literature, and writers became the true leaders of the great party that sought to overturn all of the country's social and political institutions.

Once this point has been properly grasped, the focus of the question changes. The point is to explain not how the Church of that time might have sinned as a religious institution but how it stood in the way of the impending political revolution and was, therefore, bound to be particularly troublesome for the writers who were the principal promoters of that revolution.

The very principles of church government stood opposed to the principles that the writers hoped to see prevail in civil government. The Church was founded above all on tradition; the writers professed complete contempt for any institution based on respect for the past. The Church recognized an authority superior to individual reason; the writers relied solely on individual reason. The Church was based on hierarchy; the writers favored the obliteration of all distinctions of rank. In order to reach an accommodation with the Church, both sides would have had to admit that because political society and religious society are essentially different in nature, they cannot be governed by the same principles. But agreement on that point was then a long way off, and it seemed that in order to attack state institutions, one first had to destroy the church institutions that served as their base and model.

At the time, moreover, the Church was itself the leading political power – indeed, the most detested of all, though not the most oppressive. For it had involved itself in politics when neither its vocation nor its nature compelled it to do so; it often sanctified in politics vices that it condemned elsewhere, covering them with its sacred inviolability. It seemed to want to bestow its own immortality on the other political powers as well. Any attack on the Church was sure to resonate straightaway with public passions.

In addition to these general reasons, however, writers had more specific and, as it were, more personal reasons for attacking the Church. The Church represented the part of government that was closest to them, and most directly hostile. Only occasionally did the other powers inflict themselves on writers, but the Church, with its special responsibility for supervising thought and censuring the written word, interfered with them constantly. When they defended intellectual freedom in general against the encroachments of the Church, they were fighting on their own behalf, and their first objective was to break the shackles that gripped them most tightly.

The Church, moreover, seemed to be, and indeed was, the most vulnerable and least well-defended flank of the vast edifice on which they directed their attack. It had grown weaker as temporal princes grew stronger. Having been first the princes' superior and later their equal, the Church was reduced to being their client. A certain reciprocity was established: the princes lent the Church their material strength, and it lent them its moral authority. They enforced obedience to its precepts; it preached respect for their will. This can be a dangerous bargain when revolution approaches, and is always disadvantageous to a power based not on coercion but on belief.

Although our kings still referred to themselves as eldest sons of the Church, they badly neglected their obligations to it. They exhibited far less ardor in protecting it than in defending their own government. True, they did not permit anyone to lay a hand on the Church directly, but they stood by and allowed it to be pierced from afar by a thousand arrows.

The half-measures that were imposed on the enemies of the Church at that time did not diminish their power but rather increased it. At times the oppression of writers can halt the movement of ideas; at other times it can accelerate it. But never has policing of the press of the sort attempted at this time failed to multiply its power a hundredfold.

Authors were persecuted just enough to elicit complaint but not enough to provoke fear. They were subjected to enough restraint to provoke resistance but not to the heavy yoke that might quell it. The attacks they endured were invariably drawn-out, tempestuous, and futile affairs whose purpose seemed not so much to dissuade them from writing as to spur them to it. Complete freedom of the press would have been less damaging to the Church.

In 1768, Diderot wrote to David Hume: "You think that our intolerance is more favorable to the progress of the mind than your unlimited freedom; d'Holbach, Helvétius, Morellet, and Suard do not share your opinion." It was the Scot who was right, however. Living in a free country, he knew from experience. Diderot's view was that of an author, Hume's that of a politician.

I stop the first American I meet, whether in his own country or else-where, and I ask him if he thinks religion helps to stabilize laws and achieve a well-ordered society. Without hesitation he answers that a civilized society cannot endure without religion, much less a free society. In his eyes, respect for religion is the greatest guarantee there is of the stability of the state and the security of individuals. Even those least well versed in the science of government know that much. Yet there is no country in the world in which the boldest political doctrines of the eighteenth-century *philosophes* are more widely applied than in America. Only their antireligious doctrines failed to establish a presence there, even with the advantage of unlimited freedom of the press.

I would say the same thing about the English. Our irreligious philosophy was preached in England even before most of our *philosophes* were born: It was Bolingbroke who completed Voltaire's education. Throughout the eighteenth century, unbelief found celebrated advocates in England. Clever writers and deep thinkers espoused its cause yet were never able to secure its victory as in France because all who had something to fear in revolution hastened to support established beliefs. Even those who were most deeply involved in the French society of the time, and who did not deem French philosophies to be false, nevertheless rejected them as dangerous. As is always the case in free nations, great political parties found that they had an interest in tying their cause to that of the Church. Bolingbroke himself became an ally of the bishops. The clergy, inspired by these examples and never feeling isolated, fought energetically in their own cause. The Church of England, despite the flaws in its constitution and the abuses of all kinds prevalent within it, successfully withstood the shock. Writers and orators emerged from its ranks and eagerly devoted themselves to the defense of Christianity. Theories hostile to Christian doctrine were discussed and refuted, then ultimately rejected, thanks to society's own effort, without government intervention.

But why search for examples outside of France? What French writer today would think of writing the books of Diderot or Helvétius? Who would want to read them? I would almost say, who knows their titles? The experience of public life that we have acquired over the past sixty years, though incomplete, has been sufficient to spoil our taste for this dangerous literature. See how respect for religion has gradually regained its influence among the various classes of the nation as each of them acquired public experience in the harsh school of revolution. The old nobility, which was the most irreligious class before 1789, became the most fervent after 1793. The first to be attacked, it was the first to convert. When the victorious bourgeoisie felt itself under assault, it, too, moved closer to faith. Little by little, respect for religion progressed wherever men had something to lose in popular disorder, and disbelief disappeared, or at least went into hiding, as fear of revolution manifested itself.

The situation at the end of the Ancien Régime was different. We had so completely lost our pragmatic knowledge of great human affairs, and we were so utterly oblivious of the role of religion in the government of empire, that disbelief initially took hold in the minds of the very people who had the most personal and pressing interest in maintaining order in the state and obedience in the people. They not only welcomed disbelief but, in their blindness, spread it among those below them. In their indolent lives impiety became a kind of pastime.

The Church of France, previously so fertile in great orators, thus felt it had been deserted by all who should have shared a common interest in championing its cause and therefore fell silent. For a time, it was possible to believe that as long as it was allowed to keep its wealth and its position, it was prepared to admit error as to its faith.

With those who denied Christianity raising their voices and those who still believed remaining silent, what happened was something we have often seen since that time, not only in religion but in every other area as well. People who clung to the old faith were afraid that no one else remained faithful, and, dreading isolation more than error, they joined the crowd without sharing its ideas. What was still the sentiment of only part of the nation therefore appeared to be the opinion of all, and thus seemed irresistible to the very people who created that false appearance.

The universal discredit into which all religious beliefs fell at the end of the last century undoubtedly exerted the greatest influence on our entire Revolution; it marked its character. Nothing did more to impress upon its features the terrifying expression that has so often been described.

When I try to disentangle the various effects that irreligion produced at the time in France, I find that it was far more by deranging minds than by degrading hearts or even corrupting morals that it led people to such remarkable extremes.

When religion deserted souls, it did not leave them, as so often happens, empty and debilitated. For a time they brimmed with new feelings and ideas, which temporarily took the place of religion and prevented any immediate lapse into depression.

If the French who made the Revolution were more unbelieving than we are, they retained at least one admirable belief that we do not share: they believed in themselves. They did not doubt the perfectibility or power of man. They clamored eagerly for man's glory and had faith in his virtue. They bolstered their own strength with that proud confidence that often leads to error but without which a people is capable only of servitude. They had no doubt that they had been summoned to transform society and regenerate the human race. These sentiments and passions had become for them a kind of new religion, which, by producing some of the important effects that religions have been known to produce, delivered them from individual egoism, fostered heroism and self-sacrifice, and in many cases made them indifferent to all the petty goods that possess us.

Having studied a great deal of history, I make bold to affirm that I know of no other revolution in which one finds at the start, in such large numbers of people, a more sincere patriotism, a more selfless disposition, or a more authentic grandeur. The nation exhibited the chief defect but also the chief quality of youth: inexperience and generosity.

Yet irreligion did immense public harm.

In most of the great political revolutions that had taken place previously, those who attacked established laws had respected beliefs, and in most religious revolutions, those who attacked religion had not sought at the same time to change the nature and order of all powers and to abolish the existing constitution of the government from top to bottom. Hence, even in the greatest social upheavals, there had always been a point of stability.

In the French Revolution, however, religious laws were abolished even as civil laws were overturned, so that the human mind lost its bearings altogether. It no longer knew what to hold on to or where to stop, and one witnessed the emergence of revolutionaries of a previously unknown species, who carried boldness to the point of folly, whom no innovation could surprise nor scruple slow, and who never shrank from executing any design. One must not think, moreover, that these new beings were the singular and ephemeral creations of a moment, destined to vanish when it did. They have since formed a race that has perpetuated itself and spread to all the civilized corners of the earth, a race that has everywhere retained the same appearance, the same passions, and the same character. It was in the world when we were born; it is still with us today.

III.3 – How the French Wanted Reforms Before They Wanted Liberties

One thing worth noting is that of all the ideas and sentiments that paved the way for the Revolution, the idea of, and the taste for, political liberty in the strict sense were the last to appear and the first to vanish.

The old edifice of government had been shaky for some time. It was already tottering, and the question of political liberty had yet to arise. Voltaire scarcely thought about it: three years in England had shown him what freedom looked like but had not brought him to love it. The skeptical philosophy that was freely preached in England delighted him. English political laws left him unmoved; he noticed the flaws more than the virtues. In his letters on England, which are among his masterpieces, he has less to say about Parliament than about anything else. In reality, he envied the English mainly for their literary freedom but cared little for their political freedom, as if the former could ever exist for long without the latter.

Toward the middle of the century, writers who focused especially on questions of public administration began to appear, and since they shared certain similar principles in common, they were referred to collectively as "Economists" or "Physiocrats." The Economists have left less of a mark on history than the philosophers. They may not have contributed as much to the advent of the Revolution. Yet I believe that the true nature of the event is best studied in their works. The philosophers rarely got beyond very general and very abstract ideas about government. The Economists, while clinging to their theories, nevertheless penetrated closer to facts. The former described what could be imagined, while the latter at times indicated what was to be done. All the institutions that the Revolution would abolish for good were special targets of their attacks. Not one found favor in their eyes. By contrast, all the institutions that can pass as the Revolution's own creations they heralded in advance and ardently recommended. It would be difficult to cite a single one of those institutions whose seed was not sown in one of their works. All that was most substantial in the Revolution can be found in their writings.

What is more, one can already recognize in their books the revolutionary and democratic temperament that we know so well. Not only do they hate certain privileges but diversity itself is also odious to them: They would worship equality even in servitude. Anything that stands in the way of their designs is fit only to be smashed. Contracts inspire in them little respect; private rights no consideration. Or, rather, in their eyes, private rights, strictly speaking, have already ceased to exist, and there is only public utility. Yet these were on the whole quiet men of mild manners, people of substance, respectable magistrates, and capable administrators. But the spirit peculiar to their work carried them away.

For the Economists, the past was an object of boundless contempt. "The nation has for centuries been governed by false principles," Letrosne wrote. "Everything seems to have been left to chance." Starting from this idea, they set to work. There was no institution, no matter how old or seemingly well founded, whose abolition they did not seek if it even slightly hindered their plans or disturbed their symmetry. One of them proposed to eliminate all the old territorial divisions and change the names of the provinces forty years before the Constituent Assembly actually did so.

Before the idea of free institutions dawned on them, they had already conceived of all the social and administrative reforms that the Revolution would accomplish. To be sure, they were very much in favor of free trade in commodities, of *laisser faire, laisser passer* in commerce and industry. But they did not dream of political freedoms as such, and even when by chance thoughts of such freedoms did cross their minds, they initially rejected them. Most were at first quite hostile to deliberative assemblies, local and secondary powers, and, in a general way, all the counterweights that had been established at various times in free nations everywhere to balance the central power. "The system of counterforces in government is a fatal idea," Quesnay said. And one of his friends remarked that "the speculations that have led people to imagine a system of counterweights are delusional."

The only protection they could conceive against the abuse of power was public education, for as Quesnay said, "despotism is impossible if the nation is enlightened." One of his disciples remarked that "struck by the evils engendered by the abuses of authority, men have invented a myriad of totally useless remedies and have neglected the only truly effective one, which is general and continuing public instruction in the essence of justice and the natural order." With such literary blather, they hoped to meet all needs for political safeguards.

Letrosne, who so bitterly deplored the government's neglect of the countryside and who described a rural landscape without roads, without industry, and without enlightenment, never contemplated the possibility that rural France might be better administered if the task were turned over to the inhabitants themselves.

Even Turgot, whose great soul and rare genius set him apart from the rest, had little more taste for political liberties than they did, or in any case did not acquire that taste until late in life, and when public sentiment prompted him to do so. For him, as for most of the Economists, the primary political safeguard was public education provided by the state according to certain methods and in a certain spirit. The confidence that he showed in this sort of intellectual medication, or, as one of his contemporaries put it, in the "mechanism of a principled education," was unlimited. In a memorandum to the king proposing a plan along these lines, he wrote: "Sire, I make so bold as to reply that within ten years your nation will no longer be recognizable and that by dint of education, good morals, and enlightened zeal in your service and in the service of the country, it will stand far above all other peoples. Children who are now ten will find themselves prepared for the state, devoted to their country, obedient to authority not out of fear but out of reason, helpful to their fellow citizens, and accustomed to recognize and respect justice."

Political liberty had been destroyed in France so long ago that people had almost entirely forgotten what its conditions and effects had been. What is more, the deformed vestiges that remained, and the institutions that seem to have been created to take its place, made it suspect and fomented many prejudices against it. Most of the remaining assemblies of estates preserved not just the outmoded forms but also the spirit of the Middle Ages and, far from assisting social progress, rather impeded it. The parlements, which alone occupied the place reserved for political bodies, were incapable of preventing the government from doing harm but often prevented it from doing good.

To the Economists, the idea of carrying out the revolution they imagined with the aid of all these old instruments seemed impractical. The thought of entrusting the execution of their plans to a nation now in charge of its own destiny pleased them very little, for how could an entire people be persuaded to adopt such a vast system of reform whose component parts were so intricately related? To them it seemed easier and more opportune to induce the royal administration itself to serve their designs.

This new power had not emerged from medieval institutions and did not bear their imprint. Despite its errors, the Economists were able to discern certain promising traits. It shared their natural taste for equality of conditions and uniformity of rules. Like them, it deeply detested all the old powers that stemmed from feudalism and were tending toward aristocracy. One would have searched the rest of Europe in vain for a governmental machine equally well constructed, impressive, and powerful. The existence of such a government in France struck the Economists as a singular stroke of luck. They might have called it providential, had it been as fashionable then as it is now to invoke Providence at the drop of a hat. "The situation in France," Latrosne wrote, "is infinitely better than in England, because here one can carry out reforms that change the state of the entire country in an instant, whereas in England such reforms can always be impeded by the parties."

Hence, the goal was not to destroy this absolute power but to convert it. "The state," wrote Mercier de La Rivière, "must govern in accordance with the rules of the essential order, and when it does so, it must be 'omnipotent.'" Another writer said, "Let the state understand its duty well, and then leave it free." From Quesnay to Abbé Baudeau, all shared the same temperament.

They did not count on the royal administration solely to reform the society of their time. They borrowed from it, in part, the idea of the future government they hoped to establish. Looking at one, they formed an image of the other.

In the view of the Economists, the state is responsible not only for ruling the nation but also for shaping it in a certain way. It is the state's job to fashion the minds of its citizens according to a certain preestablished model. Its duty is to fill the people's minds with certain ideas and to fill their hearts with certain sentiments, which it deems to be necessary. In reality, there are no limits to its prerogatives and no boundaries to what it can do. It not only reforms men but transforms them. It may be within its power to turn them into something utterly different from what they are. "The state makes of men whatever it wants," said Baudeau. This dictum sums up all their theories.

The immense social power that the Economists imagined was not only greater than any power they could see before them; it was also different in origin and character. It did not flow directly from God. It was not moored in tradition. It was impersonal. It was no longer called "king" but "state." It was not the legacy of a family. It was the product and representative of all, with the duty to ensure that the rights of each individual were subordinate to the will of all.

This particular form of tyranny, known as democratic despotism, of which the Middle Ages had no idea, was already familiar to the Economists: no more social hierarchy, no more well-demarcated classes, no more fixed ranks; a people composed of almost identical and entirely equal individuals, an indistinct mass recognized as the only legitimate sovereign but carefully deprived of all the faculties that might allow it to rule or even oversee its government by itself; above it, a single designated official charged with acting in its name without consulting it; to control that official, a public reason deprived of organs; to stop him, revolutions and not laws – de jure a subordinate agent but de facto a master.

Not finding anything in their vicinity that lived up to this ideal, they went looking for it in remote corners of Asia. I am not exaggerating when I say that there was not a single Economist who did not somewhere in his writings lavish fulsome praise on China. When you read their books, you are sure to come across this, if nothing else. Moreover, since little is known about China even now, there was no kind of nonsense that they did not dispense about the country. China's incompetent and barbarous government, which a handful of Europeans were able to manipulate at will, struck them as the perfect model for all nations of the world to copy. For them, China was what first England and then America would later become for all the French. They were moved and apparently delighted by a country whose sovereign, absolute but unprejudiced, plowed the earth once a year with his own hands to honor the useful arts, where all official posts were obtained through literary competitions, and where philosophy was the only religion and men of letters the only aristocracy.

People think that the destructive theories that nowadays go by the name "socialism" are of recent origin. This is a mistake: these theories were contemporaneous with the first Economists. While they employed the all-powerful government of their dreams as an instrument to change the forms of society, socialists imagined seizing the same power to under-mine its base.

Read Morelly's *Code de la nature*, and you will find, along with all the Economists' doctrines concerning the omnipotence and unlim-ited prerogatives of the state, any number of the political theories that France has lately found most frightening – theories whose birth we imag-ine having witnessed: communal property, the right to work, absolute equality, uniformity in all things, mechanical regularity in all individual movements, tyranny by regulation, and total subsumption of the citizen's individuality in the social body.

Article 1 of Morelly's Code states: "Nothing in society shall belong individually or as property to anyone." Article 2 states: "Property is detestable, and anyone who attempts to restore it shall be imprisoned for life as a madman and enemy of humanity. Each citizen shall be fed, maintained, and occupied at public expense.... All output shall be stored in public warehouses for distribution to all citizens, to meet their vital needs. Cities shall be built according to the same plan. All private buildings shall be identical. At the age of five, all children shall be taken from their families and raised in common at state expense, in a uniform fashion." The book might strike you as having been written yesterday, but it is a hundred years old. It came out in 1755, just as Quesnay was founding his school. Therein lies proof that centralization and socialism are products of the same soil. The one is to the other what the cultivated fruit is to the wild stock.

Of all the men of their time, the Economists are the ones who would seem least out of place in ours. Their passion for equality was so pro-nounced and their taste for liberty so uncertain that they give the mislead-ing appearance of being our contemporaries. When I read the speeches and writings of the men who made the Revolution, I feel as though I had been suddenly transported to a place and society with which I am unfamiliar, but when I peruse the books of the Economists, I have the feeling that I have lived with these people and talked with them only a moment ago.

In 1750, the nation as a whole was no more exigent in regard to politi-cal liberty than the Economists themselves. It had lost the taste for it, and even the idea, when it lost the use. It wanted reforms more than it wanted rights, and if there had been on the throne a prince of the stature and dis-position of Frederick the Great, I have no doubt that he would have car-ried out some of the most important reforms of society and government that the Revolution eventually achieved, and he would have done so not only without losing his crown but also with a great increase in his power. It is said that one of Louis XV's most able ministers, M. de Machault, had an inkling of this and spelled it out for his master. But projects of this sort are never undertaken on the advice of others. They can be carried out only by those capable of conceiving them.

Twenty years later, things were different: an image of political liberty had imprinted itself on the French mind, and with each passing day it became more and more attractive to the French people. Signs of the change abound. Provinces once more conceived the desire to administer themselves. The idea that the people as a whole have the right to participate in their government gained a hold in many minds. Memories of the old Estates General revived. The nation, which detested its own history, recalled this part alone with pleasure. The new current swept up the Economists themselves and forced them to complicate their unitary system with a few free institutions.

When the parlements were destroyed in 1771, the same public that had so often been obliged to suffer from their prejudices was deeply disturbed by their downfall. With them, the last barrier that might have contained royal absolutism seemed to fall.

This opposition astonished and enraged Voltaire. "Nearly the entire kingdom is in an uproar and a state of consternation," he wrote to his friends. "The ferment is as strong in the provinces as in Paris itself. Yet the edict strikes me as full of useful reforms. To end the venality of office, make justice free, avoid the need for litigants to come to Paris from the extremities of the realm only to ruin themselves, and have the king pay the fees of seigniorial judges – are these not great services to the nation? Furthermore, haven't these parlements often been barbaric persecutors? To tell the truth, I marvel at the humble 'Frenchies' who take the part of these insolent and insubordinate bourgeois. For my part, I think that the king is right, and since one must serve, I think that it is better to do so under a pedigreed lion, who is born stronger than I, than under two hundred rats of my own kind." And by way of excuse he added: "Imagine how infinitely delighted I am by the favor the king has done all the lords of the land by bearing the cost of their courts."

Voltaire, who had long been absent from Paris, thought that public opinion remained as he had left it. This was by no means the case. The French no longer limited themselves to wanting their affairs to be conducted more efficiently. They had begun to want to take charge for themselves, and it had become apparent that the great revolution to which everything was leading would take place not only with the consent of the people but also by their own hands.

From that moment on, I think that this radical revolution, which would consign all that was worst along with all that was best in the Ancien Régime to the same ruin, was inevitable. People so ill-prepared to act for themselves could hardly expect to reform everything at once without destroying everything. An absolute monarch would have been a less dangerous innovator. When I think that this revolution, which destroyed so many institutions, ideas, and habits inimical to liberty, also did away with others that liberty can hardly do without, I tend to think that had it been carried out by a despot, it might have left us less unprepared to become a free nation someday than we were after it had been carried out by the people in the name of their own sovereignty.

Anyone who wants to understand our Revolution must never lose sight of this.

When the French rediscovered their love of political liberty, they had already conceived certain ideas about government that were not only not easy to reconcile with the existence of free institutions but almost hostile to them.

They had embraced the ideal of a society in which the sole aristocracy would consist of public officials and a single, all-powerful administration would control the state and be the guardian of individuals. Although they wished to be free, they had no intention of abandoning this fundamental idea. They merely attempted to reconcile it with the idea of liberty.

Hence, they sought to combine unlimited administrative centralization with a preponderant legislative body: bureaucratic administration and representative government. The nation as a body enjoyed all the rights of sovereignty, but each individual citizen was gripped in the tightest dependency. The experience and virtues of a free people were required of the former, the qualities of a good servant of the latter.

It was this desire to introduce political liberty amid institutions and ideas that were alien or opposed to it, but to which we were either already accustomed or inclined to be drawn, that for sixty years yielded so many vain attempts at free government, followed by so many tragic revolutions that, in the end, exhausted by so much effort and repelled by such laborious and sterile labor, many of the French abandoned their second aim in order to revert to the first, reducing themselves to the thought that living as equals under a master still had a certain charm after all. And so it is that today we find ourselves much closer to the Economists of 1750 than to our fathers of 1789.

I have often asked myself what the source is of that passion for political liberty that has led in all ages to man's greatest accomplishments. In what sentiments is it rooted? From where does it draw its nourishment?

I see clearly that when nations are badly led, they readily conceive the desire to govern themselves. But this kind of love of independence, which is born only of certain specific and temporary evils that despotism brings in its wake, never lasts. It vanishes with the accident that gave it birth. People seemed to love liberty, but it turns out that they only hated the master. What a people who are made to be free hate is the evil of dependence itself.

Nor do I think that a genuine love of liberty ever arises out of the sole prospect of material rewards, for that prospect is often barely perceptible. It is indeed true that in the long run liberty always brings comfort and well-being and often wealth to those who are able to preserve it. At times, however, it temporarily hinders the use of such goods. At other times despotism alone can ensure their fleeting enjoyment. Those who prize liberty only for the material benefits it offers have never kept it for long.

What has always kindled such a powerful love of liberty in the hearts of certain men is its intrinsic attractiveness, its inherent charm, independent of its benefits. It is the pleasure of being able to speak, act, and breathe without constraint under the sole government of God and the law. Whoever seeks in liberty anything other than liberty itself is born for servitude.

Some people pursue it doggedly through peril and misery of every variety. What they love about it is not the material goods it gives them. They consider liberty itself a good so precious and so necessary that nothing else can console them for its loss, while savoring it consoles them for everything else. Others tire of it amid their riches. They allow it to be plucked from their hands without resistance for fear that any effort to hold on to it will compromise the well-being they owe to it. What do such people lack to remain free? What? The very desire to be free. Do not ask me to analyze that sublime desire; you must feel it. It finds its way unaided into great hearts that God has prepared to receive it. It fills them; it inflames them. To mediocre souls that have never felt it, one cannot hope to make it comprehensible.

III.4 – That the Reign of Louis XVI Was the Most Prosperous Era of the Old Monarchy, and How That Very Prosperity Hastened the Revolution

There can be no doubt that the depletion of the kingdom under Louis XIV began even as that monarch was triumphing over the rest of Europe. We see the first signs of this in the most glorious years of the king's reign. France was ruined well before she ceased to conquer. Who has not read the terrifying essay on administrative statistics that Vauban has left us? The reports that the intendants submitted to the duke of Burgundy at the end of the seventeenth century, even before the unfortunate War of the Spanish Succession, all allude to the nation's increasing decadence, and they do not speak of it as a very recent fact. One says that the population in his region had been decreasing rapidly for some time. Another reports that a certain city, which had once been wealthy and prosperous, is today without industry. Still another writes that once there was manufacturing in his province, but today factories lie abandoned. And in another, farmers previously derived much greater yield from their land than they do now. Twenty years before, agriculture was flourishing. Population and output have diminished by a fifth over the course of roughly thirty years, an intendant in Orléans observes at about the same time. Citizens who esteem absolute government and princes who are fond of war should be urged to read these reports.

Since the primary source of these miseries lay in flaws of the nation's constitution, neither the death of Louis XIV nor the return of peace revived public prosperity. Everyone who wrote about the country's administration or social economy in the first half of the eighteenth century agreed that the provinces did not regain their health. Indeed, many believed that they continued to decline. Only Paris, they said, gained in wealth and population. On this point intendants, former ministers, and men of affairs agreed.

I confess that I, for one, do not believe that France continued to decline in the first half of the eighteenth century, yet an opinion so widespread and shared by so many well-informed people proves if nothing else that no visible progress was being made. Among the administrative documents dealing with this period in our history, all that I have perused do indeed indicate that society had succumbed to a sort of lethargy. The government did little more than persist in old routines while creating nothing new. Cities made almost no effort to improve the comfort or health of their inhabitants. Even individuals avoided any significant undertakings.

Thirty or forty years before the Revolution erupted, things began to change. In all segments of society, it is possible to discover signs of internal agitation that were not previously apparent. Initially these signs become evident only on very diligent examination, but little by little they grow increasingly clear and distinct. Year by year this progress spread and accelerated. At length the entire nation was astir; it seemed to have been reborn. But mark this well: it was not the old life that had been restored. The spirit that moved the great body of the nation was a new spirit, and it resurrected the body only briefly before dissolving it.

Everyone became restless and dissatisfied with his situation and eager to change it. The quest for improvement was universal, but it was an impatient and irritable quest, which led people to curse the past and imagine a state of affairs utterly different from the one that lay before them.

Before long this spirit affected the government itself, transforming it from within while leaving everything outside intact. Laws were not changed, but they were applied differently.

I said earlier that the comptroller general and intendant of 1780 no longer resembled the comptroller general and intendant of 1740. The change is detailed in administrative correspondence. Yet the intendant of 1780 had the same powers, the same subordinates, and the same arbitrary authority as his predecessor; only his goals had changed. One cared about little beyond maintaining obedience in his province, recruiting for the militia, and above all collecting the taille. The other had many other concerns: his head was filled with countless plans to increase public wealth.

Roads, canals, factories, and commerce were his principal preoccupations; agriculture above all drew his attention. Sully became fashionable among administrators of that time.

It was in those days that intendants began to organize the agricultural societies that I discussed earlier. They held competitions and distributed prizes. The comptroller general issued circulars that looked more like treatises on the art of agriculture than official correspondence.

The change in the attitude of people in government is most obvious in the collection of the various taxes that filled the public coffers. The tax laws remained as inequitable, arbitrary, and harsh as in the past, but the flaws in the law were all tempered in the execution.

"When I began studying the tax laws," M. Mollien wrote in his memoirs, "I was terrified by what I found: fines, prison terms, and corporal punishments that special tribunals were allowed to impose for simple omissions; agents of tax farmers who exercised discretionary authority over nearly all property and individuals; and so forth. Fortunately, I did not limit myself to merely reading the tax code, and I soon realized that between the letter of the law and its application, the difference was the same as between the habits of the old tax officials and those of the new. The legal authorities were normally inclined to minimize offenses and moderate punishments."

"To how many abuses and irritations can the collection of taxes give rise!" observed the provincial assembly of Lower Normandy in 1787. "Nevertheless, we must acknowledge the mild and lenient practice of recent years."

Careful study of the documents fully justifies this assertion. Respect for human life and liberty is often apparent. There is above all an evidently genuine concern with the woes of the poor, for which one would have searched in vain in earlier times. The tax authorities rarely resort to violence against the miserable; tax abatements are more frequent, and help is more common. The king increased the amount of funds available for charity workshops in the countryside and aid to the indigent, and often established new funds as well. The state distributed more than 80,000 livres for these purposes to just one *généralité*, Haute Guyenne, in 1779. In 1784, 40,000 went to the *généralité* of Tours, and in 1787, 48,000 to the *généralité* of Normandy. Louis XVI did not wish to leave this aspect of government exclusively to his ministers. At times he took charge of it personally. In 1776, a council decree established damages to be paid to peasants living near royal hunting lodges whose fields had been damaged by the king's game, and the king himself drafted the introduction. Turgot tells us that this good but unfortunate monarch presented him with the text in his own hand, saying, "As you can see, I, too, have been working." If one were to portray the Ancien Régime as it was in the final years of its existence, the portrait would be quite flattering but not a very good likeness.

As these changes took place in the minds of governors and governed alike, public prosperity increased at a hitherto unprecedented pace. There were many signs of this: the population increased, and wealth increased more quickly still. War in America did nothing to slow this growth. The state went deeply into debt, but private individuals continued to grow wealthier. They became more industrious, more enterprising, and more inventive.

"Since 1774," said one contemporary administrator, "various types of industry have developed and thus increased the base of all consumption taxes." Indeed, if you compare treaties concluded in different periods of Louis XVI's reign between the state and the financial companies in charge of collecting taxes, you will find that the price on tax farms rose each time the contract was renewed, and at an increasing rate. The 1786 lease yielded 14 million livres more than the 1780 lease. "One can reckon that the combined yield of all consumption taxes is increasing at the rate of 2 million livres per year," Necker wrote in a 1781 report.

Arthur Young assures us that Bordeaux had a greater volume of trade in 1788 than Liverpool. He added: "In recent times, progress in maritime trade has been even more rapid in France than in England. It has doubled there in twenty years."

By comparing different periods, moreover, it is easy to convince oneself that in no period since the Revolution has public prosperity improved more rapidly than it did in the twenty years prior to the Revolution. In this respect, only the thirty-seven years of constitutional monarchy, which have been for us a time of peace and rapid progress, can compare to the reign of Louis XVI.

There is reason to be surprised that prosperity was already so substantial in France, and increasing so rapidly, given the many flaws of government and the many fetters still placed on industry. It may even be the case that many politicians deny the fact because they cannot explain it, believing with Molière's physician that no patient who breaks the rules can ever get better. Indeed, how could France possibly have thrived and prospered with its unequal taxation, diverse customs, internal tariffs, feudal dues, guilds, venal offices, and all the rest? Yet in spite of all that, it began to acquire wealth and develop everywhere because quite apart from the ill-constructed and ill-meshed system of gears that seemed designed to slow rather than propel the social machine, two very simple and very powerful hidden mechanisms were already holding the whole thing together and driving it toward the goal of public prosperity: a government that remained quite powerful even as it ceased to be despotic and maintained order everywhere, and a nation whose upper classes were already the freest and most enlightened in Europe, where anyone could get rich and retain his fortune once he had done so.

The king continued to speak as master, but in reality he himself was obedient to public opinion, which daily either inspired or swept him along, and which he regularly consulted, feared, and flattered. He was absolute by the letter of the law but limited by the practice. As early as 1784, Necker, in a public document, stated the following as undisputed fact: "Most foreigners find it difficult to conceive of the authority that public opinion exerts in France today. They find it hard to understand the nature of this invisible authority, which is in command even inside the palace of the king. Yet that is the way things are."

Nothing is more superficial than to attribute the greatness and power of a people to the mechanism of its laws alone, for it is less the perfection of the instrument than the power of the motors that produces this kind of result. Look at England: even today its administrative laws seem more complicated, diverse, and irregular than ours. But is there a single country in Europe in which public wealth is greater or private property more extensive, more secure, or more varied, or in which society is wealthier or sounder? This comes not from the goodness of certain particular laws but from the spirit that animates English legislation as a whole. Organs may be imperfect without preventing the organism from functioning, because life is a potent force.

As the prosperity that I have just described developed in France, people seemed to become more unsettled and anxious. Public discontent grew more bitter. Hatred of all ancient institutions increased. The nation was clearly headed for revolution.

Even more, the parts of France that were to become the principal center of that revolution were precisely those where progress was most evident. If one studies what remains of the archives of the former Île-de-France district, it is easy to see that it was in the regions around Paris that the old regime reformed itself soonest and most profoundly. There, the freedom and fortunes of the peasantry were already more effectively guaranteed than in any other *pays d'élection*. Personal labor service had disappeared long before 1789. Collection of the taille had become more regular, more moderate, and more equal than in the rest of France. In order to understand how much an intendant could do in those days to affect the prosperity or misery of an entire province, you must read the 1772 regulation that improved the system under which the taille was collected. It affected every other aspect of the tax. Every year the government sent commissioners into every parish. The community then gathered in their presence. The value of each property was publicly fixed. Each individual's resources were recorded under a process in which objections could be raised and countered. Thus, the base of the taille was established in the presence of those who would be obliged to pay it. No longer did the syndic wield arbitrary power. No longer was there pointless violence. To be sure, the taille retained all the flaws that are intrinsic to it, no matter what the system of collection. It was borne by only one class of taxpayers and affected industry as well as property. But in all other respects it differed profoundly from the tax that still bore the same name in neighboring districts.

Nowhere, by contrast, did the old regime maintain itself better than along the Loire, toward its mouth, in the marshes of Poitou and the moors of Brittany. It was precisely there that civil war flared up and spread and that the most durable and violent resistance to the Revolution occurred. Thus, one might say that the better the situation of the French became, the more unbearable they found it.

It is not always going from bad to worse that leads to revolution. What happens most often is that a people that put up with the most oppressive laws without complaint, as if they did not feel them, reject those laws violently when the burden is alleviated. The regime that a revolution destroys is almost always better than the one that immediately preceded it, and experience teaches that the most dangerous time for a bad government is usually when it begins to reform. Only a great genius can save a prince who undertakes to alleviate the lot of his subjects after a lengthy period of oppression. The evil that one endures patiently because it seems inevitable becomes unbearable the moment its elimination becomes conceivable. Then, every abuse that is eliminated seems only to reveal the others that remain, and makes their sting that much more painful. The ill has diminished, to be sure, but sensitivity to it has increased. Feudalism in the fullness of its power did not inspire as much hatred in the French as did feudalism on the verge of disappearing. The slightest instance of arbitrary rule on the part of Louis XVI seemed harder to bear than all the despotism of Louis XIV. The brief imprisonment of Beaumarchais generated more emotion in Paris than the Dragonnades.[1]

In 1780, no one was still claiming that France was on the decline. Indeed, it seemed that no limits to its further progress remained. It was at that time that the theory of man's continual and unlimited perfectibility first appeared. Twenty years earlier, the future had inspired no hope; now nothing was left to fear. The imagination, preemptively laying claim to this unprecedented impending felicity, inured people to the goods they already possessed and hastened them in pursuit of new things.

Apart from these general reasons for what took place, there were other more specific but no less powerful reasons. Although financial administration had improved along with everything else, it still suffered from flaws having to do with absolute government itself. Because financial arrangements were made in secret and carried no guarantees, some of the worst practices from the time of Louis XIV and Louis XV remained. The very steps that the government took to promote public prosperity, dispense aid and incentives, and undertake public works increased expenditures daily without enhancing receipts to the same degree. Hence, the king was every day plunged into deeper difficulties than any of his predecessors had faced. Like them, he repeatedly left his creditors in distress. Like them, he borrowed wherever he could, without open bidding or competition, and his creditors were never sure of collecting their interest. Even their capital was always at the mercy of the king's good faith.

A witness worthy of trust because he had seen what was happening with his own eyes, and was better placed to do so than anyone else, said at the time that "the French, in their relations with their own government, met with nothing but risk. If they invested their capital in loans to the government, they could never count on interest payments at fixed intervals. If they built the government's ships, repaired its roads, or clothed its soldiers, they were left without guarantees for their advances and without a date certain for reimbursement and were forced to calculate the probabilities of a contract with the ministries as they would the probabilities of a highly speculative loan." With great good sense he added: "In those days, when industry, growing rapidly, had fostered in many men a love of property and a taste and need for wealth, those who entrusted a portion

---

[1] Persecution of Protestant-dominated towns by Louis XIV after the revocation of the Edict of Nantes in 1685.

of their fortune to the state were all the more vexed when the law of contracts was violated by the one debtor who ought to have been most careful to respect it."

The French government abuses criticized here were in fact not new. What was new was the impression they created. Indeed, the flaws of the financial system had been even more glaring in earlier periods. But, since then, changes in government and society had made them infinitely more irritating than in the past.

For twenty years, the government had been far more active and engaged in all sorts of enterprises of which it had never before dreamed and had thus become the largest consumer of industrial products and the largest public works contractor in the kingdom. The number of people who did business with it, who had an interest in its loans, lived on its stipends, and speculated on its contracts, had increased prodigiously. Never had public and private fortunes been so intertwined. Poor management of public finances, which had long been only a public ill, now became for countless families a private calamity. In 1789, the state owed nearly 600 million to its creditors, nearly all of whom were debtors themselves and who, as one financier said at the time, found, in their grievances against the government, partners in everyone who suffered as they did from the fecklessness of the state. Note, moreover, that as the number of malcontents of this sort grew, so did their irritation, because the urge to speculate, the passion to get rich, and the taste for comfort spread along with the growth of business and made such evils seem unbearable to the very same people who, thirty years earlier, would have endured them without complaint.

Consequently, rentiers, merchants, industrialists, businessmen, and bankers, who usually constitute the class most hostile to political innovations and most friendly to the existing government, regardless of its nature, as well as the most obedient to the very laws that it disdains or detests, now became the most impatient and most staunchly favorable to reform. Indeed, it clamored for a complete revolution in the entire financial system, without pausing to consider that a thorough change in that part of government would bring down all the rest.

How could a catastrophe have been avoided? On one side, a nation in which the desire to get rich spread every day more widely. On the other, a government that constantly spurred this new passion but also unsettled it, that both inflamed and frustrated it, and in both respects hastened its own ruin.

III.5 – How Attempts to Relieve the People Stirred Them to Revolt

For 140 years, the people had been entirely absent from the political scene, so it was simply taken for granted that they would never be capable of putting in an appearance. Because they seemed so impassive, they were deemed to be deaf. When their fate began to arouse interest, others began to speak in front of them as if they were not there. Apparently, only those situated above the people were supposed to be able to hear what was said, and the only danger to fear was that they might not get the point.

Those who had the most to fear from the people's wrath discussed out loud, and in their presence, the cruel injustices of which the people had always been the victims. They pointed out to one another the monstrous flaws in the institutions that had oppressed the people most. They used their rhetorical skills to depict the people's misery and ill-remunerated labor. By thus attempting to relieve the people, they filled them with fury. I speak not of writers but of the government and its principal agents and of the privileged themselves.

When the king, thirteen years before the Revolution, attempted to abolish personal labor services, he said this in his preamble: "With the exception of a small number of provinces (the *pays d'états*), nearly all the roads in the kingdom were constructed free of charge by the poorest of our subjects. The full burden was thus borne by those who possess nothing but the strength in their arms and whose interest in roads is merely secondary. Those with a real interest in roads are the landowners, nearly all men of privilege, whose property values have been enhanced by the construction of highways. By forcing the poor to maintain these roads by themselves, and by obliging them to give their time and effort without wages, we deprive them of their sole resource against misery and hunger and put them to work for the benefit of the rich."

When, during the same period, an effort was made to remove from workers the fetters imposed by the system of trade guilds, a proclamation was issued in the king's name declaring "that the right to work is the most sacred of all forms of property; that any law infringing this right violates natural law and should be considered null and void; and, furthermore, that the existing guilds are bizarre and tyrannical institutions, the products of selfishness, greed, and violence." Such words were dangerous. What was even more so was to utter them in vain. A few months later, guilds and personal labor services were reinstated.

It was reportedly Turgot who put these words in the king's mouth. Most of his successors offered similar advice. In 1780, when the king announced to his subjects that increases in the taille would henceforth be publicly promulgated, he was careful to add this gloss: "Taxpayers, already harassed by the manner in which this tax has been collected, have also been vulnerable to unexpected increases, so that the proportion of the tribute paid by the poorest of our subjects has increased more rapidly than the portion paid by everyone else." When the king, not yet daring to equalize the tax burden, nevertheless attempted to equalize collection of taxes that were already shared, he said: "His Majesty hopes that wealthy individuals will not deem themselves to have been injured when, restored to the common level, they are required merely to bear a burden that they long since ought to have shared in a more equal manner."

But it was above all in times of famine that the goal of the privileged classes seems to have been to inflame the passions of the people even more than to supply their needs. One intendant, seeking to stimulate the charity of the rich, spoke "of the injustice and callousness of those landowners who owe everything they possess to the poor man's labor yet allow him to die of hunger after he has worn himself out tending the rich man's property." In similar circumstances the king said: "His Majesty wishes to defend the people against maneuvers that leave them vulnerable to shortages of basic nourishment by forcing them to supply their labor at whatever wage it pleases the wealthy to offer. The king will not tolerate a state of affairs in which some men are sacrificed to the greed of others."

Down to the end of the monarchy, struggles between different administrative powers regularly resulted in clashes of this sort, in which each of the contending parties accused the other of causing the people's misery.

This is clear, for example, in the dispute that erupted in 1772 between the Toulouse Parlement and the king concerning the transport of grain. "The government, with its mistaken measures, risks starving the poor," said the parlement. "The ambition of the parlement and the avarice of the rich are responsible for the public's distress," the king responded. Both parties to the controversy thus labored to instill in the mind of the people the idea that their woes should always be blamed on their superiors.

These statements are found not in secret correspondence but in public documents, which the government and parlement themselves were at pains to print and publish in thousands of copies. In so doing, the king had harsh words for himself and his predecessors: "The state treasury," he said one day, "has been hobbled by the profligacy of several reigns. Many of our inalienable domains have been leased at very low prices." On another occasion he was made to say the following, with more accuracy than prudence: "The trade guilds are above all a product of the fiscal greed of kings." Later he remarked that "if wasteful expenditure has been common, and if the taille has been raised unduly, it is because the financial administration, finding the taille the easiest resource to tap because of its clandestinity, relied on it even though any number of other taxes would have been less onerous for our people."

All of these statements were aimed at the enlightened segment of the nation so as to convince it of the usefulness of certain measures that had been attacked at the behest of special interests. As for the people, it was taken for granted that though they listened, they would not understand.

It has to be acknowledged that for all this benevolence, there remained a great reservoir of contempt for the wretches whose woes one so sincerely wished to alleviate. This is in some ways reminiscent of Mme Duchâtelet, who, according to Voltaire's secretary, was quite comfortable disrobing in front of her servants, in view of the absence of incontrovertible proof that valets were men.

Make no mistake: it was not just Louis XVI and his ministers who spoke in the dangerous ways I have just illustrated. The privileged individuals who were the most direct object of the people's wrath expressed themselves no differently. Admittedly, the upper classes of French society developed a concern with the fate of the poor before the poor began to inspire fear in the upper classes. They took an interest in the pauper before coming to believe that the pauper's woes might end in their ruin. That became apparent mainly in the ten years prior to 1789. During that period, pity was often expressed for the peasants. They were constantly discussed. Ways to alleviate their suffering were sought. The worst abuses from which they suffered were brought to light, and the tax laws they found most oppressive were denounced. Yet the expression of this new-found sympathy was usually as improvident as the callousness that had long preceded it.

Read the minutes of the provincial assembles that met in various parts of France in 1779 and later throughout the kingdom, and study other surviving public documents, and you will be moved by the fine sentiments they contain and surprised by the striking lack of caution in their language.

In 1787, the provincial assembly of Lower Normandy remarked that "the money that the king devoted to the highways has all too often served only to make the rich more comfortable without doing anything useful for the people. It has often been used to improve the access to a chateau, rather than facilitate the entrance of a town or village." In the same assembly, the orders of the nobility and the clergy, after denouncing the evils of compulsory road work, spontaneously offered to contribute 50,000 livres to the improvement of the provincial roads to make them practicable at no increase in cost to the people. It might have cost these men of privilege less to replace the compulsory labor system with a general tax of which they would have paid a share, yet while they were ready to forgo the benefits of unequal taxation, they chose to maintain its appearance. While willing to give up the useful part of their privilege, they insisted on keeping the odious part.

Other assemblies, composed entirely of landowners exempt from the taille, and who certainly intended to maintain their exemption, nevertheless painted the woes that this tax inflicted on the poor in the darkest of colors. They created a terrifying portrait of all its abuses and then took care to produce an unlimited number of copies. What is rather peculiar, moreover, is that to the striking expressions of interest that the people inspired in them, they occasionally added public expressions of contempt. The people had already become the object of their sympathy without yet ceasing to be the object of their disdain.

The provincial assembly of Haute Guyenne, while warmly pleading the cause of the peasants, called them "coarse and ignorant creatures, troublemakers, and uncouth, undisciplined characters." Turgot, who did so much for the people, expressed himself in largely similar terms.

These harsh expressions occurred in documents destined for the widest publicity and intended for the peasants' own eyes. It was as if one lived in one of those parts of Europe, such as Galicia, where the upper classes speak a different language from the lower and cannot be understood by them. Toward peasants subject to the *cens* and other feudal dues, eighteenth-century feudal lawyers often displayed a kindness, moderation, and sense of justice not commonly found in their predecessors, yet in certain places they still spoke of "vile peasants." Apparently, such insulting words were purely formal.

As 1789 drew near, this sympathy for the people's misery became increasingly acute and imprudent. I have held in my hands circulars that several provincial assemblies sent to the residents of various parishes in early 1788 in order to find out for themselves in detail what grievances were on the people's minds.

One of these circulars was signed by an abbé, a great lord, three nobles, and a bourgeois, all members of the assembly and acting in its name. This committee ordered the syndic in each parish to assemble all the peasants and ask them what they had to say against the way in which various taxes were assessed and collected: "We know in general terms that most taxes, especially the salt tax and taille, are disastrous for the farmer, but we are eager to learn about each abuse in particular." The provincial assembly's curiosity did not end there. It wanted to know how many people in each parish enjoyed any type of tax privileges, including nobles, ecclesiastics, and commoners, and what precisely those privileges were. What was the value of property owned by those enjoying such exemptions? Did they reside on their land or not? How much church property was there, or, as one said at the time, how much property in *mortmain*, not available for sale, and how much was it worth? All this was still not enough to satisfy them. The committee wanted to know the value of the share of taxes, including the taille, capitation, labor services, and other taxes, that would have to be borne by the privileged if equal taxation existed.

This was to inflame each and every individual by enumerating his woes and pointing a finger of blame at those responsible, thereby emboldening the victims by revealing the small number of authors of their woes, piercing their hearts to the quick, and setting them ablaze with greed, envy, and hatred. It was as if the Jacquerie,[1] the Maillotins,[2] and the Sixteen[3] had been utterly forgotten, and as if one were unaware of the fact that the

---

[1] Peasant uprising in 1358.
[2] Parisian tax revolt of 1382.
[3] Name given to the insurrectional committee of sixteen that ruled Paris during the Wars of Religion in the sixteenth century.

French, who are the gentlest and even the kindest people in the world as long as they remain in their natural state of tranquility, become the most barbarous the moment violent passions rouse them from it.

Unfortunately, I was not able to obtain all the peasants' responses to these fatal questions, but I did find some of them, and these were enough to give a general picture of their state of mind.

In these diatribes, the name of each privileged individual, noble or bourgeois, is carefully indicated. Their way of life is sometimes depicted and always criticized. A strenuous effort is made to determine the value of their property. There is much discussion of the number and nature of their privileges and even more of the harm they do to all the other inhabitants of the village. The number of bushels of wheat due them as rent is noted. Their income is enviously calculated, income from which it is said no one profits. The priest's honoraria, already referred to as "his salary," are characterized as excessive. There is bitter complaint that every service of the church must be paid for and that a pauper cannot even be buried for free. Taxes are all unfairly assessed and oppressive. Not a single one finds grace in the peasants' eyes, and they speak of all in vehement terms filled with fury.

"Indirect taxes are odious," they say. "No household is exempt from searches by the tax farmer's agent. Nothing is sacred in his eyes or to his hands. Stamp duties are crushing. The collector of the taille is a tyrant, whose greed seizes upon whatever means are available to harass the poor. The bailiffs are no better. No honest farmer is safe from their vindictiveness. Collectors are forced to ruin their neighbors lest they make themselves vulnerable to the voraciousness of these despots."

This survey does not merely herald the approach of the Revolution. The Revolution is present in it. It is already speaking its own language and baring its true face.

Among the many differences between the religious revolution of the sixteenth century and the French Revolution, one stands out. In the sixteenth century, most great nobles were quick to change religion out of calculated ambition or greed. By contrast, the people embraced change out of conviction and with no expectation of profit. In the eighteenth century, things were different. It was disinterested beliefs and generous sympathies that moved the enlightened classes and set them on the path to revolution, whereas the people were agitated by bitter grievances and a passionate desire to change their situation. The enthusiasm of the former ultimately inflamed and armed the wrath and covetousness of the latter.

III.6 – On Some Practices That Helped the Government Complete the People's Revolutionary Education

The government itself had long labored to instill in the mind of the people any number of ideas that have since been called revolutionary – ideas hostile to the individual and to private rights and friendly to violence.

The king was the first to demonstrate how contemptuous one could be toward the most ancient and apparently well-established institutions. Louis XV shook the monarchy and hastened the Revolution as much by his innovations as by his vices, as much by his energy as by his lethargy. When the people witnessed the downfall and disappearance of the parlement, which was nearly as old as the monarchy itself and previously thought to be as unshakable, they vaguely understood that a time of violence and hazard was approaching, one of those times in which everything becomes possible, when few things are so old as to be respectable or so new that they cannot be tried.

Louis XVI spoke throughout his reign of reforms to be tried. There were few institutions whose imminent ruin his words did not herald, before the Revolution arrived to sweep them all away in fact. After removing some of the worst of these from the law books, he soon put them back. It was as if his intent had been only to uproot, leaving it to others to pull down.

Among the reforms that he carried out himself, some abruptly altered ancient and respected habits without adequate preparation, at times violating established rights. They thus laid the groundwork for the Revolution, not so much by knocking down what stood in its way as by showing the people how they might do so themselves. What compounded the evil was precisely the pure and unselfish intentions of the king and his ministers, for there is no more dangerous example than that of violence exercised for good purposes by men of good will.

Much earlier, Louis XIV, through his public edicts, had taught the theory that all the land in the kingdom had belonged to the state and been leased conditionally, so that the state was the only real landowner. All others were merely tenants in possession, whose title to their land remained defective and open to challenge. This doctrine was rooted in feudal law, but it was proclaimed in France only when feudalism was dying, and the courts never accepted it. It is the central doctrine from which modern socialism descends. It is curious to find it first taking root in royal despotism.

In subsequent reigns, the administration daily taught the people in more practical terms, easier for all to grasp, that it was proper to be contemptuous of private property. In the second half of the eighteenth century, when the taste for public works, and especially roads, began to spread, the government did not refrain from seizing whatever land it needed for its projects and tearing down any houses that stood in the way. The Department of Bridges and Roads was at that time as enamored of the geometric beauty of the straight line as it is today. It carefully avoided existing roads if they were even slightly curved, and rather than make a minor detour, it would cut through a thousand inheritances. Properties devastated or destroyed in this way were almost always paid for belatedly and arbitrarily and often not paid for at all.

When the provincial assembly of Lower Normandy took over the administration from the intendant, it found that all the land taken by eminent domain for road building over the previous twenty years had yet to be paid for. The debt accumulated by the state and still unpaid in this small corner of France amounted to 250,000 livres. The number of large landowners injured by this practice was limited, but the number of small landowners hurt was large because the land had already been subdivided. Each of them had learned from his own experience that the rights of the individual merited little respect when public interest called for them to be violated, and he was careful not to forget this lesson when it came time to apply it to others for his own benefit.

In a great many parishes, there used to be charitable foundations whose purpose, as envisioned by their founders, was to come to the aid of the inhabitants of the parish in the manner indicated in the founder's will.

Most of these foundations were destroyed in the last days of the monarchy or diverted from their original purpose by mere council decrees, which is to say, by purely arbitrary decisions of the government. It was common to take funds given in this way to villages and bestow them on nearby hospitals. At about the same time, the property of these hospitals was transformed in ways that their founders never envisioned and probably would not have adopted. A 1780 edict authorized all such establishments to sell assets that had been bequeathed to them in an earlier era on condition that they be held in perpetuity; the proceeds of this sale were then transferred to the state, which paid interest on the amount. This, it was said, was to make better use of the charity of previous generations than the donors themselves had done. What was forgotten was that the best way to teach men to violate the individual rights of the living is to pay no heed to the wishes of the dead. The contempt that the administrative authorities of the Ancien Régime displayed for the dead has not been surpassed by any of the powers that have succeeded it. What is more, those authorities never displayed the rather meticulous scruples of the English, who lent each citizen the whole force of society to help him enforce his last wishes, with the result that the English show even greater respect for a man's memory than for the man himself.

Requisitions, forced sales of staples, and price controls are all governmental measures that had precedents under the Ancien Régime. In times of shortage, I discovered, administrators set prices in advance on commodities that peasants wished to sell on the marketplace, and when the peasants, afraid of being forced to sell at those prices, failed to turn up on market day, warrants were issued to compel them to appear or else face fines.

But no form of instruction was more pernicious than the application of certain forms of criminal justice to the people. The poor man already enjoyed better safeguards than one might imagine against the depredations of richer and more powerful citizens, but in his dealings with the state, as I indicated earlier, he had no choice but to contend with special courts, biased judges, summary or sham procedures, and injunctions to pay damages from which no appeal was permitted: "The provost of marshals and his lieutenant are hereby summoned to prepare for any disturbances or gatherings that may occur in connection with the grain situation. It is hereby ordered that the case be judged and the verdict rendered by the provost without possibility of appeal. His Majesty forbids any other court of justice to take jurisdiction in this case." This council decree enjoyed the force of law throughout the eighteenth century. From the marshals' records we know that in these circumstances, suspect villages were encircled by night, homes were entered before dawn, and designated peasants were arrested without warrants. Those arrested often remained in prison for lengthy periods before being allowed to speak to a judge, despite the fact that there were edicts ordering that anyone accused of a crime be interrogated within twenty-four hours. This provision of the law was no less categorical than it is today, nor was it any more respected.

So it was that a mild and well-established government daily taught the people a criminal justice code most appropriate to revolutionary times and most convenient to tyranny. Its school was always open. To the end, the Ancien Régime bestowed this dangerous education on the lower classes. Even Turgot faithfully imitated his predecessors in this respect. In 1775, when his new law on grain met with resistance in parlement and rioting in the countryside, he persuaded the king to issue an order that deprived the regular courts of jurisdiction and delivered the mutineers to the provost's court, "whose primary purpose is to suppress popular upheaval when it is useful to set an example without delay." In addition, any peasant who left his parish without signed permission from the priest and syndic was to be pursued, arrested, and tried in the provost's court as a vagabond.

To be sure, in the eighteenth-century monarchy, the forms of punishment were terrifying but the penalties were almost always moderate. One preferred to frighten rather than harm, or, rather, one was arbitrary and violent out of habit and indifference, and mild by temperament. But the taste for summary justice took hold all the more readily as a result. The lighter the punishment, the more easily forgotten was the way in which judgment was pronounced. The mildness of the sentence concealed the horror of the procedure.

Being in possession of the facts, I make so bold as to say that many of the procedures employed by the revolutionary government derived from precedents and examples of measures adopted against the lower classes in the final two centuries of the monarchy. The Ancien Régime provided the Revolution with any number of its formal procedures; the Revolution added only the savagery of its spirit.

III.7 – How a Great Administrative Revolution Preceded the Political Revolution, and on the Consequences It Had

Nothing had yet changed in the form of government, yet most of the secondary laws that govern the lives of individuals and the administration of affairs had already been abolished or amended.

The destruction of the guilds, followed by their partial and incomplete reinstatement, had profoundly altered all existing relations between worker and master. These were not only different but also uncertain and strained. The regulations governing Sunday work were abolished. State oversight was not yet firmly established, and the artisan, placed in a difficult and ambiguous position between the government and the employer, had no idea which of the two could protect him or was supposed to monitor him. The uncomfortable and anarchical state to which the entire urban lower class had been reduced in one fell swoop had immense consequences the moment the people began to return to the political scene.

A year before the Revolution, a royal edict turned the system of justice upside down. Several new jurisdictions were created, a host of others were abolished, and all jurisdictional regulations were changed. Now, in France, as I noted previously, the number of people involved either in judging or enforcing judicial decisions was immense. In truth, the entire bourgeoisie was directly or indirectly dependent on the courts. The immediate effect of the law was therefore to threaten the position and fortune of thousands of families, who suddenly found themselves on a new and more precarious footing. The edict was scarcely less unfortunate in its effects on litigants, who in the midst of this judicial revolution had difficulty identifying which law applied to them and which court was supposed to judge them.

But it was above all the radical reform to which the government itself was subjected in 1787 that first threw public affairs into disarray and then wreaked havoc among citizens, disrupting even their private lives.

As we have seen, in the *pays d'élection*, which is to say in nearly three-quarters of France, districts were governed by a single individual, the intendant, who acted not only without oversight but without advice.

In 1787, a provincial assembly was established at the intendant's side, and this assembly became the real administrator of the district. In every village, an elected municipal body also took the place of the old parish assembly and, in most cases, of the syndic.

The new law, so contrary to what had gone before, and which changed not only the order of affairs but also the relative position of individuals, was supposed to be applied everywhere at once, and in almost the same manner, without any regard for previous practice or for the distinctive situation of each province. Such was the extent to which the unitary spirit of the Revolution had already taken hold of the old government, which the Revolution was soon to bring down.

It then became clear how important a role habit plays in the interaction among political institutions, and how much easier it is for people to make do with obscure and complicated laws with which they have long been familiar than with simpler laws that are new to them.

In France under the Ancien Régime there were all sorts of powers, which varied endlessly from province to province, and none of which had fixed or well-defined limits, so that the field of action of each of them overlapped with that of several others. Despite this, a regular and rather uncomplicated order of business had ultimately been established, whereas the new powers, which were fewer in number, carefully limited, and similar to one another, immediately became entangled in the greatest confusion and often reduced one another to impotence.

Furthermore, the new law contained a major flaw, which by itself would have been enough, especially at the beginning, to make its application difficult: all the powers that it created were collective.

Under the old monarchy, there had been only two methods of government. In places where government was entrusted to a single individual, that individual acted without the assistance of any assembly. Where assemblies existed, as in the *pays d'états* and the cities, executive power was not entrusted to anyone in particular. The assembly not only governed and oversaw the administration but also administered in its own name or through temporary commissions that it appointed.

Since these methods were the only ones known, as soon as one was abandoned, the other was adopted. It is rather strange that in so enlightened a society, in which public administration had long since played such a major role, it never occurred to anyone to combine the two systems and distinguish without separating the executive power from the power to oversee and prescribe. This idea, which seems so simple, never emerged. It was not discovered until this century. In a sense, it is the only major discovery in the realm of public administration that we can claim as our own. We shall soon see the consequences of the contrary practice: in carrying administrative habits over into politics, and obeying the traditions of the Ancien Régime while at the same time detesting it, the National Convention applied the system that the provincial estates and municipal councils of the towns had followed, and what had previously been merely an encumbrance to the transaction of official business overnight became the breeding ground of the Terror.

Thus, the provincial assemblies of 1787 were authorized to administer on their own in most circumstances in which the intendant had previously acted alone. On the authority of the central government, they were charged with apportioning the taille and overseeing its collection, deciding what public works projects to undertake, and managing the execution of those projects. They were in direct command of all agents of the Department of Bridges and Roads, from inspectors on down to laborers. They were supposed to tell these subordinates what to do, report to the minister on their work, and tell him what compensation they deserved. Oversight of local governments was placed almost entirely in the hands of these assemblies. They had initial jurisdiction in all litigation that had previously been handled by the intendant, for example. Many of these new functions were ill-suited to a collective power that could not be held accountable for its actions, in addition to which the duties in question were to be discharged by people who had no previous administrative experience.

What ultimately confused matters still further was the fact that although the intendant was thus reduced to impotence, he was allowed to remain in his post. He was deprived of the absolute power to do as he pleased, only to be assigned the duty to help the assembly and oversee whatever it might do, as if a functionary stripped of power can ever enter into the spirit of the legislation that dispossesses him and facilitate its implementation.

What was done to the intendant was done to his subdelegate as well. Alongside him, in the place he had only recently occupied, a district assembly was established. Its action was to be guided by the provincial assembly and based on similar principles.

Everything that we know from the legislative acts and minutes of the provincial assemblies that were created in 1787 tells us that immediately after coming into being, they engaged in silent and often even open warfare with the intendants, who in turn used their superior experience only to hinder the actions of their successors. Here we find an assembly complaining of the effort required to wrest essential documents from the hands of the intendant. Elsewhere it was the intendant who accused the members of the assembly of wishing to usurp prerogatives that, in his view, the edicts had left to him. He appealed to the minister, who frequently did not answer, or prevaricated, because the matter was as new and obscure to him as to everyone else. In some cases, the assembly concluded that the intendant had not done his job well, that the roads he had built were badly laid out or poorly maintained. He had permitted the ruin of communities that he had overseen. Assemblies were often puzzled by the obscurities of little-known laws. They consulted with others near and far and received a steady stream of advice. The intendant of Auch claimed that he had the right to challenge a provincial assembly that had authorized a commune to assess its own taxes. The assembly asserted that in this matter, the intendant henceforth had the power only to give advice, not to issue orders, and it asked the provincial assembly of Île-de-France for its opinion.

Amid these recriminations and consultations, the work of the administration often slowed and sometimes ground to a halt. Public life then seemed to hang in suspense. "Affairs are at a complete standstill," said the provincial assembly of Lorraine, which in so doing merely echoed the complaints of any number of other assemblies. "All good citizens find this distressing."

In other instances, the new administrations sinned through an excess of assiduousness and self-confidence. All were filled with restless, disruptive zeal, which led them to want to change old methods all at once and hastily correct the longest-standing abuses. On the pretext that it was henceforth their job to oversee the towns, they sought to manage communal affairs themselves. In short, in seeking to improve everything, they ended up creating turmoil everywhere.

Consider, if you will, the vast role that the public administration in France had played for a very long time. Consider the multitude of interests that it affected every day, that depended on it or needed its cooperation. Think of the way in which individuals depended more on it than on themselves to succeed in their own ventures, to promote their industry, to secure their subsistence, to plan and maintain their roads, to keep their peace and guarantee their well-being. Think of all these things and you will have some idea of the infinite number of people who must have been affected personally by the ills from which the administration suffered.

But it was above all in the villages that the flaws of the new organization were felt. There, it not only disturbed the relation of powers to one another but abruptly changed the relative standing of individuals and brought all classes into confrontation and conflict.

When Turgot, in 1775, proposed to the king a reform of the way in which the countryside was administered, the greatest difficulty he faced, as he himself tells us, arose from the unequal apportionment of taxes. Since the principal affairs of a parish involved the assessment, collection, and use of taxes, how could he bring the people of the parish together to deliberate on these matters and act in common when they were not all subject to paying those taxes in the same manner, and some were exempt altogether? In each parish there were nobles and clerics who did not pay the taille, peasants who were partially or totally exempt, and others who paid the full amount. These comprised three distinct parishes, each of which would have required its own administration. The difficulty was insoluble.

Nowhere, in fact, were differences of taxation more visible than in the countryside. Nowhere was the population more divided among different groups, which were often hostile to one another. To give villages a collective administration and free government of their own, it would first have been necessary to subject everyone to the same taxes and reduce the distance between the classes.

This was not done when this reform was at last attempted in 1787. Within the parish, the old separation of orders was maintained, as was the inequality with respect to taxation that was its principal sign, yet the entire task of administration was turned over to elective bodies. This led directly to some quite bizarre consequences.

Take the electoral assembly that was supposed to choose municipal officials. The priest and lord were not allowed to participate because they belonged to the order of the nobility or clergy; in this case, it was primarily up to the Third Estate to elect its representatives.

Once the municipal council was elected, however, the priest and lord were ex officio members because it would not have seemed proper to exclude two such prominent residents from the government of the parish. The lord even presided over the same municipal council whose members he had not been permitted to elect, yet he was prohibited from participating in most of its decisions. When it came time to assess and apportion the taille, for instance, the priest and lord were not allowed to vote. Were they not both exempt from this tax? By the same token, the municipal council had nothing to do with their capitation. It was still determined by the intendant, who relied on special procedures for the purpose.

For fear that the presiding lord, though isolated from the body he was supposed to direct, might nevertheless exert some indirect influence over it inimical to the interest of the order of which he was not a member, a request was made that the votes of his farmers should not count. Consulted on this point, the provincial assemblies found the request fully justified and entirely in keeping with their principles. Other nobles living in the parish were not allowed to sit on the commoners' municipal council unless they were elected by the peasants, in which case they were entitled, as duly noted in the regulation, only to represent the Third Estate.

The lord, therefore, appeared before the council only to be treated in every way as a subordinate of his own former subjects, who had overnight become his masters. He was their prisoner rather than their leader. The goal of bringing these people together in this way seemed to be not so much to bring them closer as to make them see clearly how they differed and how much their interests were opposed.

Was the syndic still the discredited functionary who did his duty only when coerced, or had his status improved along with that of the community whose principal agent he remained? No one knew for sure. I found a letter dated 1788 from a certain local bailiff who was outraged to discover that he had been elected syndic. "This," he said, "is incompatible with all the privileges of my office." The comptroller general responded that it would be necessary to change this man's ideas "and make him understand that he should consider it an honor to have been chosen by his fellow citizens, and that in any case, the new syndics would be nothing like the officials who had previously worn that name and should count on being treated with greater respect by the government."

We also find important residents of the parish and even nobles suddenly seeking closer relations with peasants once the peasants had become a power to be reckoned with. The lord and high judge of one village on the outskirts of Paris complained that the edict prevented him from taking part as an *ordinary resident* in the operations of the parish assembly. Others, by their own account, consented "out of devotion to the public good to serve even in the post of syndic."

It was too late. As men from the wealthy classes approached the people of the countryside and sought to mingle with them, the people withdrew into the isolation to which they had been relegated and threw up their defenses. Some parish assemblies refused to accept the lord as a member. Others resorted to all sorts of chicanery before admitting even commoners, if they happened to be rich. "We have learned," the provincial assembly of Lower Normandy remarked, "that several municipal assemblies have refused to admit commoners who own land in the parish but are not domiciled there, even though there is no doubt that these people are entitled to membership. Other assemblies have even refused to accept farmers who did not own property within their territory."

Consequently, everything to do with secondary laws already involved novelty, obscurity, and conflict even before the principal laws dealing with government of the state itself had been touched. What remained standing had been shaken loose from its foundations, and it seemed that not a single regulation was left whose abolition or imminent modification had not been announced by the central government itself.

This vast, sudden overhaul of all rules and administrative customs, which in France preceded the political revolution but is seldom talked about today, was nevertheless already one of the greatest disruptions that had ever occurred in the history of a great nation. This first revolution exerted a prodigious influence on the second and made the latter different from all other events of a similar kind either before or since.

The first English revolution, which stood the country's whole political constitution on its head and even abolished the monarchy, had only a very superficial impact on secondary laws and virtually no effect on customs and usages. The courts and administration remained unchanged in form and went about their business as they had always done. At the height of the civil war, England's twelve judges reportedly still made the rounds of the assizes twice a year. The effects of the revolution were circumscribed, and English society, though disturbed in its upper reaches, remained on a firm footing.

Since 1789, we ourselves have seen in France a number of revolutions that have changed the structure of our government from top to bottom. Most were quite sudden and achieved by force, in open violation of existing laws. Nevertheless, the ensuing disorder did not last long, nor was it widespread. Much of the nation scarcely felt any effect and at times was scarcely aware that a revolution was taking place.

The reason is that since 1789, the administrative constitution has always remained intact amid the ruins of one political constitution after another. The country changed rulers, or changed the form of the central government, but the daily course of business continued undisturbed, without interruption. In the petty affairs in which they were involved, individuals continued to be subject to the familiar rules and customs. They relied on the secondary powers with which they had long been in the habit of dealing, and usually they dealt with the same agents, for although every revolution decapitated the administration, its body remained intact and alive. The same functions were performed by the same functionaries. These officials perpetuated the same spirit and method through the diversity of political laws. They judged and administered at first in the name of the king, then in the name of the Republic, and finally in the name of the emperor. Then, as the wheel of fortune came full circle, they began once again to administer and judge for the king, for the Republic and for the emperor, still the same people they had always been, with the same methods. For what did the name of the master matter to them? Their business was less to be citizens than to be good administrators and good judges. Therefore, once the initial shock had passed, it seemed that nothing in the country had changed.

When the Revolution erupted, this part of the government, which, though subordinate, had daily affected the lives of every citizen and exerted the most constant and effective influence on the well-being of all, had just been turned completely upside down. All the agents of the public administration had been replaced overnight, and all its principles had changed. At first, the state appeared not to have been greatly affected by this vast reform, but everyone in France had experienced a small private upheaval. Everyone's situation had been disturbed, everyone's habits disrupted, everyone's work impeded. In the broadest, most important affairs, a certain regularity persisted, but in the lesser matters that constitute the daily business of society, already no one knew any longer whom to obey, to whom to turn, or how to behave.

With no part of the nation secure in its foundations, one final blow was enough to upset the entire edifice and initiate the greatest upheaval in history and the most dreadful confusion that ever existed.

III.8 – How the Revolution Emerged Naturally from the Foregoing

I want to conclude by bringing together some of the features that I have thus far described separately, to see how the Revolution emerged naturally from the Ancien Régime whose portrait I have just painted.

When we reflect that it was in France that the feudal system most completely lost its ability to protect or serve without losing its capacity to harm or vex, it becomes less surprising that the Revolution that would so violently sweep away the old European constitution should have erupted here rather than elsewhere.

When we note that the nobility, having lost its former political rights and having ceased, more than anywhere else in feudal Europe, to administer and lead the population, nevertheless not only preserved but greatly increased its pecuniary immunities and individual advantages; and that, while becoming a subordinate class, it remained privileged and closed, or, as I put it earlier, became less and less of an aristocracy and more and more of a caste; it will come as no surprise that its privileges should have seemed so inexplicable and detestable to the French, or that democratic envy should have flared up in the French heart so intensely that it still burns there today.

When we observe, finally, that this nobility, separated from the middle class that it had rejected from its bosom, and from the people whose heart it had allowed to escape, was utterly isolated in the nation's midst, apparently at the head of an army but in reality a corps of officers without soldiers, we can understand how, after having stood for a thousand years, it could have been toppled in one night.

I showed how the royal government, after abolishing provincial liberties and supplanting all local powers across three quarters of France, took charge of all public business, from the smallest affairs to the largest. Elsewhere I showed how, as an inevitable consequence of this, Paris made itself the master of a country of which it had previously been only the capital, or, rather, how Paris itself became the entire country. These two facts, which were peculiar to France, could by themselves suffice to explain why a riot was able to completely destroy a monarchy that had for centuries withstood so many violent shocks, and which on the eve of its downfall still seemed unshakable to the very people who would overthrow it.

Since France was, among European countries, one of those in which all political life had been most completely snuffed out for the longest time, and in which private citizens had most fully lost touch with public affairs, the ability to interpret events, familiarity with popular movements, and almost the very notion of the people, it is easy to imagine how the French could have fallen all at once into an awful revolution without seeing it, with those most threatened by the Revolution marching at the head of the column and taking it upon themselves to blaze and broaden the trail that led them to their doom.

Since there were no longer any free institutions and therefore no political classes, functioning political bodies, or organized and disciplined parties, and since, in the absence of regular political forces such as these, public opinion, once it revived, fell exclusively under the influence of philosophers, it was to be expected that the Revolution would be led less by the light of certain specific facts than in accordance with abstract principles and quite general theories. One might expect that instead of attacking bad laws one by one, the revolutionaries would attack all laws and seek to replace France's ancient constitution with an entirely new system of government conceived by these writers.

Since the Church was, of course, mixed up with all the old institutions that were to be destroyed, there could be no doubt that the Revolution, in the course of toppling the civil government, would disrupt religion as well. From this point on, it was impossible to say what extraordinary acts of recklessness the innovators might perpetrate once their minds were freed from all the restraints that religion, custom, and law normally impose on man's imagination.

And anyone who had carefully studied the state of the country could easily have foreseen that no act was so reckless that it could not be attempted and no violence so extraordinary as to be inadmissible.

Burke, in one of his eloquent pamphlets, exclaims: "I never yet heard that a single man could be named of sufficient force or influence to answer for another man, much less for the smallest district in the country.... We see every man that the Jacobins choose to apprehend taken up in his village or house, and conveyed to prison without the least shadow of resistance, whether he is suspected of Royalism, Federalism, Moderantism, Democracy Royal or any other of the names of faction which they start by the hour."[1] Burke had little notion of the conditions in which the monarchy he mourned had left us to face our new masters. The administration of the Ancien Régime had deprived the French in advance of both the ability and the desire to help one another. When the Revolution came, one would have searched in vain in most of France for ten men accustomed to acting together in a disciplined way and defending themselves. The central government alone was supposed to take charge of defending them all, so that when the royal administration lost control of that central government to a sovereign and unaccountable assembly, and this once-complacent body turned terrifying, nothing could stop it or even slow it for a moment. The same cause that had brought the monarchy down so easily made everything possible after its fall.

Never had religious tolerance, moderation in the exercise of power, humanity, and even kindness been more widely preached or apparently more fully accepted than in the eighteenth century. The law of war, which is the last refuge of violence, had itself been pared down and softened. Yet from such mild mores the most inhumane revolution was soon to emerge. Nevertheless, all this softening of mores was not mere sham, for no sooner had the fury of the Revolution abated than one saw this same mildness spread at once throughout the law and suffuse all political habits.

The contrast between the benign character of the theories and the violence of the acts, which was one of the strangest features of the French Revolution, will not surprise anyone who observes that the groundwork for the Revolution was laid by the most civilized classes of the nation and carried out by the coarsest and most uncultivated. Since the men of the former group had no preexisting ties among themselves, no experience of reaching an understanding, and no hold on the people, the people took charge almost immediately once the old powers had been destroyed.

---

[1] Edmund Burke, "Remarks on the Policy of the Allies," in *The Works of the Right Honorable Edmund Burke* (Boston: Little Brown, 1869), p. 416.

Where the people themselves did not govern, they nevertheless imparted their spirit to the government. And if, moreover, one thinks of the way in which the people lived under the Ancien Régime, it is easy to imagine how they became what they became.

The peculiarities of the people's situation had equipped them with several rare virtues. Having been freed from serfdom early on and having long since become owners of part of the land, isolated rather than dependent, they had proven themselves to be temperate and proud. They were inured to suffering, indifferent to life's amenities, resigned to the greatest ills, and steadfast in the face of danger. They constituted a simple, virile race, which soon would fill the ranks of the powerful armies to which Europe would succumb. But the same cause made them a dangerous master. For centuries they had borne the whole burden of abuses almost alone. They had lived apart, nursing their prejudices, jealousy, and hatred in silence, hardened by the rigors of their fate, and they had become capable of both enduring anything and inflicting every kind of suffering.

It was in this condition that the people seized control of the government and sought to complete the work of the Revolution. Books had provided the theory. The people took charge of the practice, and they altered the ideas of the writers to suit their own rage.

Those who, in reading this book, have studied eighteenth-century France attentively will have witnessed the inception and development of two main passions that did not exist simultaneously or always tend toward the same goal.

One, older and more deeply rooted, was the violent, inextinguishable hatred of inequality. This was ignited and fueled by the sight of inequality itself, and with constant and irresistible force it had long driven the French to seek to destroy, down to the very foundations, whatever remained of the institutions of the Middle Ages, and once the ground was clear, to build upon it a society in which men would be as similar and conditions as equal as humanity would allow.

The other, more recent and less deeply rooted, made them want to live not just as equals but as free men.

Toward the end of the Ancien Régime, these two passions were equally sincere and seemed equally vigorous. At the beginning of the Revolution, they came together. They briefly mingled and merged, each lending heat to the other, and ultimately inflamed the heart of all of France. This was 1789, a time of inexperience, no doubt, but also of generosity, enthusiasm, virility, and grandeur, a time of immortal memory toward which men will gaze with admiration and respect long after all who witnessed the event, as well as we who came after them, have vanished from the earth. At that time, the French were proud enough of their cause and of themselves to believe that they could live in freedom as equals. Alongside democratic institutions they therefore created free institutions everywhere. Not only did they reduce to dust the superannuated legislation that divided men into castes, guilds, and classes and made their rights even more unequal than their conditions; they also abrogated at one stroke more recent laws, achievements of the monarchy that had deprived the nation of its free enjoyment of itself and placed each Frenchman under the watchful eye of the government, which served as his teacher, guardian, and, if need be, oppressor. With absolute government, centralization also fell.

But when the vigorous generation that had launched the Revolution was destroyed or exhausted, as generally happens to generations that attempt such enterprises, and when, in keeping with the natural course of events of this kind, love of liberty lost heart and languished amid anarchy and popular dictatorship, and a bewildered nation began to grope after its master, the rebirth and reestablishment of absolute government proved marvelously easy, owing to the genius of the man who was both the continuator of the Revolution and its destroyer.

The Ancien Régime had in fact contained any number of modern institutions, which, not being hostile to equality, easily found a place in the new society yet offered remarkable assistance to despotism. One searched for these institutions amid the debris of all the others, and there they were. They had previously fostered habits, passions, and ideas that tended to keep men divided and obedient; these were now revived and put to use. Centralization was salvaged from the ruins and restored. And because it was raised up again, while everything that had once kept it in check still lay in ruins, what suddenly emerged from the entrails of a nation that had just overthrown the monarchy was a power more extensive, more minute, and more absolute than our kings had ever exercised. The enterprise seemed extraordinarily bold and its success unprecedented because people thought only of what they saw and forgot what they had seen. The oppressor fell, but what was most substantial in his work remained standing. His government died but his administration lived on, and since then, whenever anyone has tried to topple absolute power, he has merely placed Liberty's head on a servile body.

On several occasions between the beginning of the Revolution and the present, the passion for liberty has died out, then revived, then died out again and been reborn again. And so it will continue for a long time to come: always inexperienced and ill-disciplined, easy to discourage, frighten, and vanquish, superficial and fleeting. During this same period, the passion for equality has continued to dwell deep within the hearts it was first to capture. There it has fastened onto the feelings we hold most dear. While one passion is constantly changing in appearance, diminishing, growing, strengthening, or waning in response to events, the other remains the same, constantly pursuing the same goal with the same stubborn and often blind ardor, prepared to sacrifice everything to those who permit its satisfaction and to provide any government willing to foster and flatter it with the habits, ideas, and laws that despotism needs in order to rule.

The French Revolution must remain obscure to those unwilling to look beyond it. One must look to the preceding period for the light that is alone capable of illuminating it. Without a clear view of the previous society, of its laws, its flaws, its prejudices, its miseries, and its grandeur, one can never understand what the French did in the sixty years that followed its downfall. But such understanding alone still would not suffice if one failed to grasp the essential nature of France.

When I think of the French nation in itself, I find it more extraordinary than any of the events of its history. Has there ever been another nation on this earth so full of contrasts, so extreme in each of its acts, more driven by its sensations, or less guided by its principles; doing therefore better or worse than expected, at times below the common level of humanity, at times well above; a people so unalterable in its principal instincts that we recognize it in portraits two or three thousand years old, and yet so changeable in its daily thoughts and tastes as to have become a surprising spectacle in its own eyes, often as astonished as foreigners by the sight of what it has just done; more wedded to home and routine than any other people when left alone, but ready when wrenched from hearth and habit to march to the ends of the earth and dare all; indocile by temperament, yet more amenable to the arbitrary and even violent rule of a prince than to the free and lawful government of leading citizens; today the sworn enemy of all obedience, tomorrow serving with a passion that not even the nations most gifted for servitude can match; led by a thread as long as no one resists, ungovernable as soon as an example of resistance is set somewhere; thus always deceiving its masters, who fear it either too much or too little; never so free that one must give up hope of subjugating it, nor so subjugated that it cannot still smash the yoke; apt in everything but excelling only in war; worshipping chance, force, success, brilliance, and bluster more than true glory; more capable of heroism than of virtue, of genius than of common sense; given to conceiving immense designs rather than completing great enterprises; the most brilliant and most dangerous of European nations, and the most likely to become by turns an object of admiration, hatred, pity, and terror, but never indifference?

Only this nation could have given birth to a revolution so sudden, so radical, so impetuous in its course, and yet so full of retreats, contradictory events, and contrary examples. Without the reasons I have stated, the French would never have done it. Yet it must be granted that all these reasons together would not suffice to explain such a revolution anywhere but in France.

Thus, I come to the threshold of this memorable Revolution. For now I will not cross it. Soon, perhaps, I will be able to do so. Then I will set aside its causes and examine only the Revolution in itself, and I will dare at last to offer a judgment upon the society that emerged from it.

Appendix

On the *Pays d'états*, and in Particular Languedoc

It is not my intention here to examine in detail how things were done in each of the *pays d'états* that still existed at the time of the Revolution.

I merely wish to note their number and to identify those that retained an active local existence, as well as to describe their relations with the royal administration, in what respects they departed from the common rules I set forth earlier and in what respects they did not, and, finally, by taking one of them as an example, to show what they all might easily have become.

Estates had at one time existed in most of the provinces of France. In other words, each province had been administered, under the auspices of the royal government, by the "people of the three estates," as people used to say. This expression should be understood to mean an assembly composed of representatives of the clergy, the nobility, and the bourgeoisie. This provincial constitution, like other medieval political institutions, could be found with identical features in almost all civilized parts of Europe, or at any rate in all those influenced by Germanic mores and ideas. In many German provinces, estates persisted right up to the French Revolution. Where they had vanished, they had done so only in the course of the seventeenth and eighteenth centuries. Everywhere, for two centuries, princes had waged war on them, at times covertly, at times openly, but without interruption. Nowhere did they seek to improve the institution in accordance with the progress of the times. They preferred rather to destroy it or, if nothing worse was possible, to deform it.

In France in 1789, estates still existed in only five provinces of any size, as well as in a few small districts of no significance. There was no real provincial liberty to speak of except in two of those provinces, Brittany and Languedoc. Everywhere else the institution had been utterly sapped of its virility and reduced to a mere semblance of its former self.

I will take Languedoc as an example for closer examination.

Languedoc was the largest and most populous of the *pays d'états*. It contained more than two thousand *communes*, or "communities," as they were called at the time, and boasted a population of nearly two million. It was, moreover, the best organized and most prosperous as well as the largest of these provinces. Languedoc is, therefore, a good case to study in order to see what provincial liberty could be like under the Ancien Régime and to what extent it had been subordinated to royal power even in those regions where it remained strongest.

In Languedoc, the estates could meet only on express orders of the king and only after each member had received an individual letter of convocation. Accordingly, a rebel of the time remarked: "Of the three bodies that make up our estates, one, the clergy, is appointed by the king, who chooses those who are to hold bishoprics and benefices, and the other are as good as chosen by the king, since an order from the court can ban any member whom the king wishes to exclude. There is no need to exile or try the person; it suffices simply not to invite him."

The estates were required not only to convene but also to disperse on specific days chosen by the king. A council decree fixed the ordinary length of a session at forty days. The king was represented in the assembly by commissioners, who always had the right to attend upon request. and who were charged with stating the wishes of the government. Furthermore, the estates operated under strict supervision. They could not make a decision of any importance or promulgate a financial measure of any kind until their deliberations had been approved by a council decree. For a tax, a loan, or a lawsuit, the express permission of the king was required. All of their general regulations, including those governing their own meetings, had to be authorized before they could take effect. All receipts and expenditures – what would today be called their budget – were subject to annual review.

Moreover, the central government exercised the same political powers in Languedoc as everywhere else. Whatever laws it chose to promulgate, whatever general regulations it issued, as it did constantly, and whatever general measures it decided on were applicable there just as they were in the *pays d'élection*. It also performed all the natural functions of government. It employed the same police and the same agents as everywhere else. And as was the case everywhere, from time to time it created a host of new functionaries, whose offices the province was obliged to purchase at great expense.

Languedoc, like the other provinces, was governed by an intendant. This intendant had subdelegates in each district who corresponded with community leaders and directed their work. The intendant exercised administrative oversight, exactly as in the *pays d'élection*. Not even the smallest, most remote village in the gorges of the Cévennes could make the slightest expenditure unless authorized from Paris by a council decree. Administrative tribunals formed no less extensive a part of the judicial system in Languedoc than in the rest of France; indeed, they were even more extensive. The intendant had primary jurisdiction over all issues to do with highways; he heard all suits involving roads and, in general, decided all cases in which the government had, or believed it had, an interest. The government was no less diligent there than elsewhere in protecting its agents from troublesome litigation by citizens with whom they interfered.

What, then, was special about Languedoc that distinguished it from other provinces and made it an object of their envy? Three things sufficed to make it entirely different from the rest of France:

1. An assembly composed of men of substance who enjoyed the confidence of the population and the respect of the royal government. No functionary of the central government, or, as one said at the time, "no officer of the king," could belong to this body, which convened annually to discuss the particular interests of the province freely and seriously. The mere existence of this enlightened body was enough to ensure that the royal administration exercised its privileges in a very different way and that, even though it employed the same agents and possessed the same instincts, it did not resemble the royal administration in other parts of the country.

2. In Languedoc there were many public works that were carried out at the king's expense and by his agents. There were others for which the central government provided a portion of the funds and managed a large part of the work. But most projects were financed exclusively by

the province. Once the king had approved the design and authorized the expenditure, the work was overseen by officials chosen by the estates and inspected by commissioners chosen among the members of the assembly.

3. Finally, the province had the right to levy by itself, and by whatever method it chose, a portion of the royal taxes and all other taxes that it was allowed to establish to provide for its own needs.

We shall see what benefits Languedoc was able to derive from these privileges. This is a matter worthy of close scrutiny.

What is striking about the *pays d'élection* is the virtually complete absence of local taxes. General taxes were often oppressive, but these provinces spent almost nothing on themselves. In Languedoc, by contrast, the annual cost of public works was enormous; in 1780 it exceeded 2 million livres.

At times, the central government found such a high level of expenditure troubling. It feared that the province would exhaust itself in such efforts and be unable to meet its obligation to the central government. It criticized the estates for not moderating their expenditure. I read one report in which the assembly responded to these criticisms. What I am about to quote verbatim from this report will portray better than anything else the spirit that animated this provincial government.

The report acknowledged that the province had indeed planned and carried out vast public projects. It made no excuses for this but, instead, stated that if the king were not opposed, it would continue with more of the same. The province had already improved or straightened the course of the main rivers flowing through its territory and had taken it upon itself to extend the Languedoc Canal, which dated from the time of Louis XIV and was no longer adequate, by adding new stretches through Lower Languedoc via Cette and Agde and on to the Rhône. It had made the port of Cette suitable for commerce and maintained it at considerable expense. The report pointed out that all of these expenditures were more national than provincial in character. Nevertheless, the province that profited most from the work had accepted the need to pay for it. It was also in the process of draining the marshes at Aigues-Mortes and making them once again suitable for agriculture. But roads were its primary interest: it had built or improved all the roads that connected it with the rest of the kingdom and repaired even those that simply connected cities and towns within Languedoc. All of these various roads were kept in excellent condition, even in winter, and stood in stark contrast to the hard, rough, and poorly maintained roads in most of the nearby provinces, including Dauphiné, Quercy, and the *généralité* of Bordeaux (a *pays d'élection*, as the report noted). On this point it cited the opinions of businessmen and travelers, and the judgment it offered was accurate, as evidenced by a comment made by Arthur Young when he traveled through the region ten years later: "Languedoc, *pays d'états*; good roads, built without forced labor."

The report continued: If the king did not object, the estates would go further still. They would undertake to improve the secondary roads, which were no less important than the others, "for if the farmer's produce cannot be moved from his storehouse to the market, what does it matter that it can be transported to more distant places?" Furthermore, "the doctrine of the estates concerning public works has always been that what should count is not the grandeur of the project but rather its utility." Rivers, canals, and roads that enhance the value of all the products of the soil and of industry by allowing them to be transported at low cost in all seasons to wherever there is a need for them, and by means of which commerce can insinuate itself into every corner of the province, enriches the region regardless of the cost. What is more, such projects, if judiciously undertaken at a roughly equal level in all parts of the province simultaneously, support the wage level everywhere and help the poor. "The king has not needed to bear the cost of charity workshops in Languedoc, as he has had to do in the rest of France," the report concluded with a note of pride. "We do not ask for such favor. The useful works that we ourselves undertake year after year make it unnecessary and provide everyone with productive employment."

The more I study the measures that the estates of Languedoc took, with the king's permission but not usually at his behest, in those areas of public administration that were left to their discretion, the more I admire the wisdom, fairness, and mildness that they demonstrated, and the more I find that the methods of local government were superior to those employed in the regions directly administered by the king.

The province was divided into communities (towns and villages), administrative districts called "dioceses," and, finally, into three large sectors known as *sénéchaussées*. Each of these parts had a distinct representation and a small government of its own, which operated under the guidance of either the estates or the king. Where public works touching on the interests of one of these small political bodies were concerned, projects were undertaken only at their request. If work done by a community might be useful to the diocese as a whole, it would be expected to contribute something toward defraying the cost. If the interests of the *sénéchaussée* were served, it too would be expected to help. Finally, the diocese, *sénéchaussée*, and province would be expected to aid the community even if only its own interests were involved, provided that the work was necessary and exceeded the capacity of the community itself. As the estates said repeatedly: "The fundamental principle of our constitution is that all the parts of Languedoc are inextricably intertwined and must consistently help one another."

Projects carried out by the province required lengthy preparation and were supposed to be carefully examined by all of the subordinate levels of government that would be expected to contribute to them. They could be undertaken only if there was money to pay for them. Compulsory labor was unknown. In the *pays d'élection*, as we have seen, land taken for public works was always poorly or belatedly compensated, if it was paid for at all. This was one of the major complaints of the provincial assemblies when they met in 1787. Some even complained that their ability to discharge debts contracted in this way was compromised because the property taken was destroyed or altered before its value could be estimated. In Languedoc, every parcel of land taken from its owner had to be carefully evaluated before work was begun *and paid for during the first year of work.*

The rules that the estates of Languedoc applied to public works projects, from which I have taken these details, were so well designed that the central government admired them, though it did not imitate them. The King's Council, after authorizing the implementation of the rules, had copies printed up by the Royal Press and ordered that these be distributed to all intendants as a standard reference.

What I have said about public works applies all the more to another and no less important aspect of provincial administration: the collection of taxes. On this score especially, it is difficult, on moving from kingdom to province, to believe that one is still in the same state.

As I noted earlier, the procedures for levying and collecting the taille in Languedoc were, to some extent, the same as those we use for collecting taxes today. I will say no more about this subject here, beyond adding that the province was so pleased with the superiority of its own methods in this regard that whenever the king created a new tax, the estates never hesitated to pay dearly for the right to levy the tax in their own way and with their own agents.

Despite all the expenditures that I have enumerated, Languedoc's affairs were in such good order, and its credit was so firmly established, that the central government frequently relied on it, borrowing money in the name of the province that it could not have obtained on equally good terms itself. I discovered that toward the end of the monarchy, Languedoc guaranteed 73,200,000 livres in loans on the king's behalf.

Nevertheless, the government and its ministers took a very dim view of these particular liberties. Richelieu first curtailed and then abolished them. The pliable and indolent Louis XIII, who liked nothing, detested them. All provincial privileges so horrified him, according to Boulainvilliers, that he became incensed at the mere mention of them. The energy that weak souls can muster in hatred of anything that forces them to make an effort can never be gauged. All their remaining virility is lent to the purpose, and they nearly always turn out to be strong in this regard, even if feeble in all others. Fortunately, Languedoc's ancient constitution was restored during the childhood of Louis XIV. The king, looking upon it as his own work, respected it. Louis XV suspended it for two years but subsequently allowed it to be reinstated.

The creation of municipal offices subjected the province to dangers that were less direct but no less great. This detestable institution not only destroyed city constitutions but also contributed to the denaturing of provincial constitutions. I do not know if the deputies of the Third Estate in the provincial assemblies were ever elected, but they certainly had not been elected for quite some time. Municipal officials in the towns were the only legal representatives of the bourgeoisie and people.

The absence of a special mandate, granted with an eye to the interests of the moment, went relatively unnoticed as long as the towns elected their own officials freely by universal suffrage, and usually for a very short term. Within the estates, the mayor, consul, or syndic then represented the will of the people in whose name he spoke as faithfully as if the people had chosen him expressly for the purpose. Obviously, this was not the case when a person used his money to purchase the right to administer his fellow citizens. Such a person represented nothing but himself, or at most the petty interests and passions of his coterie. Yet those who purchased their powers at auction retained the same prerogatives that elected officials had previously possessed. This immediately changed the whole character of the institution. The nobility and the clergy, instead of sitting in the provincial assembly alongside or opposite representatives of the people, encountered only isolated, timid, and impotent bourgeois, and the Third Estate played an increasingly subordinate role in the government, even as it grew steadily wealthier and more powerful in society. This was not the case in Languedoc, however, as the province had always been at pains to purchase from the king any offices that he established. In one year alone, 1773, the province borrowed more than 4 million livres for this purpose.

Other, more powerful causes also helped to infuse these old institutions with the new spirit and made the estates of Languedoc incontestably superior to all the others.

In Languedoc, as in much of the south, the taille was a real as opposed to a personal tax: in other words, it was set according to the value of the property and not the status of the owner. True, some land was exempt from the tax. This land had once belonged to the nobility, but with the passage of time and economic progress, some of it had fallen into the hands of commoners. Meanwhile, nobles had become the owners of many properties subject to the taille. The transfer of the privilege from persons to things was no doubt more absurd, but it was less acutely felt because, though still vexing, it had ceased to be humiliating. Since it was no longer inextricably linked to the idea of class and did not create for one class an interest alien or hostile to the interests of the other classes, it did not stand in the way of allowing all classes to share in the work of government. In Languedoc more than anywhere else, all classes did in fact participate in government on a footing of perfect equality.

In Brittany, every nobleman enjoyed the right to appear in person at the estates, which, therefore, often resembled the Polish Diet. In Languedoc, nobles participated in the estates only through representatives. Twenty-three of them stood for all the rest. The clergy was represented by twenty-three of the province's bishops. Especially worthy of note is the fact that the towns had as many votes as the first two orders combined.

Since the assembly met together as a single body and votes were counted not by order but by head, the Third Estate naturally acquired considerable importance. Little by little, its peculiar spirit imbued the entire body. What is more, the three magistrates known as syndics general, who were delegated by the estates to take charge of routine affairs, were always men of the law, which is to say, commoners. Although the nobility was strong enough to maintain its status, it was no longer strong enough to rule by itself. At the same time, the clergy, though largely composed of nobles, maintained close contact with the Third Estate. It enthusiastically supported most of the latter's projects, worked with it to enhance the material prosperity of all citizens and to promote commerce and industry, and thus placed its great knowledge of men and rare dexterity in the handling of affairs at the service of the Third Estate. A clergyman was nearly always chosen to go to Versailles for debates with ministers involving controversial issues related to conflicts between royal authority and the estates. It is fair to say that throughout the last century, Languedoc was administered by bourgeois under the supervision of nobles and with the help of bishops.

Thanks to Languedoc's unusual constitution, the spirit of the new age could quietly infuse this old institution and change it utterly without destroying it.

It could have been the same everywhere else. A small part of the perseverance and energy that France's kings put into abolishing or deforming the provincial estates would have sufficed to improve them as in Languedoc and adapt them to the needs of modern civilization, if only those monarchs had ever wanted anything other than to become and remain masters of their realms.

Notes

Page 22, line 11
POWER OF ROMAN LAW IN GERMANY – WAY IN WHICH IT HAD
REPLACED GERMANIC LAW

At the end of the Middle Ages, Roman law became the principal and virtually the only subject of study for German legal scholars. At that time, most of them even obtained their education outside Germany, in Italian universities. Since these scholars, who had no political power but bore responsibility for explaining and applying the laws of their society, could not abolish Germanic law, they sought to force it into a Roman law framework. They applied Roman laws to every aspect of Germanic institutions that bore the slightest similarity to the Justinian Code. They introduced a new spirit and new customs into the laws of the nation, which were gradually transformed to the point of unrecognizability. By the seventeenth century, no one could understand German law. It had been replaced by something I cannot describe, which was still German in name but Roman in fact.

I have reason to believe that the work of these scholars worsened the situation of many people in the old Germanic society, most notably the peasants. Many who had managed to retain some or all of their liberties and possessions now lost them because scholars had equated their status with that of Roman slaves or tenants.

This gradual transformation of national law was clearly at work in the history of Wurtemberg, which also reveals futile efforts to oppose it.

From the country's inception in 1250 to the creation of the duchy in 1495, the laws were entirely indigenous. They consisted of customary laws, local laws made by towns or seigniorial courts, and statutes promulgated by the estates. Only ecclesiastical matters were regulated by foreign legislation, specifically, canon law.

After 1495, the character of the law changed. Roman law began to make inroads. The *doctors*, as those who had studied law in foreign schools were called, entered government and took control of the high courts. In the first half of the fifteenth century, political society opposed them, much as it did in England during the same period, but with very different results. In the Diet of Tubingen in 1514, as well as in subsequent diets, representatives of the feudal lords and deputies from the towns protested what was happening in a variety of ways. They attacked the legal scholars who had gained ascendancy in the courts and altered the spirit as well as the letter of all existing customs and laws. At first, the advantage seemed to lie with the opposition. It won from the government a promise that appointments to the high courts would henceforth be limited to honorable and enlightened men chosen from the duchy's nobility and the estates; the doctors were to be excluded, and a committee composed of agents of the government and representatives of the estates was to draft a code that could be applied throughout the country. Wasted effort! Before long, Roman law had entirely supplanted national law in many areas and firmly implanted itself even where it allowed national law to remain.

A number of German historians attribute this triumph of foreign law over native law to two things: 1) a general intellectual tendency at that time to turn toward the languages and literatures of antiquity, coupled with a contempt, to which this tendency gave rise, for the fruits of the German spirit; and 2) an idea that had always fascinated medieval Germans and influenced the laws they made even at that time, to wit, that the Holy Roman Empire was the continuation of the Roman Empire, whose legal system it had inherited.

By themselves, however, these factors cannot explain why Roman law spread throughout the continent at this time. In my view, this happened because absolute monarchies were established upon the ruins of Europe's ancient liberties everywhere, and because Roman law, a law of servitude, was marvelously well adapted to absolutist thinking.

Roman law, which everywhere raised civil society to a pitch of perfection, also degraded political society everywhere because it was, on the whole, the work of a highly civilized but thoroughly subjugated people. Kings therefore embraced it eagerly and instituted Roman law wherever they ruled. Throughout Europe, the interpreters of Roman law became their ministers and principal agents. Legal scholars provided kings with legal support, when needed, against the law itself. And from that time on, they have continued to do so on numerous occasions. Wherever a monarch violated the law, it was rare that a legal scholar did not step forward to offer him assurance that what he was doing was perfectly legitimate, and learned proof that violence was just and the oppressed were in the wrong.

Page 23, line 33
THE TRANSITION FROM FEUDAL MONARCHY TO DEMOCRATIC MONARCHY
Since all monarchies became absolute at about the same time, there is little evidence in favor of the hypothesis that this change was related to some particular circumstance that by chance happened to exist everywhere at the same time, and one has to concede that all these similar and contemporary events must have been the result of a general cause equally and simultaneously at work everywhere.

This general cause was the transition from one social state to another, from feudal inequality to democratic equality. The nobles had already been cut down to size and the people had not yet risen; the former were still too low and the latter not yet high enough to impede the actions of the state. The result was what might be called the golden age of monarchy, and it lasted 150 years, during which absolute monarchs enjoyed both stability and omnipotence – two things that are ordinarily mutually exclusive: they were as sacred as hereditary feudal princes and as absolute as the rulers of democracy.

Page 24, line 15
DECADENCE OF FREE CITIES IN GERMANY. – IMPERIAL CITIES
(*REICHSSTÄDTE*)
According to German historians, these cities achieved the apogee of their splendor in the fourteenth and fifteenth centuries. They were then repositories of wealth, art, and learning and the mistresses of European commerce, hegemonic centers of civilization. Ultimately, especially in the north and south of Germany, urban centers joined forces with powerful nobles in their vicinity to form independent confederations, just as Swiss cities had allied themselves with peasants.

In the sixteenth century these cities were still prosperous, but decadence had begun to set in. The Thirty Years' War completed their ruin. Virtually none escaped destruction or devastation in its wake.

The Treaty of Westphalia nevertheless treated the German cities as independent states subordinate only to the emperor. Yet their sovereignty was quite narrowly limited, on the one hand by neighboring sovereigns and on the other by the emperor, whose power after the Thirty Years' War was largely limited to these minor vassals of the empire. In the eighteenth century, fifty-one independent German city-states still remained. They occupied two benches in the diet, where they spoke with a distinctive voice, but in fact they no longer exerted any control over general policy.

All bore a crushing load of debt. This was partly because they continued to pay imperial taxes at a level determined by their former splendor and partly because they were very poorly governed. What is particularly worthy of note is that bad government seems to have been a secret malady common to all, regardless of the form of their constitution. Whether aristocratic or democratic, the complaints were, if not identical, at least equally acute. If aristocratic, the government was said to have become the coterie of a small number of families: favor and special interests ruled. If democratic, intrigue and venality were everywhere. In both cases, governments were accused of dishonesty and partiality. The emperor was constantly compelled to intervene in the affairs of the imperial city-states to restore order. Urban populations declined, and the cities fell into misery. They ceased to be the centers of German civilization. The arts abandoned them and took their brilliance to new cities, created by sovereigns and typical of the new world. Commerce turned elsewhere. The old energy and patriotic vigor of the German burgs disappeared. Hamburg, virtually alone among them, remained a major center of wealth and learning, but for reasons peculiar to itself alone.

Page 31, line 7
Date of the Abolition of Serfdom in Germany
As the following list shows, the abolition of serfdom in most parts of Germany took place at a quite recent date. Serfdom was not abolished

1. In Baden until 1783;
2. In Hohenzollern in 1798;
3. In Schleswig and Holstein in 1804;
4. In Nassau in 1808.
5. Prussia. Frederick William I ended serfdom on his estates in 1717. As we have seen, the code of Frederick the Great claimed to abolish it throughout the kingdom but in reality eliminated only its harshest form, *Leibeigenschaft*. It preserved the milder form, *Erbuntertänigkeit*. It was not until 1809 that it ended entirely.
6. In Bavaria, serfdom vanished in 1808.

7. A Napoleonic decree issued in Madrid in 1808 abolished serfdom in the grand duchy of Berg and various other minor territories, such Erfurt, Bayreuth, etc.
8. In the kingdom of Westphalia, the end of serfdom dates from 1808 and 1809.
9. In the principality of Lippe-Deltmold, from 1809.
10. In Schomburg-Lippe, from 1810.
11. In Swedish Pomerania, also from 1810.
12. In Hesse-Darmstadt, from 1809 and 1811.
13. In Würtemberg, from 1817.
14. In Meckenburg, from 1820.
15. In Oldenburg, from 1814.
16. In Saxony, for Lusatia, from 1832.
17. In Hohenzollern-Sigmaringen, only from 1833.
18. In Austria, from 1811. As early as 1782 Joseph II had ended *Leibeigenschaft*, but serfdom in the milder form of *Erbuntertänigkeit* endured until 1811.

Page 31, line 7
Parts of territories that are today German, such as Brandenburg, old Prussia, and Silesia, were originally populated by Slavs and conquered and partially occupied by Germans. In these regions, serfdom was much harsher even than in Germany, and it left still deeper traces in the late eighteenth century.

Page 32, line 8
FREDERICK THE GREAT'S CODE
Among the works of Frederick the Great, the least well known, even in his own country, and the least spectacular is the code of law that he ordered to be drafted and that his successor promulgated. Yet I am not sure that anything else sheds more light on the man himself and on his time or better reveals the mutual influence of each on the other.

This code is a veritable constitution in the sense normally attributed to that word. Its purpose is to regulate relations not only between citizens but also between citizens and the state: it is at once a civil code, a criminal code, and a charter.

It rests, or, rather, appears to rest, on certain general principles set forth in a very philosophical and highly abstract form, which in many respects are similar to those contained in the Declaration of the Rights of Man in the Constitution of 1791.

The document states that the welfare of the state and its inhabitants is the purpose of society and limit of the law, that laws can restrict the liberty and rights of citizens only to enhance the common utility, that each member of the state must work for the general good in proportion to his position and fortune, and that the rights of individuals must give way to the general good.

Nowhere is there any mention of the hereditary right of the prince or his family or even of a special right distinct from that of the state. The word "state" is already the only one that is used to denote the royal power.

By contrast, the code does speak of the general rights of men: the general rights of men are based on the natural freedom to seek one's own good without harming the rights of others. Any action that is not prohibited by natural law or by some positive law of the state is permitted. Any inhabitant of the state may demand that it defend his person and his property, and he has the right to defend himself by force if the state fails to come to his aid.

Having set forth these great principles, the lawmaker, instead of deriving from them the dogma of popular sovereignty and the organization of a popular government in a free society, as in the Constitution of 1791, stops short and moves on to another, equally democratic but illiberal consequence: he regards the prince as the sole representative of the state and bestows on him all the rights that have just been granted to society. In this code, the sovereign is no longer the representative of God; he is only the representative of society, its agent and servant, as Frederick made explicitly clear in all his works. But he is its sole representative and alone exercises all powers. As stated in the introduction, the chief of state, to whom is given all power to produce the general good, which is the sole purpose of society, is authorized to direct and regulate all individual acts to that end.

Among the principal duties of this all-powerful agent of society I find the following: to maintain peace and public security domestically and to protect every individual from violence. Abroad, it is up to him to make peace and war; he alone must give laws and keep order. He alone has the right to pardon and to quash criminal prosecutions.

All associations that exist within the state and all public establishments are subject to his inspection and direction, in the interest of peace and general security. In order for the head of state to fulfill these obligations, he needs certain revenues and revenue-producing dues (*droits utiles*). He therefore has the power to establish taxes on private fortunes, on persons, and on their professions, commerce, production, and consumption. The public functionaries who act in his name must be obeyed as he himself would be in all things falling within the scope of their office.

Beneath this quite modern head there emerged, as we shall now see, a quite Gothic body. Frederick merely saw to it that anything that might hinder the action of his own power was removed from that body to yield a monstrous whole, which seemed to be a transition from one state of creation to another. In this strange production, Frederick demonstrated as much contempt for logic as solicitude for his own power; he also demonstrated his desire not to create unnecessary difficulties for himself by attacking that which still had the strength to defend itself.

The inhabitants of the countryside, with the exception of a few districts and localities, were placed in hereditary servitude, which was not limited to compulsory labor and services inherent in the possession of certain pieces of land but extended, as we have seen, to the person of the possessor.

Most landowner privileges were consecrated anew by the code. One can even say that they were consecrated against the code, since it was stated that in case local custom differed from the new law, the former should be obeyed. It was formally declared that the state may not destroy any of these privileges without compensation and adherence to proper judicial formalities.

To be sure, the code made it clear that serfdom in the personal sense (*Leibeigenschaft*) was abolished, but the hereditary subjection (*Erbuntertänigkeit*) that replaced it was still a kind of servitude, as is clear from the text.

The same code continued to maintain a careful distinction between bourgeois and peasant. Between the bourgeoisie and the nobility, a sort of intermediate class was recognized: it consisted of non-noble high officials, ecclesiastics, and professors in schools of higher learning, gymnasia, and universities.

Although separate from the rest of the bourgeoisie, these bourgeois were not confused with nobles. On the contrary, they remained in an inferior status. They could not in general purchase knightly properties or obtain the highest positions in the civil service. Nor were they *Hoffähig*, which is to say, they could not be presented at court except in rare cases, and never with their families. As in France, this inferiority was all the more hurtful because this class was daily becoming more enlightened and influential, and while bourgeois state officials may not have held the most brilliant posts, they already filled those that had the most to do and did the most useful things. Irritation with noble privileges, which in France contributed so much to the Revolution, in Germany paved the way for the approval with which the Revolution was initially greeted. Although the chief drafter of the code was a bourgeois, he was no doubt following the orders of his master.

In this part of Germany, the old constitution of Europe had yet to be demolished sufficiently for Frederick to believe, despite the contempt it inspired in him, that the time had come to clear away the debris. On the whole, he confined himself to depriving nobles of the right to assemble and administer as a body, while allowing each individual nobleman to retain his privileges. He merely limited and regulated their use. That is why this code, drafted on orders issued by a student of our French *philosophes* and put into force after the French Revolution had broken out, is the most recent and authentic legislative document establishing a legal foundation for the very feudal inequalities that the Revolution would soon abolish throughout Europe.

In it, the nobility is declared to be the principal body of the state. Noblemen are to be preferred, the code states, for all honorific posts when they are capable of filling them. They alone may own noble lands, create entailments, and enjoy the hunting rights and judicial powers inherent in noble estates, along with rights of patronage over churches. Only they may take the name of land they own. Bourgeois may, exceptionally, receive express authorization to own noble lands but enjoyed only those rights and honors of ownership explicitly set forth in the authorization. A bourgeois who owns a noble property may leave it to a bourgeois heir only if that heir is of the first degree. If there is no such heir and there are no other noble heirs, the property must be sold.

One of the most characteristic sections of Frederick's code is the appendix on criminal law applicable to political offenses.

Despite the feudal and absolutist provisions of the code described here, Frederick the Great's successor, Frederick William II, thought he saw revolutionary tendencies in his uncle's work and therefore suspended publication until 1794, at which point his scruples were said to have been overcome by the fact that the code included a fine array of criminal penalties, which corrected for its wicked principles. Indeed, there has never been a more comprehensive schedule of punishments, before or since. Not only are revolts and conspiracies punished with the utmost severity; disrespectful criticisms of government actions are also quite harshly repressed. The purchase and distribution of dangerous writings are strictly prohibited; printer, publisher, and distributor are jointly and severally responsible for the author's act. Balls, masquerades, and other amusements are declared to be public meetings and must be authorized by the police. Even meals in public places require authorization. Freedom of the press and speech are subject to strict and arbitrary surveillance. It is forbidden to bear arms.

Throughout this work, half-borrowed from the Middle Ages, one finds provisions so extreme in their centralizing spirit that they border on socialism. For instance, it is stated that it is incumbent upon the state to provide food, work, and wages for all who cannot sustain themselves and are not entitled to help from some lord or village. Such people must be provided work suited to their strength and capabilities. The state must establish institutions to aid the poor. Furthermore, the state is authorized to eliminate charitable institutions that tend to encourage idleness and distribute any funds they may possess to the poor.

The theoretical boldness and innovativeness and practical timidity of Frederick's great work are everywhere apparent. On the one hand, it proclaims the great principle of modern society, that everyone must be equally subject to taxation. On the other, it lets stand provincial laws containing exemptions from this rule. It is asserted that any lawsuit involving a subject and the sovereign shall be judged according to the same formalities and regulations set forth for other lawsuits. In fact, this rule was never obeyed when it conflicted with the king's interests or passions. The mill at Sans-Souci was proudly displayed, while in any number of other circumstances the courts were quietly cowed into submission.

What proves that this code, so innovative in appearance, was not very innovative in reality, and what makes it so very interesting to study if one wants to know the true state of society in this part of Germany at the end of the eighteenth century, is the fact that the Prussian nation seems barely to have noticed its publication. Only legal scholars studied it, and many educated people today have never read it.

Page 33, Line 22
PEASANT PROPERTY IN GERMANY

There used to be many free peasant landowners, but the family property was subject to a kind of permanent entail. Whatever land the family owned was indivisible. One son became the sole heir. This was usually the youngest – a custom observed in certain parts of England as well. The heir's only obligation was to offer his brothers and sisters a dowry.

Peasant *Erbgüter* (hereditary properties) were fairly common through-out Germany. Nowhere was all the land held under feudal tenure. Even in Silesia, where the nobility has to this day maintained possession of vast estates encompassing most villages, some villages were wholly owned by their inhabitants and entirely free. In some parts of Germany, such as the Tyrol and Frisia, peasant *Erbgüter* predominated.

In the vast majority of German regions, however, this type of property was the exception, more common in some places than in others. In villages where it existed, small landowners of this type constituted a kind of aristocracy among the peasants.

Page 33, line 28
POSITION OF THE NOBILITY AND DIVISION OF LAND
ALONG THE RHINE

From information gathered on the spot and from individuals who lived under the Ancien Régime, it emerges that in the electorate of Cologne, for example, there were a large number of villages without lords, admin-istered by agents of the prince. In places where the nobility did exist, its administrative powers were quite limited. The position of nobles (at least as individuals) was more brilliant than it was powerful. The nobil-ity enjoyed many honors and accepted princely appointments but did not exercise real, direct power over the people. I also ascertained that in this same electorate, property was extensively divided and a very large num-ber of peasants owned land, a situation that can be attributed specifically to the fact that a significant proportion of noble families had long lived in straitened or semi-impoverished circumstances, as a result of which they were constantly selling off small portions of their land, which the peasants acquired in exchange for rent or cash. I found one document recording the population of the bishopric of Cologne at the beginning of the eighteenth century, which listed the status of each piece of land at that time. It showed that a third of the land already belonged to peasants. These circumstances gave rise to a range of sentiments and ideas that brought the people of the Rhineland much closer to revolution than those who lived in other parts of Germany, where these specific conditions had yet to develop.

Page 34, line 3
HOW THE LAW ON INTEREST-BEARING LOANS
HASTENED THE DIVISION OF THE SOIL

Laws prohibiting interest-bearing loans, no matter what the rate, were still in force at the end of the eighteenth century. Turgot tells us that such laws could still be found in many places in 1769. These laws remained on the books, he said, despite being frequently violated. Consular judges allowed interest to be paid as long as there was no alienation of capital, whereas ordinary courts condemned this practice. One finds dishonest debtors bringing criminal charges against their creditors for having lent them money without alienation of the capital.

Apart from the effects that such legislation inevitably had on the nation's commerce and, more generally, on its industrial mores, it had a considerable effect on the division of the land and land tenure. It gave rise to an enormous number of perpetual rents, both on land and on other forms of property. Instead of borrowing in times of need, ancient land-owners were forced to sell small portions of their estates for a price paid partly in capital and partly in the form of perpetual rent. This greatly contributed to division of the land, on the one hand, and, on the other, to burdening small holdings with a multitude of perpetual charges.

Page 36, line 23
EXAMPLE OF THE PASSIONS ALREADY AROUSED BY
THE TITHE TEN YEARS BEFORE THE REVOLUTION

In 1779, an obscure attorney from Lucé complained bitterly, and in a style that already smacked of the Revolution, that priests and other major recipients of the tithe were charging farmers an exorbitant price for straw that came to them via the tithe and that farmers desperately needed for compost.

Page 36, line 23
EXAMPLE OF THE WAY IN WHICH THE CLERGY ALIENATED
THE PEOPLE BY EXERCISING ITS PRIVILEGES

In 1780, the prior and canons of the priory of Laval complained about being subjected to payment of a tariff on items of consumption and materials needed for the repair of their buildings. They claimed that because this tariff was the equivalent of the taille, from which they were exempt, they owed nothing. The minister advised them to apply to the local authorities (*élection*) and to appeal to the Cour des Aides if not given satisfaction.

Page 36, line 26
FEUDAL DUES OWNED BY PRIESTS. ONE OF A THOUSAND
EXAMPLES. ABBEY OF CHERBOURG (1753)

The abbey at this time owned seigniorial rents payable in cash or in kind in nearly all the parishes around Cherbourg. One parish owed 306 bushels of wheat. The abbey owned the barony of Sainte-Geneviève, the barony and seigniorial mill of Bas-du-Roule, and the barony of Neuville-au-Plein, from which it was separated by at least ten leagues. In addition, it received tithes from a dozen parishes on the peninsula, several of which were quite some distance away.

Page 38, line 22
IRRITATION CAUSED BY FEUDAL DUES AMONG PEASANTS, AND, IN PARTICULAR, BY THE FEUDAL DUES OWED TO PRIESTS

Here is a letter written shortly before the Revolution by a farmer, addressed to the intendant. It does not constitute authoritative proof of the facts it alleges, but it does accurately portray the state of mind in the class to which the letter writer belonged. The letter reads as follows:

> Although we have little nobility in this region, do not believe that properties here are less burdened with rents. On the contrary, nearly all the fiefs belong to the cathedral, the archbishopric, the collegiate church of Saint-Martin, the Benedictines of Noirmoutiers and Saint-Julien, and other ecclesiastics, to whom payments never end and who are forever coming up with musty old parchments fabricated by God knows who!
>
> The whole region is infected with rents. Most land owes a seventh of the wheat grown annually per acre, while other land owes wine. One orchard owes the manor a quarter of the fruit it produces, another a fifth, and so on, and that is after deduction for the tithe; still another owes a twelfth and another a thirteenth. These dues vary so widely that I can cite examples from a fourth down to a fortieth.
>
> What to think about all these rents, payable in various forms, including grains, vegetables, cash, poultry, labor, wood, fruits, and candles? I am aware of other, still more unusual forms of payment, such as bread, wax, eggs, headless pigs, wreaths of roses, bouquets of violets, gilt spurs, and what have you. There are a host of other seigniorial dues as well. Why hasn't someone rid France of all these extravagant charges? At long last, people have begun to open their eyes, and much is to be expected from the wisdom of the present government. It will extend a helping hand to impoverished victims of the exactions of the old fiscal regime known as seigniorial dues, which can never be alienated or sold.
>
> And what to think of the tyrannical exaction known as *lods et ventes*? A buyer goes to great lengths to make a purchase and is obliged to pay huge fees for assessments, contracts, closing, transcripts, stamps, title registration, the hundredth penny, eight sous

per livre, etc., and on top of all that he must show his contract to his lord, who will make him pay *lods et ventes* on the principal of his purchase. Some charge a twelfth, others a tenth. Some claim a fifth, others a fifth plus a fifth of the fifth. There are some at all prices, and I even know some who charge a third of the principal. No, not even the fiercest, most barbarous nations in the world ever conceived of exactions like these, which our tyrants piled in such great number on the heads of our forebears. [This philosophical and literary tirade was written without regard for the rules of spelling.]

What! The late king allowed the commutation of rents on town property but did not include country property? He should have begun with the latter. Why not allow poor farmers to break their shackles, to commute and free themselves from the host of seigniorial dues and ground rents that do so much harm to vassals and bring so little profit to their lords? There should have been no distinction between town and country or between lords and commoners when it came to commutations.

At each change of title, the stewards of those holding title to church properties pillage and loot all the tenants. We can mention a very recent example. The steward of our new archbishop gave notice upon his arrival that all the tenants of his predecessor, M. de Fleury, would have to leave. He declared all leases that they had contracted with the latter null and void and banished all who were not willing to double their rents and pay large bribes, which they had already done with M. de Fleury's steward. They were thus deprived of the seven or eight years remaining on their leases, which had been publicly agreed to, and obliged to leave immediately, on Christmas Eve, the most critical time of the year because of the difficulty of feeding the animals, without knowing where they were going to live. The king of Prussia could have done no worse.

Indeed, it appears to be true that for clerical property, leases issued by the previous title holder created no legal obligation for his successor. The author of the letter is quite correct in saying that feudal rents could be commuted in the towns but not in the countryside. Here, then, is further proof of the abandonment of the peasant, in contrast to the way in which everyone above him somehow managed to take care of his own interests.

Page 38, line 22

Any long-dominant institution, after establishing itself in its natural sphere, extends its influence beyond that sphere until ultimately it exerts great influence on parts of the legal structure in which it is not paramount. Although the feudal system fell primarily under the head of political law, it transformed all of civil law and profoundly altered the status of property and human beings in all things pertaining to private life. It influenced inheritances through unequal division of estates, a principle that extended down as low as the middle class in certain provinces (witness Normandy). It encompassed all landed property, for there was scarcely any land to which it did not apply or whose owners were not affected by feudal laws. It affected the property not only of individuals but also of municipalities. It touched industry by levying charges on it. It affected incomes by taxing them unequally and affected pecuniary interests in general in almost every type of human affairs: landowners paid dues, rents, and labor services; farmers were affected in a myriad of ways, among them monopolies, ground rents, *lods et ventes*, etc.; merchants paid market fees; traders paid tolls, etc. By bringing feudalism down, the Revolution made its presence visible and palpable, as it were, at every point where private interest was susceptible.

Page 45, line 27
PUBLIC CHARITY DELIVERED BY THE STATE. FAVORITISM
In 1748, the king made a grant of 20,000 pounds of rice (it was a year of great misery and famine, of which there were so many in the eighteenth century). The archbishop of Tours claimed that it was he who had obtained the assistance and that said assistance was to be distributed only by him and in his diocese. The intendant maintained that the aid had been granted to the entire tax district and was to be distributed by him to all the parishes. After a prolonged struggle, the king, in order to settle the dispute, doubled the amount of rice for the district so that the archbishop and intendant might each distribute half. Both agreed, moreover, that the distributions would be done by parish priests. Neither lords nor syndics were to be involved. The correspondence between the intendant and the comptroller general reveals that, according to the former, the archbishop wanted rice to be distributed only to his protégés, and in particular he wanted most of it to be distributed in parishes belonging to Mme la duchesse de Rochechouart. Furthermore, the same packet of documents contains letters from great lords who requested rice particularly for their parishes, as well as letters from the comptroller general designating the parishes of certain individuals.

Legal charity gives rise to abuses, no matter what the system. But it is unworkable when it is handled, as in this case, from afar, without public scrutiny, by the central government.

Page 45, line 29
EXAMPLE OF THE WAY IN WHICH THIS LEGAL
CHARITY WAS HANDLED
In a report made to the provincial assembly of Haute Guyenne in 1780, we read: "Of the sum of 385,000 livres granted to this district by His Majesty since 1773, when the charity works were established, through 1779, the *élection* of Montauban, seat and residence of Monsieur l'Intendant, has alone received more than 240,000 livres, the greater part of which has been spent in the community of Montauban itself."

Page 45, line 38
POWERS OF THE INTENDANT TO REGULATE INDUSTRY
Intendants' archives are filled with documents pertaining to the regulation of industry.

Industry in those days was subject not only to fetters placed on it by state bodies, guilds, and so on but also to the whims of government, usually in the form of general regulations issued by the King's Council, as well as specific applications of those regulations by the intendants. One discovers that intendants were endlessly concerned with the measurement of cloth, the fabrics to be selected, methods to be used, and errors to be avoided in manufacturing. Serving under them, in addition to the subdelegates, were local inspectors of industry. In this respect, centralization was even more extensive then than it is today. It was more capricious and arbitrary. It led to a rapid increase in the number of public officials and gave rise to habits of submission and dependence of all sorts.

Note that these habits were instilled primarily in the bourgeois, mercantile, and commercial classes, which were soon to triumph, rather than in the classes that were about to be defeated. Hence, the Revolution, rather than destroy the habits in question, guaranteed their predominance and spread them everywhere.

The preceding remarks are prompted by my reading of numerous letters and documents classified under the head "Manufacturing and Workshops, Cloth, Chemicals." These can be found among the papers in the archives of the intendance of Île-de-France. The same archive contains the frequent and detailed reports that inspectors sent to the intendant concerning their visits to manufacturers to ensure that the rules laid down for manufacturing were obeyed, as well as various council decrees issued at the behest of the intendant in order to prohibit or permit manufacturing in certain places or of certain fabrics or using certain methods.

What stands out in the observations of the inspectors, who are quite disdainful of the manufacturers, is the idea that it is the state's right and duty to force them to do their best, not only in the public interest but in the interest of the manufacturers themselves. Hence, they feel obliged to force the manufacturers to adopt the best method and to discuss the smallest details of their craft, while handing out a large number of violations and imposing enormous fines.

Page 47, line 9
SPIRIT OF THE GOVERNMENT OF LOUIS XI

No document gives a better idea of the true spirit of the government of Louis XI than the many constitutions that he granted to towns. I had the opportunity to study quite closely those that he granted to most of the towns of Anjou, Maine, and Touraine.

All of these constitutions are based more or less on the same model and reveal the same designs with perfect clarity. From them emerges an image of Louis XI rather different from the one with which we are familiar. This king is commonly regarded as the enemy of the nobility but at the same time as a sincere, if somewhat brutal, friend of the people. Here, he is seen to harbor the same hatred for the political rights of both the people and the nobility. He also uses the bourgeoisie to diminish what stands above it and to repress those who lie below. He is at once antiaristocratic and antidemocratic: the bourgeois king par excellence. He heaps privileges upon the notable citizens of the towns, seeking to increase their importance. He lavishes them with noble titles, thereby reducing the value of nobility, while at the same time destroying the popular, democratic character of town administration, and he restricts the government to a small circle of families attached to his reform and tied to his power by the vast benefits they derive from it.

Page 47, line 24
A TOWN ADMINISTRATION IN THE EIGHTEENTH CENTURY

I take from a 1764 survey of town administration the file pertaining to Angers. There, one finds the constitution of the town by turns analyzed, attacked, and defended by the presidial, the municipal corporation, the subdelegate, and the intendant. Since the same views can be found in a great many other places, the picture that emerges from this file must be seen as anything but an individual portrait.

Report of the presidial on the current state of the municipal constitution of Angers and the reforms to be enacted. "Since the municipal corporation of Angers almost never consults the general population, even for the most important projects, unless it is obliged by special orders to do so, this administration is unknown to all who are not members of the municipal corporation, including the temporary aldermen, who have only a superficial grasp of town affairs." [Indeed, all of these restricted bourgeois oligarchies tended to consult as little as possible with what is here referred to as the "general population."]

According to a regulation of March 29, 1681, the municipal corporation comprised twenty-one officials:

A mayor, who acquired ex officio nobility and whose term of office was four years.

Four temporary aldermen, who served for two years.

Twelve aldermen councilors, who served for life once elected.

Two town prosecutors.

One prosecutor by hereditary right.

One clerk of the court.

They enjoyed various privileges, including the following: their capitation was fixed and modest; they were exempt from the obligation to quarter, equip, supply, and maintain troops; they were exempt from the tax on double and triple subdivision of housing, old and new local duties, and supplementary tax on foodstuffs, and even from the "free gift," from which, according to the presidial, they believed they were entitled to exempt themselves on their own private authority. In addition, they received allowances for candles, and some of them were granted a salary and free housing.

These details make it clear that at this time, it was a good thing to be an alderman in Angers with life tenure. Note how this system bestowed tax exemptions on the wealthiest individuals at all times and in all places. Later in the same report, we read: "These positions are coveted by the wealthiest residents, who hope thereby to obtain a considerable reduction in the capitation, the heavy burden of which then falls on others. There are currently several municipal officials whose capitation is fixed at 30 livres but who should pay 250 to 300 livres. There is one who, in view of his fortune, could pay a capitation of at least 1,000 livres." In another part of this report, we find this: "Among the wealthiest residents we find more than forty officials or widows of officials (owners of offices), whose positions confer the privilege of not contributing to the significant capitation with which the town is burdened. The burden of this capitation falls on untold numbers of poor artisans, who feel that they are overburdened and constantly protest the heavy taxes they must pay, yet these protests are almost always without justification, because there is no inequality in the apportionment of what remains of the town's obligation."

The general assembly consists of seventy-six[1] individuals:

The mayor.
Two deputies of the chapter.
A syndic of clerics.
A lieutenant general of police.
Four aldermen.
Two aldermen councilors.
A royal prosecutor attached to the presidial.
A town attorney.
Two deputies of the Department of Waters and Forests.
Two from the *élection*.
Two from the salt storehouse.
Two from the customs office.
Two from the mint.
Two from the lawyers' guild.
Two judge consuls.
Two notaries.
Two from the corporation of merchants.
Finally, two deputies from each of sixteen parishes.

The latter were supposed to represent the people in the strict sense, and in particular the guilds. Clearly, things were arranged to ensure that the guilds were permanently in the minority.

When a place in the municipal corporation became vacant, the general assembly selected three subjects to fill the vacancy. Most town hall positions were not assigned to particular corporations, as I have seen in other municipal constitutions; that is, the voters were not required to choose either a magistrate or an attorney or what have you, a system that members of the presidial deemed quite ill-advised.

---

[1] Actually they only add up to seventy-four.

According to the same presidial, which seems to have been animated by extreme jealousy of the municipal corporation, and which I strongly suspect found fault with the town constitution only to the extent that it deemed its own privileges insufficient, "the general assembly, which is too large and made up in part of not very intelligent individuals, should be consulted only in cases involving alienation of the communal estate, loans, establishment of tariffs, and election of municipal officers. All other affairs could be deliberated in a smaller assembly, composed solely of notables. Membership in this assembly could be limited to the lieutenant general of police, the royal prosecutor, and twelve other notables chosen from six corporations – the clergy, the magistracy, the nobility, the university, commerce, and the bourgeoisie – and others not belonging to said corporations. The choice of notables could be left initially to the general assembly and subsequently to the assembly of notables or to the corporation from which each notable is to be drawn."

All these state officials, who joined the municipal corporations of the Ancien Régime as owners of offices or notables, resembled the officials of today as to the titles of the functions they exercised, and sometimes even the nature of those functions, but differed profoundly as to position – a circumstance to which careful attention must always be paid in order to avoid drawing erroneous conclusions. Nearly all were, in fact, notables of the city before being invested with public functions, or else they coveted public functions in order to become notables. They had no idea of leaving their offices and no hope of rising to higher positions, and, because of these two facts alone, they were quite different from the officials with whom we are familiar today.

Report of municipal officials. From the report, we learn that the municipal corporation was created by Louis XI in 1474 on the ruins of the town's old democratic constitution, and already on the model described previously, in that most political rights were limited to the middle class, the popular element was excluded or enfeebled, the number of officials was large so that more people would have a stake in the reform, and the segment of the bourgeoisie that took part in town administration was rewarded with lavish grants of hereditary nobility and privileges of all sorts.

The same report contains letters patent issued by Louis XI's successors, who recognized the new constitution and further restricted the power of the people. We learn that in 1485, letters patent issued for that purpose by Charles VIII were attacked before parlement by residents of

Angers, in exactly the same way that one might bring suit in an English court if a dispute arose involving a town charter in England. In 1601, it was again a decree of parlement that defined the political rights created by the royal charter. From that time on, however, the report refers only to the King's Council.

The report reveals that not just the position of mayor but all other positions in the municipal corporation were filled by the king, who chose from among three candidates presented by the general assembly under the provisions of a council decree of June 22, 1738. It is also revealed that in virtue of council decrees of 1733 and 1741, the merchants of the town had the right to a post of alderman or councilor (as the permanent aldermen were known). Finally, we learn that in those days, the municipal corporation was charged with apportioning the amounts to be raised from the capitation, military equipment tax, military lodging tax, and assessments for poor relief, troops, coast guards, and foundlings.

This is followed by a very long list of the duties of municipal officials, which in their eyes fully justified their privileges and life tenure – favors that we can see they were very afraid of losing. Several of the justifications they gave of their activities are rather odd, including this one: "Their most essential occupation is to audit the ever more numerous financial issues connected with the constant expansion of sales taxes, salt taxes, stamp and registry fees, illegally collected registry fees, and francs-fiefs. Because the activities of the financial companies provoke constant challenges to the various taxes, town officials have been forced to argue cases on behalf of the town before various jurisdictions, including parlement and the King's Council, in order to resist the oppression to which they have been subjected. Thirty years' experience and service have taught them that a lifetime is scarcely sufficient to learn to avoid the traps and pitfalls that the various agents of the tax farms are forever putting in the way of citizens in order to preserve their commissions."

What is curious is that all these things were written to the comptroller general himself, to win his favor for maintaining the privileges of those who wrote them, so habituated were they to viewing the companies charged with collecting taxes as an adversary that could be attacked from every angle without raising anyone's hackles. As this habit spread and gained in intensity, it ultimately cast the royal treasury itself in the light of an odious and deceitful tyrant – not the agent of all but everyone's common enemy.

The report continues: "All offices were combined in the municipal corporation for the first time by a council decree of Sept. 4, 1694, in exchange for a sum of 22,000 livres," meaning that the offices were then redeemed for that sum. By a decree of April 26, 1723, the municipal offices created by the edict of May 24, 1722, were added to the town corporation. In other words, the town was allowed to purchase them. Yet another decree, of May 24, 1723, allowed the town to borrow 120,000 livres to acquire the aforementioned offices. Another decree of July 26, 1728, allowed the town to borrow 50,000 livres to purchase the offices of the town registrar and secretary. According to the report, "the town paid these sums to preserve its free elections and ensure that its elected officials could enjoy the various prerogatives associated with their offices for two years in some cases and for life in others." Because some municipal offices were reestablished by the edict of November 1733, the council, at the request of the mayor and aldermen, issued a decree on January 11, 1735, whereby the redemption price was set at 170,000 livres, for the payment of which the town was permitted to extend the collection of local customs duties for a period of fifteen years.

This is a fair sample of town administration in the Ancien Régime. Towns were induced to take on debt and then authorized to levy special temporary taxes to liquidate that debt. And then later these temporary taxes were made permanent, as I frequently discovered, and the central government, of course, claimed its share.

The report continues: "Town officials were not deprived of the important judicial powers granted to them by Louis XI until royal courts were established. Before 1699 they had jurisdiction over disputes between masters and workers. An accounting of local customs fees was delivered to the intendant, as specified in all the decrees creating and extending such fees."

The report also shows that the deputies of the sixteen parishes discussed earlier, who participated in the general assembly, were chosen by companies, guilds, and communities and were strictly representatives of the group that chose them. They received binding instructions on every issue.

Finally, the entire report demonstrates that in Angers as everywhere else, expenditures of any kind had to be authorized by the intendant and council. Clearly, when the administration of a town is given to certain individuals as their own property, and those men, instead of being remunerated for their services in specified amounts, are granted privileges that exempt them personally from any consequences that their administration may have on the private fortunes of their fellow citizens, administrative oversight may be seen as a necessity.

The whole report, besides being badly done, reveals an extraordinary fear on the part of officials of seeing any change in the existing state of affairs. They advance a host of reasons, both good and bad, in the interest of maintaining the status quo.

The subdelegate's report. The intendant, after receiving these two contradictory reports, sought the advice of his subdelegate. He, too, prepared a report.

"The municipal councilors' report is not worth dwelling on," he wrote. "Its only purpose is to justify the privileges these officials enjoy. The report of the presidial contains useful information, but there is no reason to grant these magistrates all the prerogatives they are asking for."

According to this subdelegate, the town's constitution had long been in need of improvement. In addition to the immunities with which we are already familiar and which the municipal officials of Angers possessed, he tells us that the mayor, while in office, was entitled to housing worth at least 600 francs in rent, plus 50 francs in salary and 100 francs in franking privileges, plus attendance fees. The prosecutor syndic also received housing, as did the town clerk. In order to exempt themselves from sales taxes and local customs fees, an estimated level of consumption was established for each municipal official. Each of them was entitled to import so many barrels of wine per year without paying any fees, and the same privilege applied to all other items of consumption.

The subdelegate did not propose that municipal councilors be deprived of their tax exemptions, but he did suggest that the intendant set the amount of their capitation each year instead of leaving it fixed at a very inadequate level. He also felt that the same officials should be subject, as other citizens were, to the "free gift," from which they had exempted themselves on the basis of who knows what precedent.

The report further states that municipal officials are responsible for drawing up the capitation rolls for the town's inhabitants. Because they are careless and arbitrary in performing this task, the intendant is annually besieged with a large number of claims and petitions for relief. It would be desirable if, in the future, this assessment were made by the members of each company or community in their own interest and in accordance with fixed general rules. Municipal officials would retain responsibility only for assessing the capitation of bourgeois and others who are not members of any organized body, such as certain artisans and the domestic servants of all the privileged.

The subdelegate's report confirmed what the municipal officials had already said: that the town had redeemed its municipal offices in 1735 for the sum of 170,000 livres.

Letter from the intendant to the comptroller general. With all these documents in hand, the intendant wrote to the minister. "It is important," he said, "for the sake of the residents and the public good to reduce the size of the municipal corporation, whose superfluity of members is an enormous burden on the public owing to the privileges they enjoy."

"I am struck," he added, "by the enormous sums that were paid at various times to redeem Anger's municipal offices. Had these sums been put to productive use, they would have redounded to the profit of the town, which instead has felt only the burden of authority and of the privileges of these officials."

"The internal abuses of this administration deserve the council's full attention," the intendant went on. "Apart from attendance fees and the candle allowance, which consume an annual total of 2,127 livres [this was the sum indicated for these types of expenses in the normal budget, which the king periodically imposed on the towns], public monies have been wasted and put to clandestine uses at the whim of these officials, and the royal prosecutor, who has owned his office for the past thirty or forty years, so dominates the administration, whose inner workings only he knows, that the residents have been unable at any time to obtain the slightest information about the use of the communal revenues." The intendant therefore asked the minister to reduce the town council to a mayor who would serve for four years, six aldermen who would serve six years, a royal prosecutor who would serve eight years, and a clerk and tax collector, who would serve permanently.

What is more, the same intendant proposed the same constitution for the town of Tours. In his view, the following steps were necessary:

1. Preserve the general assembly, but only as an electoral body charged with electing the municipal officials;
2. Create an extraordinary council of notables, which would have to fulfill all the functions that the edict of 1764 appeared to assign to the

general assembly. This council was to consist of twelve members, who would be elected for a term of six years not by the general assembly but by the twelve so-called notable bodies (each body electing its own representative). He listed the following notable bodies:

The presidial.
The university.
The *élection* [which conducted annual visitations of each locality to ensure fair assessment of taxes].
The officials of the Department of Waters and Forests.
The salt warehouse.
The tax collectors.
The mint.
The attorneys and prosecutors.
The judge consuls.
The notaries.
The merchants.
The bourgeois.

Clearly, nearly all these notables were public officials, and all public officials were notables, from which it follows, as is also clear from a thousand other places in the records, that the middle class was as avid for public office then as it is today, and as little inclined to look elsewhere for its livelihood. The only difference, as I wrote in the text, was that then people purchased what little importance such jobs could confer, whereas today's job seekers ask to be given it free of charge.

This proposal makes it clear that all real municipal power lay with the extraordinary council, which allowed a very small bourgeois coterie to capture the town government. The only assembly in which common people still had a voice had no function other than to elect municipal officials and was no longer permitted to offer those officials its advice. Note, too, that the intendant was more restrictive and antipopular than the king, who seemed in his edict to bestow the main functions of government on the general assembly, while the intendant was much more liberal and democratic than the bourgeoisie, to judge at least by the report that I cited in the text, a report in which the notables of another town sought to exclude the people even from the election of municipal officials, a power that the king and intendant were willing to grant.

The reader will have noticed that the intendant uses the terms bourgeois and merchants to refer to distinct categories of notables. It is perhaps worth pausing to give precise definitions of these two words in order to show how the bourgeoisie was sliced up into many small pieces and vexed by many small vanities.

The word bourgeois had a general meaning and a more narrow meaning: it indicated members of the middle class, and, in addition, it designated a certain group of people within that class. "The bourgeois are those enabled by birth and fortune to live decently without engaging in gainful employment," according to one of the reports generated by the survey of 1764. The remainder of the report shows that "bourgeois" was not meant to apply to anyone who was a member of an industrial company or guild, but to say precisely to whom it did apply is more difficult. "For," the same report notes, "among those who claimed the title of bourgeois, one often finds individuals to whom it applies solely by virtue of their idleness, while in other respects they are without fortune and leading uncultivated, obscure lives. By contrast, the bourgeois should always be distinguished by fortune, birth, talents, manners, and way of life. The artisans who make up the guilds have never enjoyed the rank of notables."

In addition to the bourgeois, the merchants were a second type of person who did not belong to either a company or guild. But what were the limits of this tiny class? The report continues: "Should we classify merchants of low birth and retail commerce along with wholesalers?" To resolve these difficulties, the report proposed having the aldermen draw up a list of notable merchants every year, which list would then be given to their leader or syndic so that he might invite only those included therein to join in deliberations at the town hall. Care would be taken to ensure that this list would not include any domestic servants, peddlers, carters, or others engaged in lowly trades.

Page 50, line 20

One of the most prominent characteristics of eighteenth-century town government was not so much the abolition of all public representation and intervention in town affairs as it was the extreme variability of the rules to which such government was subjected, because powers were granted, rescinded, restored, increased, reduced, and modified in a myriad of ways, and constantly. There is no better indication of how debased these local liberties had become than the perpetual fluidity of the law, to which no one seems to have paid attention. This fluidity alone would have sufficed to preclude any distinctive local ideas, any attachment to the past, and any local patriotism in the institution that was most apt to foster these things. This laid the groundwork for the vast destruction of the past that the Revolution would carry out.

Page 50, line 27
A VILLAGE GOVERNMENT IN THE EIGHTEENTH CENTURY, DRAWN FROM THE PAPERS OF THE INTENDANCY OF L'ÎLE-DE-FRANCE
 The affair of which I am about to speak was chosen from among many others as an example of some of the forms adopted by parish administrations, in order to understand why the workings of parish government were often so slow and to show what the general assembly of a parish looked like in the eighteenth century.

 The issue was one of repairing the rectory and steeple of a rural church in Ivry, Île-de-France. To whom could one turn to get such repairs done? How was the apportionment of expenditures determined? How was the necessary sum to be raised?

1. The parish priest petitioned the intendant, informing him that the steeple and rectory were in urgent need of repair, and that his predecessor, having attached useless additions to the rectory, had completely altered and deformed it, so that it was up to the residents of the village, who had allowed this to be done, to bear the cost of putting things back in order, unless they could collect the sum from the heirs of the previous priest.

2. His Excellency the intendant issued an order (on August 29, 1747) instructing the syndic to convene a general assembly to deliberate on the need for the requested repairs.

3. The residents, upon due deliberation, declared that they were not opposed to repairing the rectory but were opposed to repairing the steeple, which stood above the choir, and the priest, as the recipient of the tithe, was responsible for repairs to the choir. [A council decree from the end of the previous century (April 1695) did indeed assign responsibility for repairs to the choir to the person entitled to the parish tithe, the parishioners themselves being responsible only for the maintenance of the nave.]

4. A new order from the intendant, who, in view of the contradictory facts of the case, sent an architect, Sieur Cordier, to inspect the rectory and steeple, prepare an estimate of needed repairs, and conduct an inquiry.

5. A report of these efforts indicated that a number of people who owned land in Ivry appeared before the representative of the intendant. Among

them were apparently nobles, bourgeois, and peasants of the village, who wished to go on record either for or against the priest's claims.

7. [*sic*] A further order from the intendant indicated that the estimates of repairs drawn up by the architect representing him should be presented to a new general assembly of landowners and residents, to be convened by the syndic.

8. A new parish assembly was convened as a result of this order, during which the residents stood by what they had said previously.

9. An order issued by His Excellency the intendant prescribed the following: 1) that contracts should be awarded for the work indicated in the estimates, with the award to be made by his subdelegate in Corbeil, at his official residence, in the presence of the priest, syndic, and principal residents of the parish, and 2) that in view of the fact that the church was in danger of collapse, a tax would be levied on all the residents, except that those who continued to believe that the steeple was part of the choir and should be repaired by the recipient of the tithe would be allowed to appeal this decision before the regular courts.

10. All parties were summoned to the home of the subdelegate in Corbeil for an auction and award of contracts.

11. The parish priest and several residents petitioned that the fees for the administrative procedure not be assigned to the contractor, as would normally be the case, because these fees were very high and would make it impossible to find a contractor.

12. The intendant ordered that the fees incurred in the award of the contract be reckoned by the subdelegate, so that this amount might be included in the contract fee and tax.

13. Certain notable residents granted Sieur X the power to attend the award of the contract and give his consent in keeping with the architect's estimates.

14. The syndic certified that the usual announcements and advertisements had been made.

15. A copy of the contract:
Amount of repairs to be done .... 487 l.
Expenses incurred in awarding the contract .. 237 l. 18 s. 6 d.

16. Finally, a council decree was issued (on July 23, 1748) authorizing a tax to cover this sum.

The reader may have noticed that the parish assembly was convened several times in the course of this procedure. Here are the minutes of one of these assemblies, as an example of how such meetings were generally conducted. It is a notarized document:

> Today, at the conclusion of the parish mass, in the usual and customary place, after the ringing of the bell, there appeared in the assembly convened by the residents of said parish, in the presence of X, notary of Corbeil, undersigned, and the witnesses named hereafter, Sieur Michaud, vintner, syndic of said parish, who had the intendant's order read to the assembly and commanded that its instructions be complied with.
>
> At this point a resident of said parish appeared, who stated that the steeple was erected above the choir and therefore the responsibility of the priest. Several others also appeared [and the names of several other individuals prepared to grant the priest's request were duly noted].... Then fifteen peasants, laborers, masons, and vintners came forward in support of what the previous witnesses had said. Sieur Rambaud, vintner, also appeared, and said that he was entirely prepared to accept whatever His Excellency the intendant decided. Sieur X, doctor of the Sorbonne and priest, also appeared and maintained what he had previously stated and requested in his petition. Of which, as of all the foregoing, those in attendance took note. Done and heard at Ivry, opposite the cemetery of said parish, in the presence of the undersigned, who was engaged in the drafting of the present document from 11 in the morning until 2 in the afternoon.

We see that this parish assembly was nothing but an administrative inquiry but with the formalities and costs of a judicial inquiry. It never resulted in a vote and thus in an expression of the will of the parish. It included only individual opinions and in no way constrained the will of the government. Indeed, we know from many other documents that the parish assembly was intended to inform the intendant's decision, not to block it, even though the issue involved only the interests of the parish itself.

The same documents tell us that this affair resulted in three separate inquiries: one before the notary, another before the architect, and a third before two notaries in order to determine whether or not the residents stood by their previous statements.

The tax of 524 livres 10 sous imposed by the decree of July 23, 1748, was to be borne by all property owners, privileged and nonprivileged alike, as was almost always the case in expenditures of this sort, but the basis used to determine the share of each group was different. Those subject to the taille were taxed in proportion to their taille, while the privileged were taxed on the basis of their presumed wealth, which gave the latter a great advantage over the former.

Finally, in this same case, the assessment of the sum of 524 l. 10 s. was done by two tax collectors, both residents of the village and neither elected nor chosen by turn, as was usually the case, but rather selected by the subdelegate and intendant.

Page 51, line 25

The pretext that Louis XIV used to destroy the liberty of the towns was their poor management of their finances. Yet, as Turgot rightly points out, this same mismanagement persisted and grew worse after the king introduced his reforms. Most towns, he added, are substantially indebted today, partly for funds that they lent to the government and partly for expenses and decorations on which town officials, who managed other people's money and did not have to account to anyone or take instruction from anyone, spent lavishly in order to distinguish themselves and in some cases to enrich themselves.

Page 54, line 24

THE STATE WAS THE OVERSEER OF THE CONVENTS AS WELL AS THE VILLAGES. EXAMPLE OF THIS OVERSIGHT

The comptroller general, in authorizing the intendant to pay 15,000 livres to the convent of the Carmelites, to which damages were owed, recommended that he make sure that this capital was invested wisely. Numerous similar instances could be cited.

Page 59, line 14

HOW IT WAS THAT IN CANADA IT WAS POSSIBLE TO JUDGE THE ADMINISTRATIVE CENTRALIZATION OF THE ANCIEN RÉGIME MOST ACCURATELY

It was in the colonies that it was possible to judge the character of metropolitan government most accurately because there, the features of that government were magnified and thus easiest to see. If I want to judge the character of the administration of Louis XIV and discover its flaws, I must go to Canada. There one sees the deformity of the specimen as under a microscope.

In Canada, the development of the government's thinking was not impeded by a multitude of obstacles overtly or covertly placed in its way by prior circumstances or a former social state. There was virtually no nobility, or at any rate what nobility there was had few roots. The Church no longer enjoyed a dominant position. Feudal traditions had vanished or lapsed into obscurity. Judicial power was not rooted in old institutions and customs. The central government was free to indulge its natural predilections, and its guiding spirit shaped all legislation. In Canada, no vestige of municipal or provincial institutions remained; there was no legitimate collective force, no permissible individual initiative. An intendant there enjoyed far greater power than his counterparts in France. The central administration was involved in far more things in Canada than in the metropolis, and it insisted on managing everything from Paris, despite the 1,800 leagues that separated the capital from the colony. It never accepted the great principles that can make a colony populous and prosperous but, rather, relied on meddlesome, artificial procedures and petty, tyrannical regulations to increase and spread the population: it required certain plantings; asserted exclusive administrative jurisdiction over all lawsuits arising from land grants, from which it excluded the local administration; prescribed techniques of cultivation; obliged citizens to live in one place rather than another, etc. All this took place under Louis XIV; the edicts were countersigned by Colbert, but one could easily believe that they were the work of a full-blown modern, centralized regime operating in, say, Algeria. Indeed, what was done in Canada was a faithful image of what we have long since witnessed in Algeria. In both places, we find an administration with a staff almost as large as the population, overweening, active, and prone to regulate, restrict, and plan everything. The government assumes full responsibility for all that happens and knows more about the interests of its subjects than they do themselves. Its efforts are as tireless as they are bootless.

In the United States, by contrast, the English system of decentralization was carried to an extreme: villages became virtually independent municipalities, democratic republics. The republican element, which formed, as it were, the core of the English constitution and English mores, developed unimpeded in the United States. In England, the government as such does little, while private individuals do a great deal. In America, the government no longer does anything, as it were, and individuals, joined together in associations, do everything. The absence of an upper class, which left the individual Canadian more subject to the government than was the individual Frenchman in the same period, made the citizen of the English provinces increasingly independent of the central government.

In both colonies, a fully democratic society was established, but in Canada, at least as long as it belonged to France, equality was combined with absolute government; in the United States it combined with freedom. As for the material consequences of the two colonial methods, we know that in 1763, at the time of the conquest, the population of Canada was 60,000, whereas that of the English provinces was 3 million.

Page 60, line 16
One Example among Many of the General Regulations
That the Council of State Was Constantly Making,
Which Had Force of Law Throughout France and Created
Special Offenses That Could Be Judged Only by the
Administrative Courts

I will take the first examples that come to hand: a council decree of April 29, 1779, which ordered that, in the future, throughout the kingdom, anyone who kept or sold sheep must mark the animals in a certain way or pay a fine of 300 livres. His Majesty commanded his intendants to oversee the execution of this order, which meant that it was up to the intendant to impose the penalty for violation. Another example: the council decree of December 21, 1778, which prohibited haulers and carters from warehousing their cargo or pay a fine of 300 livres. His Majesty ordered the lieutenant general of police and intendants to enforce this order.

Page 68, line 23
The provincial assembly of Haute Guyenne loudly called for the establishment of new brigades of mounted police, in much the same way as the general council of Aveyron or Lot might call for the establishment of a new brigade of gendarmes today. The idea remains the same: the police force stands for order, and order can come with the police only from the government. The report adds: "Complaints are heard daily about the absence of police in the countryside [how could it have been otherwise? The nobles turned their backs on the problem, the bourgeois lived in the towns, and the village, represented by some coarse peasant, had no power in any case], and it must be granted that, except in a few cantons where just and benevolent lords use the prestige and power over their vassals, derived from their situation to prevent the acts of violence to which rural residents are naturally inclined by the crudeness of their manners and harshness of their characters, there is almost no other way to restrain these ignorant, coarse, and angry men."

Such was the way in which the nobles of the provincial assembly allowed themselves to be talked about, and in which the members of the Third Estate, who by themselves accounted for half the assembly, spoke about the common people in public documents.

Page 69, line 14

Tobacco licenses were as eagerly sought under the Ancien Régime as they are today. Important personages solicited them for their protégés. I have found some that were awarded on the recommendation of ladies of high rank. Others were awarded at the behest of archbishops.

Page 69, line 36

The extinction of all public life at the local level had gone farther than one might think possible. One of the roads from Maine to Normandy was impassable. Who was to request repairs? The district of Touraine, through which the road passed? The province of Normandy or the province of Maine, which had interests in commerce in livestock that depended on this route? Or some canton especially injured by the poor condition of the road? The district, province, and cantons had no voice. The dealers who used the road and bogged down on it had to take it upon themselves to make the central government aware of its condition. They wrote to the comptroller general in Paris and begged him to come to their aid.

Page 78, line 6

THE GREATER OR LESSER IMPORTANCE OF SEIGNIORIAL
RENTS OR DUES, DEPENDING ON THE PROVINCE

Turgot says in his works: "I should point out that these kinds of dues are of another order of magnitude in most of the wealthy provinces, such as Normandy, Picardy, and the Paris region. In these places, wealth consists primarily in the product of the land itself, with plots combined into large farms whose owners derive considerable rents from them. The seigniorial rents of the largest estates constitute only a very modest portion of the revenue, and this item is considered almost an honorific payment. In the less wealthy provinces, where the principles of farming are different, lords and nobles own almost no land of their own. Inherited lands, which have been extensively divided, are burdened with very heavy rents in kind, for which the cotenants are jointly responsible. These rents frequently absorb most of what the land produces, and the income of the landlords comes almost entirely from this source."

Page 83, line 34
ANTICASTE INFLUENCE OF COMMON DISCUSSION OF AFFAIRS
The relatively less important works of eighteenth-century agricultural societies give us an idea of the anticaste influence of common discussion of common interests. Although these meetings took place thirty years before the Revolution, at the height of the Ancien Régime, and although they were concerned solely with theories, the mere fact that questions of interest to the various classes of society were debated and discussed in common immediately makes us aware of the way in which people of different classes were brought together and mingled. We see how ideas for reasonable reform appealed to the privileged and nonprivileged alike, even though only issues of conservation and agriculture were at stake.

I am convinced that only a government like that of the Ancien Régime, which never looked for support outside itself and always dealt with individuals one at a time, could have maintained the ridiculous and senseless inequality that existed in France at the time of the Revolution. The slightest contact with *self-government* [in English in the original] would have profoundly altered it and rapidly transformed or destroyed it.

Page 83, line 34
Provincial liberties can subsist for a time without national liberty when those liberties are ancient and linked to habit, mores, and memories, while despotism is new. But it is unreasonable to think that one can create local liberties at will or even maintain them for long if general liberty is suppressed.

Page 84, line 32
Turgot, in a report to the king, summarized, quite accurately in my view, the true extent of noble privilege in regard to taxes:

1. The privileged can claim full exemption from the taille for a farm of four plows, which, in the Paris region, would ordinarily pay 2,000 francs in taxes.
2. The same privileged individuals pay absolutely nothing for woods, pastures, vineyards, or ponds, or for enclosed land contiguous to their chateaus, no matter how extensive. There are cantons whose principal production is from pastures or vineyards, in which case the absentee landlord is exempt from all taxes, the burden of which falls on those subject to the taille. This second advantage is immense.

Page 85, line 4

INDIRECT PRIVILEGE WITH RESPECT TO TAXATION: DIFFERENCE
IN COLLECTION EVEN WHEN THE TAX IS COMMON

Turgot also describes this in a way that, having read the documents,
I believe to be correct:

> The privileged enjoy very substantial advantages with respect to the
> capitation. The capitation is by nature an arbitrary tax. It is impossi-
> ble to distribute among all citizens except blindly. It has been deemed
> more convenient to use the rolls of the taille as a basis, since these
> were readily available. A special roll was created for the privileged, but
> since they were able to defend themselves while those subject to the
> taille had no one to speak for them, the capitation of the former was
> gradually reduced in the provinces to an unreasonably small amount,
> while that of the latter was almost equal to the principal of the taille.

Page 85, line 4

ANOTHER EXAMPLE OF INEQUALITY IN THE COLLECTION
OF A COMMON TAX

We know that local taxes were levied on everyone. Council decrees ordering these kinds of expenditures said that "said sums shall be levied on all
subjects, both exempt and nonexempt, privileged and nonprivileged, with
no exceptions, in conjunction with the capitation, or in proportion to it."

Note that since the capitation of those subject to the taille, which was
linked to the taille itself, was always higher in relative terms than the capitation of the privileged, the inequality was reproduced even in those taxes
that seemed to exclude it most.

Page 85, line 4

Same subject: In a proposed edict from 1764, which was intended to
establish equal taxation, I found all sorts of provisions intended to preserve the special position of the privileged in regard to collection. Among
other things, I found that where the privileged were concerned, all measures whose purpose was to assess the value subject to taxation could be
applied only in their presence or that of their authorized proxies.

Page 85, line 6

HOW THE GOVERNMENT ITSELF RECOGNIZED THAT THE PRIVILEGED
WERE FAVORED IN COLLECTION EVEN WHEN THE TAX WAS COMMON

"I see," the minister wrote in 1766, "that the taxes that are most difficult to collect are always those owed by nobles and other privileged
individuals, because the collectors of the taille feel obliged to make

adjustments on their behalf, and because of this they have long been in arrears at far too high a level in regard to their capitation and *vingtièmes* [the taxes they paid in common with other people]."

Page 94, line 13

One finds, in the *Travels of Arthur Young* in 1789, a small portrait in which the state of these two societies is so pleasantly depicted and so nicely framed that I cannot resist the urge to include it here.

Young, who traveled across France in the wake of the initial reaction to the taking of the Bastille, found himself stopped in a certain village by a crowd of people who, on noticing that he was not wearing a cockade, proposed to throw him in jail. To save himself, he hit on the idea of delivering the following short speech:

> I did not like my situation at all, especially on hearing one of them say that I ought to be secured till somebody would give an account of me. I was on the steps of the inn, and begged they would permit me a few words; I assured them that I was an English traveler, and to prove it, I desired to explain to them a circumstance in English taxation, which would be a satisfactory comment on what Mons. l'Abbé had told them, to the purport of which I could not agree. He had asserted that the impositions must be paid as heretofore. That the impositions must be paid was certain, but not as heretofore, as they might be paid as they were in England. Gentlemen, we have a great number of taxes in England, which you know nothing of in France; but the *tiers état*, the poor do not pay them; they are laid on the rich; every window in a man's house pays; but if he has no more than six windows, he pays nothing; a Seigneur, with a great estate, pays the *vingtièmes* and *tailles*, but the little proprietor of a garden pays nothing; the rich for their horses, their voitures, and their servants, and even for liberty to kill their own partridges, but the poor farmer nothing of all this, and what is more, we have in England a tax paid by the rich for the relief of the poor. Hence the assertion of Mons. l'Abbé that because taxes existed before they must exist again, did not at all prove that they must be levied in the same manner; our English method seemed much better. There was not a word of this discourse they did not approve of. They seemed to think that I might be an honest fellow, which I confirmed by crying, *vive le tiers, sans impositions*, when they gave me a bit of a huzza and I had no more interruption from them. My miserable French was pretty much on a par with their own *patois*.[2]

---

[2] Arthur Young, *Travels in France During the Years 1787, 1788, 1789* (London: George Bell and Sons, 1890), pp. 213–14.

Page 95, line 34

The church of X in the Chollet district had fallen into ruins. It was to be repaired in the manner indicated in the decree of 1684 (Dec. 16), that is, with the help of a tax levied on all the inhabitants. When the collectors attempted to collect this tax, the marquis de X., lord of the parish, stated that because he alone had assumed responsibility for repairing the choir, he did not wish to participate in this tax. The other residents replied, with considerable justice, that as lord and major recipient of the tithe (he was no doubt entitled to the feudal tithes), he was obliged to repair the choir at his own expense, so that responsibility could not exempt him from the common tax. At this point, the intendant issued an order dismissing the marquis's claim and authorizing the collectors to collect the tax. The file contains more than ten letters from the marquis, each more urgent than the last, emphatically insisting that the rest of the parish should pay in his place and deigning, in order to get what he wanted, to address the intendant as *monseigneur* and even to *beg* him.

Page 96, line 34

EXAMPLE OF THE WAY IN WHICH THE GOVERNMENT OF THE ANCIEN RÉGIME RESPECTED ACQUIRED RIGHTS, FORMAL CONTRACTS, AND THE LIBERTIES OF TOWNS AND ASSOCIATIONS

A royal declaration "suspends in wartime reimbursement of all loans made by cities, towns, colleges, communities, hospital administrations, charity homes, trade guilds, and other associations, which are paid out of the receipts from local duties or other dues granted by us for the purpose, while interest on said loans shall continue to run."

This not only suspended repayment of the loan by the date indicated in the contract with the creditor but also threatened the collateral pledged to guarantee the loan. Such measures, which were commonplace under the Ancien Régime, would never have been accepted under a government subject to scrutiny by the public or by assemblies. Compare this state of affairs with the way these kinds of things have always been done in England and even in America. Here, contempt for the law is as flagrant as contempt for local liberties.

Page 98, line 5

The case cited in the text is far from the only one in which the privileged realized that the feudal dues that weighed on the peasant also affected their own interests. Here is what one agricultural society composed entirely of privileged individuals said thirty years before the Revolution:

Unamortizable rents, whether ground rents or feudal rents, when levied on a landed estate and if fairly substantial in amount, become so onerous to the debtor that they cause his ruin and consequently that of the estate itself. He is forced to neglect the estate because he cannot find a way to borrow on already overencumbered collateral, nor can he find buyers if he wishes to sell. If the rents were amortizable, the ruined rentier would not want for occasions to borrow in order to pay them down nor would he lack for buyers in a position to reimburse both the collateral and the rent. One is always comfortable maintaining and improving a free property when one feels tranquil in one's ownership. It would be a great encouragement to agriculture if a practical way could be found to make these kinds of rents amortizable. Many lords of fiefs, convinced of this truth, would be eager to enter into such arrangements. It would therefore be of great interest to discover and set forth practical ways of extinguishing ground rents in this manner.

Page 99, line 17

All public functions, even the office of tax farmer, were compensated with immunities from taxation, a privilege granted by the ordinance of 1681. In 1682, an intendant sent a letter to a minister stating that "among the privileged there is no class as numerous as the employees of the salt tax franchise, the *traits*, the *domaines*, the post office, the *aides*, and various other administrative departments. There are few parishes without such employees, and any number of them have two or three."

The purpose of this letter was to persuade the minister not to propose to the council a degree extending tax immunities to the employees and domestics of these privileged agents, immunities which the farmers general were constantly demanding, according to the intendant, so as to free themselves from the need to pay their own employees.

Page 99, line 17

Such offices were not absolutely unknown elsewhere. In Germany a few minor princes had introduced them, but they were few in number and confined to relatively unimportant parts of the public administration. Only in France was the system extensively adopted.

Page 103, line 5

It should come as no surprise, though it may seem and is in fact quite strange, to find public officials of the Ancien Régime, many of whom worked for the government proper, pleading in parlement to determine the extent of their various powers. The reason for this becomes clear when

we realize that such questions were not only questions of public administration but also of private property. What one takes to be an encroach-
ment by the judicial power was merely a consequence of the error that
the government committed when it sold public offices. Since offices were
privately owned and each official was remunerated on the basis of actions
performed, it was impossible to change the nature of the function without infringing a right that had been purchased from the previous owner.
To cite one example among many: the lieutenant general of police of Le
Mans engaged in a lengthy lawsuit against that city's finance office in
order to prove that since he was in charge of maintaining order in the
streets, he was also responsible for all actions pertaining to their paving
and entitled to the price of performing those actions. This time it was
not the King's Council that decided. Because it was primarily a matter
of the interest on the capital invested in the purchase of the office, it was
the parlement that rendered judgment in the case. An administrative case
was transformed into a civil suit.

Page 104, line 8
ANALYSIS OF THE GRIEVANCE BOOKS OF THE NOBILITY IN 1789
The French Revolution is, I believe, the only revolution in which
the various classes of society were able separately to give voice to the
ideas and sentiments that animated them at the beginning, before the
Revolution itself had distorted or modified them. As everyone knows,
this authentic testimony was set down in the grievance books that each
of the three orders compiled in 1789. These books, or reports, were
drafted in complete freedom, in very public circumstances, by each of
the orders. They were discussed at length among the interested parties and earnestly reflected upon by their drafters, for when government
appealed to the nation in those days, it did not take it upon itself to supply both questions and answers. Once the grievance books were drafted,
the most important parts were collected in three volumes, which one can
find in any library. The originals were placed in the National Archives,
and with them can be found the minutes of the assemblies that drafted
them and some of the correspondence between M. Necker and his
agents about those meetings. This collection comprises a lengthy series
of folio volumes. It is the most precious document that old France has
bequeathed to us, and one that must be consulted constantly by anyone
interested in what our forefathers were thinking at the outbreak of the
Revolution.

I had thought that the three-volume digest to which I alluded above might have been the work of a party and might not accurately reflect the character of this vast survey, but on comparing one with the other, I found that the smaller copy faithfully reflected the larger canvas.

The summary of the grievances of the nobility that I will give in the following accurately conveys the feelings of the vast majority of that order. We can see clearly which of its old privileges the nobility stubbornly insisted on retaining, which it was not far from giving up, and which it offered to sacrifice voluntarily. Above all, we learn a great deal about how the nobility felt about political liberty. A strange and melancholy portrait!

Individual rights. Above all, the nobles asked for an explicit declaration of the rights that belong to all men, acknowledging their freedom and ensuring their security.

Personal freedom. They wanted serfdom to be abolished where it still existed, and they wanted to look for ways to abolish the trade in Negroes as well as slavery. Everyone should be free to travel and to settle wherever he wished, inside or outside the kingdom, without arbitrary interference. They wanted an end to the abuse of police regulations and asked that questions of law and order subsequently be placed in the hands of judges, even in cases of riot. They argued that no one should be arrested or judged except by his natural judges and, therefore, requested that state prisons and other illegal places of detention be abolished. Some asked for the demolition of the Bastille. The nobility of Paris particularly insisted on this point.

All *lettres closes* and *lettres de cachet* were to be prohibited. If some danger to the state made it necessary to arrest a citizen without turning him over immediately to the ordinary courts of justice, steps should be taken to prevent abuse, either by informing the Council of State of the arrest or by some other means.

The nobility wanted all special commissions, all special and exceptional courts, all privileges of *committimus*, all reprieves, etc., to be abolished and asked that anyone who issued or executed an arbitrary order be severely punished. The nobility further requested that in the ordinary courts, which were the only tribunals that were to be maintained, the necessary steps should be taken to protect the freedom of individuals, especially in criminal matters. Justice should not have to be paid for, and useless courts should be abolished. "Magistrates are established for the people and not the people for magistrates," one *cahier* stated. There was even a request to establish in each district free legal counsel and public defenders for the poor. The prosecution's case was to be public, and each defendant had to be free to defend himself. In criminal cases, the accused should be provided with counsel, and at every stage of the proceedings the judge should be assisted by a certain number of citizens of the same order as the accused, whose responsibility it would be to render judgment on the crime or misdemeanor with which the defendant was charged. They referred on this point to the constitution of England. The punishment should be proportional to the crime and equal for all. The death penalty should become more rare, and all corporal punishment, torture, etc., abolished. Finally, the conditions of detention should be improved, particularly for the accused awaiting trial.

The grievance books also called for finding ways to respect the freedom of individuals in the conscription of recruits for the army and navy. It should be possible to pay for exemption from compulsory military service, and recruitment by lottery should not be allowed except in the presence of a deputation in which all three orders were represented. Finally, military discipline and subordination were to be combined with the rights of the citizen and free man. Punishment by beating with the flat of a saber should be abolished.

Liberty and inviolability of property. The nobility asked that property be inviolable and not subject to confiscation except in cases of essential public utility. In that case, the government should pay a high indemnity without delay. Confiscation should be abolished.

Freedom of commerce, labor, and industry. Freedom of industry and commerce must be ensured. Master's licenses and other privileges awarded to certain guilds were therefore to be eliminated. Customs boundaries were to be moved to the country's frontiers.

Freedom of religion. The Catholic religion was to be the sole dominant religion in France, but each individual was to be allowed freedom of conscience, and non-Catholics permitted to have their civil status and property restored.

Freedom of the press, inviolability of the mail. Freedom of the press shall be assured, the grievance books stated, and a law shall establish in advance the restrictions that may be imposed in the general interest. No one should be subject to ecclesiastical censorship except in the case of books dealing with dogma. As for other books, it would be enough to take steps to ensure that the identities of authors and printers were known.

Several of the grievance books requested that press offenses be subject to judgment by juries only.

Above all, the grievance books unanimously insisted that the secrecy of the mail must remain inviolable, so that letters could not become counts in indictments or grounds for prosecution. They bluntly stated that the opening of letters is the most odious form of espionage, because it is a violation of the public trust.

Teaching, education. The grievance books of the nobility merely requested that active efforts be made to encourage education, which should be offered in both town and countryside and based on principles compatible with the anticipated future of each child. Above all, the children should receive a national education in the form of instruction in their duties and rights as citizens. The books also asked for the drafting of a catechism that would bring the main points of the constitution within the children's reach. Beyond this, they did not specify what means should be employed to facilitate and expand instruction. They confined themselves to asking that educational institutions be established for the children of indigent nobles.

Care that must be taken of the people. A large number of grievance books insisted that greater concern be shown for the people. Several of the books alleged abuses of police regulations, which, they said, led to the arbitrary imprisonment, without regular judgment, of a host of artisans and other useful citizens, often for misdemeanors or merely on suspicion of wrongdoing, thereby infringing natural liberty. All the grievance books asked for the permanent abolition of compulsory labor services. A majority of districts wanted to allow the redemption of dues for milling and highway tolls. A large number asked for a reduction of a number of feudal dues and abolition of the *franc-fief*. According to one grievance book, the government has an interest in facilitating the purchase and sale of land. This was precisely the reason that would later be given for abolishing all seigniorial dues at one stroke and for putting up for sale all property subject to *mainmorte* [that is, reversion of ownership to the lord upon the death of the person in possession]. Many grievance books asked that dovecote dues be reduced to a level less prejudicial to agriculture. As for *capitaineries*, or royal game preserves, the grievance books called for their immediate abolition as infringements on the rights of property. They also asked that existing taxes be replaced by taxes less onerous to the people.

The nobility called for efforts to spread prosperity and well-being to the countryside; for the establishment of facilities to spin and weave coarse cloth in the villages in order to keep country people occupied during the winter months; for the creation of public granaries in every district, with inspection by the provincial authorities, to prevent famine and maintain the price of staples at a certain level; for the perfection of agriculture and improvement of conditions in rural areas; for an increase in public works, especially for the draining of marshes and the prevention of floods, etc; and finally, for measures to encourage commerce and agriculture in all provinces.

The grievance books called for the division of hospitals into small institutions in each district; for the elimination of poorhouses and their replacement by charity workshops; for the establishment of relief funds under the supervision of the provincial estates and for the assignment of surgeons, physicians, and midwives to the various districts, at the expense of the provinces, to provide free care for the poor; for guarantees that justice would always be free of charge for common people; and finally, for plans to provide institutions for the care of the blind, the deaf and mute, foundlings, etc.

In regard to all these matters, moreover, the noble order on the whole limited itself to expressing its desires for reform in general without going into great detail about how specific reforms were to be carried out. It is clear that the nobility had spent less time than the lower clergy living among the lower classes and, having had less contact with their misery, had devoted less thought to the means of remedying it.

On acceptability for public office, the hierarchy of ranks, and the honorific privileges of the nobility. It was especially, or, rather, it was only in regard to the hierarchy of ranks and status differences that the nobility departed from the general spirit of requested reforms. Although it offered some important concessions, it clung to the principles of the Ancien Régime. It felt that, on this score, it was fighting for its very existence. Its grievance books, therefore, insisted that the clergy and nobility be maintained as distinct orders. They even called for finding ways to preserve the noble order in all its purity. They asked for a ban on the purchase of noble titles. They called for a halt to the practice of granting nobility as an attribute of certain offices and asked that titles be granted only in exchange for long years of useful service to the state. They proposed that false nobles be tracked down and prosecuted. Finally, all the grievance books insisted that nobles should retain all their honorific privileges. Some asked that nobles be granted a distinctive mark that would facilitate identification by outward appearance.

It is impossible to think of a demand more characteristic of the nobility or more apt to demonstrate the perfect similarity that already existed between the noble and the commoner, despite the difference in their status. Generally speaking, the grievance books of the nobility showed a fair amount of flexibility with respect to practical rights yet clung anxiously to honorific privileges. Nobles already felt so overwhelmed by the tide of democracy and so afraid it would engulf them that they sought to preserve all the privileges they had, while inventing others they had never possessed. Remarkably, they sensed this danger instinctively without perceiving it clearly.

As for the distribution of public posts, the nobles demanded that the sale of judicial offices be eliminated. The nation should be able to propose, and the king to appoint, any citizen regardless of rank, subject only to conditions of age and fitness for office. The majority believed that the Third Estate should not be excluded from officer ranks in the military and that any soldier who deserved to be rewarded by his country should be eligible for the most eminent positions. Several grievance books stated that "the order of the nobility does not approve of any of the laws that deny the order of the Third Estate access to military employments." The nobles simply asked that right to join a regiment as an officer without having risen through the lower ranks be reserved for them alone. Furthermore, nearly all the grievance books asked that fixed rules, applicable to everyone, be established for the distribution of army ranks, that these should not be awarded simply on the basis of favor, and that ranks other than those of senior officer should be awarded on the basis of seniority.

As for clerical functions, the nobles asked that elections be restored for the distribution of benefices, or at least that the king create a committee to advise him on the matter.

Finally, they recommended that pensions be distributed more carefully, that they not be limited to certain families, that no citizen be allowed to receive more than one pension or a salary for more than one position at a time, and, finally, that inheritable pensions should be abolished.

Church and clergy. When the nobility's own rights and internal constitution were not at stake and the issue was, rather, the privileges and organization of the Church, the nobility was less demanding. It saw abuses quite clearly.

Nobles asked that the clergy not be granted any tax privileges and that they be required to pay their debts rather than transfer them to the nation. They also requested extensive reforms of the monastic orders. A majority of the grievance books expressed the view that these orders had deviated from the spirit in which they were founded.

A majority of districts asked that tithes be made less prejudicial to agriculture. Many even called for abolition of the tithe. One grievance book said that "the bulk of the tithe goes to those priests who contribute the least to the spiritual well-being of the people." Clearly, the second order showed no mercy in its comments on the first. Nobles were scarcely more respectful toward the Church itself. Several districts formally acknowledged the right of the Estates General to abolish certain religious orders and put their property to other uses. Seventeen districts held that the Estates General had the power to impose discipline. Several contended that there were too many holidays and that this was inimical to agriculture and encouraged drunkenness, so that many holidays ought to be abolished or celebrated on Sunday as in the past.

Political rights. As for political rights, the grievance books recognized that all French citizens have the right to participate in government either directly or indirectly, that is, the right to elect and be elected, but that the hierarchy of ranks must be preserved, so that no one can appoint or be appointed except within his order. With this principle in mind, the system of representation should be designed so as to guarantee that all orders of the nation be able to contribute materially to the management of the affairs of government.

As to the manner of voting in the Estates General, opinions were divided. Most preferred that each order vote separately. Some felt that votes on taxation should be an exception to this rule, while others insisted that the exception should become the rule. "Votes shall be counted by head and not by order," said the latter, "this being the only reasonable method of voting and the only way to eliminate and destroy the selfishness of certain estates, the sole source of all our woes, while bringing people together and leading them to the result that the nation has every right to expect from an assembly in which patriotism and other important virtues are fortified by enlightenment." Yet because this innovation, if introduced too abruptly, could have been dangerous in the state of mind then current in the nation, several of the grievance books expressed the view that it should not be adopted without precautions and that the assembly should consider whether it might not be wiser to postpone voting by head until the next Estates General. In all cases, the nobility requested that the dignity that was every Frenchman's due be respected and, consequently, called for the abolition of the humiliating customs to which the Third Estate had been subjected under the Ancien Régime, such as the requirement to kneel before others of higher rank: "The sight of a man on his knees before another man is an affront to human dignity and signifies, between beings equal by nature, an inferiority incompatible with their essential rights," as one grievance book put it.

On the system of government to be established and the principles of the constitution. As to the form of government, the nobility called for maintaining the monarchical constitution, with legislative, judicial, and executive powers continuing to reside in the person of the king, while at the same time establishing fundamental laws for the purpose of guaranteeing the rights of the nation in the exercise of those powers.

Consequently, all the grievance books proclaimed the right of the nation to assemble in Estates General composed of a number of members sufficiently large to assure their independence. They asked that the estates meet henceforth at fixed intervals, as well as upon each new succession to the throne, with no need whatsoever for letters of convocation. Many districts even stated that it would be desirable for this assembly to become permanent. If the convocation of the Estates General did not take place within the time limit set forth by law, the people should have the right to refuse to pay taxes. A small number wished that in the interval between two meetings of the estates, an interim commission be established to monitor the administration of the kingdom, but the overwhelming majority of the grievance books were strictly opposed to the establishment of such a commission on the grounds that it would be entirely contrary to the constitution. The reason that they gave for this was rather odd: they were afraid that such a small body left to deal with the government alone might succumb to governmental pressure.

The nobility did not want ministers to have the right to dissolve the assembly and asked that any ministers who formed cabals to interfere with its activities be subject to legal sanctions. No official or other individual dependent on the government in any way could serve as deputy. Deputies should be inviolable in their persons and not subject to prosecution for the opinions they might express. Finally, meetings of the assembly should be public, and in order to involve the nation more deeply in its deliberations, these should be communicated by way of the press.

The nobility unanimously requested that the principles that were supposed to guide the national government be applied to the governments of the various parts of the country. Hence, in each province, each district, and each parish, assemblies should be organized, with members freely elected for a limited period of time.

Several grievance books expressed the view that the offices of intendant and general tax collector should be abolished. All maintained that provincial assemblies should henceforth bear sole responsibility for assessing taxes and safeguarding the particular interests of each province. They intended that the same idea should apply to district and parish assemblies, which should henceforth cease to be subordinate to any body other than the provincial estates.

Separation of powers. Legislative power. As for the separation of powers between the nation assembled and the king, the nobility asked that no law take effect unless it had the consent of both the Estates General and the king and had been recorded in the registers of the courts responsible for enforcing it. The nobles also asked that the Estates General be granted the exclusive right to establish and assess taxes and that consent to the payment of any amount last only until the next meeting of the estates. Any tax collected or established without the consent of the estates should be declared illegal, and any minister or tax collector who ordered or received any such tax should be prosecuted for embezzlement.

Similarly, the nobility requested that no borrowing by the state be approved without the consent of the Estates General. The estates should simply establish a line of credit, upon which the government could draw in case of war or other major calamity, with the proviso that a meeting of the Estates General be convened as soon as possible.

All national reserves should be subject to scrutiny by the Estates General, which should be empowered to set the budget for each department. Reliable methods should be established to ensure that expenditures did not exceed the allocated amounts.

Most of the grievance books called for elimination of the vexatious taxes known as *droits d'insinuation, centième denier,* and *entérinements* and joined together under the designation *Régie des domaines du roi*: "The designation *régie* would by itself be enough to wound the nation, because it asserts a royal title to things that are really the property of citizens," said one grievance book. The nobles asked that all nonalienated royal domains be placed under the administration of the provincial estates and that no financial prescription or edict regarding them be issued without the consent of the three orders of the nation.

Clearly, the idea of the nobility was to bestow upon the nation full responsibility for financial administration, in regard to both the regulation of loans and taxes and the collection of taxes, via the intermediary of general and provincial assemblies.

Judicial power. Similarly, in the organization of the judiciary, the nobility was, on the whole, inclined to make the power of judges subordinate to the nation assembled. So, for example, several grievance books contained statements like this: "Magistrates shall be responsible in their duties to the nation assembled." They may not be removed from office without the consent of the Estates General. No court may be hampered in the exercise of its duties on any grounds whatsoever without the consent of the estates. Derelictions of duty by the appellate court and parlements shall be judged by the Estates General. According to a majority of the grievance books, judges were not to be appointed by the king unless nominated by the people.

Executive power. Executive power was reserved exclusively for the king, but the nobility proposed necessary limits to prevent abuses.

For instance, in regard to the administration, the grievance books requested that the accounts of the various government departments be printed and publicly divulged and asked that ministers be made responsible to the nation assembled. Similarly, they asked that the king, before using troops to defend against foreign enemies, make his precise intentions known to the Estates General. Internally, troops could not be used against citizens except upon requisition by the Estates General. The size of the army was to be limited, and in ordinary times only two-thirds of the troops should remain on active duty. Any foreign troops that the government might employ should be removed from the center of the kingdom and sent to the frontiers.

What is most striking in reading the grievance books of the nobility, which no excerpt can convey, is the degree to which these nobles were men of their time: they have the spirit of the age and use its language fluently. They speak of "the inalienable rights of man" and of "principles inherent in the social pact." When the subject is the individual, they are usually concerned with his rights, and when it is society, with its duties. The principles of politics seem to them "as absolute as those of morality, and both have a common basis in reason." They want to abolish what remains of serfdom: "The goal is to root out the last traces of the degradation of humankind." They sometimes refer to Louis XVI as "a citizen king" and several times refer to the crime of "*lèse-nation*," of which they would so often be accused in the future. In their eyes, as in the eyes of everyone else, there was nothing that public education could not achieve, and it should be controlled by the state. One grievance book maintained that "the Estates General shall take care to inspire a national character by changing the education of children." Like the rest of their contemporaries, they demonstrated a sustained and pronounced taste for uniformity of legislation, except for legislation affecting the existence of orders. They wanted administrative uniformity, uniformity of weights and measures, etc., as much as the Third Estate. They indicated all sorts of reforms, and they intended for those reforms to be radical. In their view, all taxes should be abolished or transformed, without exception. The entire system of justice should be changed, except for the manorial courts, which simply needed to be improved. For them as for all other Frenchmen, France was an experimental laboratory, a kind of "model farm" in the sphere of politics, where everything could be plowed up and anything attempted, provided that nothing was disturbed in the small corner where their special privileges grew. And to their credit, it must be said that they did not spare even that. In short, reading the grievance books of the nobles leads to the conclusion that they might have made the Revolution themselves had they only been commoners, for that was the only ingredient they lacked.

Page 104, line 36
EXAMPLE OF RELIGIOUS GOVERNMENT IN AN ECCLESIASTICAL
PROVINCE IN THE MIDDLE OF THE EIGHTEENTH CENTURY

1. The archbishop.
2. Seven vicars general.
3. Two ecclesiastical courts, called "officialities." One, called the "metropolitan officiality," had jurisdiction over judgments of suffragan bishops; the other, called the "diocesan officiality," had jurisdiction over a) individual lawsuits between clerics and b) the validity of marriages as to the sacrament. The latter court was composed of three judges. Associated with it were various notaries and attorneys.
4. Two fiscal courts.

One of the fiscal courts, called the "diocesan bureau," had initial jurisdiction in all cases pertaining to taxes on the clergy in the diocese. (The clergy set its own taxes.) This court, presided over by the archbishop, was composed of six other priests. The other court judged on appeal cases brought before other diocesan bureaus in the ecclesiastical province. All of these courts admitted attorneys and heard pleas.

Page 105, line 23
SPIRIT OF THE CLERGY IN THE PROVINCIAL ESTATES
AND ASSEMBLIES

What I say at this point in the text about the Estates of Languedoc also applies to the provincial assemblies that met in 1779 and 1787, most notably in Haute Guyenne. In this provincial assembly, the members of the clergy were among the most enlightened, active, and liberal participants. It was the bishop of Rodez who proposed making the assembly's minutes public.

Page 106, line 7

The liberal political disposition of priests, which was evident in 1789, was not solely a product of the excitement of the moment. It was already apparent in a much earlier period. In particular, it was on display in Berry in 1779, when the clergy offered 68,000 livres in voluntary gifts on the sole condition that the provincial government be maintained.

Page 107, line 29

Note well that the bonds of political society had yet to be established, while those of civil society remained intact. Class ties still existed. In addition, something remained of the close tie that had once existed between the class of lords and the people. Although this state of affairs existed within civil society, its consequences were felt indirectly in political society. Although people bound to one another by such ties formed irregular and disorganized groups, they nevertheless remained refractory to government control. When the Revolution broke these social bonds without establishing political bonds in their place, it created the conditions for servitude as well as equality.

Page 108, line 22
EXAMPLE OF THE WAY IN WHICH THE COURTS EXPRESSED
THEMSELVES IN THE FACE OF CERTAIN ARBITRARY ACTS

From a report submitted to the comptroller general in 1781 by the intendant of the Paris district, it emerges that it was customary there for each parish to have two syndics, one elected by the residents in an assembly presided over by the subdelegate, the other chosen by the intendant, whose job was to oversee the other syndic. In the parish of Rueil, a quarrel erupted between the two syndics, and the elected syndic refused to obey the appointed syndic. The intendant persuaded M. de Breteuil to incarcerate the elected syndic at La Force for fifteen days, and the syndic, after being duly arrested, was removed from office and replaced by another person. Whereupon the parlement, upon petition of the imprisoned syndic, initiated a proceeding of which I have been unable to locate further records, in which it was said that the imprisonment of the appellant and the overturning of his election could only be regarded as "arbitrary and despotic acts." Justice in those days was in some cases rather poorly muzzled.

Page 110, line 37

Under the Ancien Régime, the educated and wealthy classes were a long way from being oppressed and subjugated. Indeed, all of them, including the bourgeoisie, were far too free to do as they pleased, since the royal government did not dare to prevent members of those classes from setting themselves apart, to the detriment of the people, and nearly always felt obliged to abandon the people to their mercy in order to win their indulgence or quell their opposition. It is fair to say that in the eighteenth century, a French member of those classes would often have found it easier to resist the government and force it to spare his interests than would an Englishman in the same situation. In many cases, the French government felt obliged to tread more carefully and move more cautiously than an English government would have felt in regard to a subject of the same category. It is a mistake to confuse independence with freedom. There is nothing less independent than a free citizen.

Page 110, line 38

THE REASON WHY THE ABSOLUTIST GOVERNMENT OF THE ANCIEN RÉGIME WAS OFTEN FORCED TO TAKE A MODERATE COURSE

In ordinary times, there is hardly anything other than increasing old taxes or, even more, creating new ones that can cause great trouble for the government or arouse the people. Under the old financial constitution of Europe, when a prince had expensive passions, or embarked upon an adventurous policy, or allowed his finances to become chaotic, or needed money to maintain himself in power by offering large profits or unearned salaries to many people in order to win their support, or maintained large armies, or undertook major public works, etc., he immediately had to raise taxes, which aroused and agitated all classes of society, and especially the class that is behind all violent revolutions, namely, the people. Today, in the same situation, the government takes out a loan, the immediate effects of which often go unnoticed, while the ultimate consequences will be felt only by the next generation.

Page 111, line 6

As one example of this among many others, I found that the principal estates in the Mayenne district were leased to farmers general, who took as tenants poor, humble sharecroppers who had nothing of their own and had to be given everything they needed, down to the most essential tools. Obviously, these farmers general were not obliged to be lenient with the tenants or debtors of the former feudal landlord, who had put them in his place, and feudalism as they practiced it could often seem harsher than in the Middle Ages.

Page 111, line 8

ANOTHER EXAMPLE

The residents of Montbazon had included on the rolls of the taille the stewards of a duchy owned by the prince de Rohan, even though those stewards acted only on behalf of the prince. The prince (who was certainly quite wealthy) not only put an end to *this abuse*, as he called it, but succeeded in winning restitution of the sum of 5,344 livres 15 sous, which had been wrongly charged to him and would now be imputed to the residents.

Page 115, line 4

EXAMPLE OF THE WAY IN WHICH MONEY RENTS DUE THE CLERGY ALIENATED THE HEARTS OF PEOPLE WHOSE ISOLATION SHOULD HAVE DRAWN THEM TOGETHER

The parish priest of Noisai claimed that the residents of the parish were obliged to repair his barn and press and asked for a local tax to cover the expense. The intendant replied that the residents were required only to repair the rectory. The barn and press would remain the responsibility of the pastor, who was more concerned with his rents than with his flock (1767).

Page 116, line 29

In a response submitted by a group of peasants to a survey conducted by a provincial assembly in 1788 – a response clearly written and moderate in tone – we find the following: "In addition to abuses in the collection of the taille, there is also abuse by the sheriff's deputies. They usually make five visits during the collection of the taille. They are often disabled veterans or Swiss mercenaries. On each visit they spend four or five days in the parish, for which the taille collection office assesses a fee of 36 sous per day. As for the apportionment of the taille, we will say nothing about the arbitrariness of the process, which is already well known, or about the evil effects of the tax rolls drawn up by officials who are often incapable and almost always partial and vindictive. These have nevertheless been the source of disturbances and disputes. They have given rise to lawsuits very costly to the parties and very advantageous to the district towns in which the courts are located."

Page 117, line 23
SUPERIORITY OF THE METHODS ADOPTED IN THE *PAYS D'ETATS* ACKNOWLEDGED BY OFFICIALS OF THE CENTRAL GOVERNMENT ITSELF

A confidential letter dated June 3, 1772, from the director of taxes to the intendant reads as follows: "In the *pays d'états*, taxes are assessed as a fixed percentage, so that each taxpayer is subject to taxation and actually pays. When the king asks for a tax increase, the fixed percentage is increased proportionately to the total increase demanded by the king (1 million livres, say, instead of 900,000). This is a simple operation. By contrast, in districts elsewhere, assessments are individual and in a sense arbitrary. Some pay what they owe; others pay only half, still others one-third, one-quarter, or nothing at all. How can an increase of one-ninth then be apportioned?"

Page 119, line 25
ON THE WAY IN WHICH THE PRIVILEGED INITIALLY UNDERSTOOD THE PROGRESS OF CIVILIZATION IN TERMS OF ROADS

The comte de X. complained in a letter to the intendant that the government was showing no haste in building a road adjacent to his property. This, he said, was the fault of the subdelegate, who was not energetic enough in the discharge of his duties and did not force the peasants to do their compulsory labor service.

Page 119, line 30
ARBITRARY IMPRISONMENT FOR COMPULSORY LABOR

Example: A letter from a chief provost in 1768 contains the following: "Yesterday, at the request of M.C., the deputy engineer, I ordered three men imprisoned for failing to perform their compulsory labor duties. This caused a disturbance among the women of the village, who shouted: 'Look at that! They think of us poor when they need laborers, but when it comes to keeping us alive, they couldn't care less.'"

Page 119, line 35

Resources for building roads were of two kinds: 1) The more important was compulsory labor for all major works that required nothing but labor; and 2) the less important was a general tax, the proceeds of which were made available to the Department of Bridges and Roads to subsidize works of engineering. The privileged, which is to say the major landowners, who had a greater interest in building roads than anyone else, did not contribute labor service, and what is more, since the bridge and road tax is associated with the taille and collected along with it, the privileged were again exempt.

Page 120, line 2

EXAMPLE OF COMPULSORY LABOR FOR TRANSPORTING CONVICTS

A letter sent to the intendant in 1761 by a policeman in charge of chain gangs reveals that peasants were forced to convey the convicts in wagons, which they did quite unwillingly, and they were often mistreated by the guards, "because the guards are coarse and brutal people and the peasants, who perform this service against their will, are often insolent."

Page 120, line 7

Turgot described the disadvantages and burdens imposed by the use of forced labor to transport military equipment, and on the basis of my reading of the files, his accounts do not seem exaggerated. Among other things, he says that the first drawback of the practice was the extreme inequality in the apportionment of a very onerous burden. It fell almost entirely on a small number of parishes made vulnerable by their location. The distance to be covered was often as much as five or six leagues and sometimes even ten or fifteen. A round trip then took three days. The payment allocated to landowners amounted to only a fifth of their cost. This compulsory labor service was almost always required during the summer, at harvest time. The oxen were nearly always exhausted and often returned sick from their labor, so that many landowners chose to pay 15 or 20 livres, rather than supply a wagon and four oxen. Finally, disorder inevitably reigned: peasants were constantly exposed to violence by the soldiers. The officers almost always demanded more than they were due. Sometimes they ordered saddle horses to be hitched to carriages at the risk of laming them. Soldiers insisted on riding on wagons that were already very heavily laden. Sometimes they became impatient that the oxen were moving so slowly and stuck them with their swords, and woe unto the peasant who dared to complain.

Page 120, line 12
EXAMPLE OF THE WAY IN WHICH COMPULSORY LABOR
WAS APPLIED TO EVERYTHING

The naval intendant in Rochefort complained about the poor attitude of peasants who were forced to haul wood for shipbuilding purchased by naval suppliers in various provinces. The correspondence reveals that peasants were still forced to provide this service in 1775, with compensation set by the intendant. The minister of the navy, who passed this letter on to the intendant of Tours, told him that he must ensure that the requisitioned wagons were provided. The intendant, M. Du Cluzel, refused to authorize labor drafts of this kind. The minister of the navy then sent him a threatening letter, saying that his recalcitrance would be reported to the king. The intendant responded at once, on December 11, 1775, stating firmly that in the ten years he had served as intendant of Tours, he had never agreed to authorize such labor drafts because of the inevitable abuses to which they led, abuses that were not alleviated by the compensation offered for the use of the wagons, "for often," he said, "the animals are crippled by the weight of the enormous pieces they are required to pull along roads that are as bad as the seasons in which they are requisitioned." What made the intendant reply in such a firm tone was apparently a letter from M. Turgot, attached to the documents and dated July 30, 1774, from the time he became minister, stating that he had never authorized such labor drafts in Limoges and adding that he approved of M. Du Cluzel's decision not to do so in Tours.

From other parts of this correspondence, it emerges that the wood suppliers often demanded labor drafts even when they were not authorized to do so by their contracts with the government, because doing so saved them at least a third of the transportation cost. One subdelegate offered an example of this source of profit: "The distance to haul timber from the place where it was cut to the river, via almost impassable roads, six leagues; time for round trip, two days. The forced laborers are paid at the rate of six liards per league per cubic foot, which comes to 13 fr. 10 s. for the journey, which is barely enough to cover the expense of the small landowner, his helper, and the oxen or horses that he needs to hitch to his cart. His time and effort and the labor of his animals – all are lost for him." On May 17, 1776, a direct order from the king to draft the needed labor was passed to the intendant by the minister. M. Du Cluzel having died in the interim, his successor, M. Lescalopier, hastened to obey and published an order announcing that "the subdelegate will distribute the burden among the parishes, and those drafted from each parish shall be obliged to appear at the place and time designated by the syndics, proceed to the place where the timber is found, and haul it at a price to be determined by the subdelegate."

Page 129, line 15

It has been said that the philosophy of the eighteenth century was a sort of worship of human reason, characterized by unlimited confidence in the power of reason to transform laws, institutions, and mores at will. To be frank, it was not so much human reason that some of these philosophers worshiped as their own reason. No one ever showed less confidence in the common wisdom of mankind than they did. I could cite any number of them who despised the crowd almost as much as they despised God. To God they displayed the pride of rivals, while to the crowd they displayed the pride of parvenus. True and respectful submission to the will of the majority was as alien to them as was submission to the will of God. Nearly all of the revolutionaries exhibited this double character. They were a long way from sharing the respect of the English and Americans for the sentiments of the majority of their fellow citizens. With them, reason is proud and self-confident but never insolent. So it has led to liberty, whereas our reason has accomplished little more than to invent new forms of servitude.

Page 139, line 10

Example of the Way in Which the Peasants Were Often Dealt With

1768. The king granted a 2,000 franc reduction of the taille to the parish of La Chapelle-Blanche, near Saumur. The parish priest proposed using part of this sum to build a steeple so as to move the bells farther from the rectory and thus save him from their irritating noise. The residents resisted and petitioned for relief. The subdelegate decided in favor of the priest and, one night, ordered the arrest and imprisonment of the town's most prominent residents.

Another example: A woman insulted two mounted policemen. The king ordered her jailed for two weeks. Another order mandated two weeks in prison for a stocking weaver who had dared to criticize the mounted police. To this second order, the intendant responded by informing the minister that he had already jailed the man; the minister vociferously approved. The insulting remarks about the police had followed the violent arrest of a number of beggars, an arrest that seems to have disgusted the population. When the subdelegate had the weaver arrested, he warned the public that anyone who continued to insult the police would be severely punished.

The correspondence between this intendant and his subdelegates (1760–70) makes it clear that arrests were ordered not to bring troublesome individuals to justice but to keep them under lock and key. One subdelegate asked the intendant for authority to impose life sentences on two dangerous beggars he had arrested. A father protested the arrest of his son who had been arrested on charges of begging because he was traveling without papers. A landowner in X asked for the arrest of his neighbor, a man who had come to live in his parish, to whom he had offered help but who subsequently behaved badly toward him and caused him grief. The intendant of Paris asked the intendant of Rouen to order this arrest as a favor to the landowner, who was a friend of his.

To a person who asked that the imprisoned beggars be freed, the intendant responded "that the poor house should be regarded not as a prison but merely as a facility for the *administrative correction* of beggars and vagabonds." This idea even influenced the Penal Code, because in this respect the traditions of the Ancien Régime had been very well preserved.

Page 140, line 12

Frederick the Great wrote in his *Memoirs*: "The Fontenelles and Voltaires, the Hobbeses, Collinses, Shaftesburys, and Bolingbrokes – these great men dealt a mortal blow to religion. Men began to examine what they had stupidly worshiped. Reason destroyed superstition. People felt disgust for myths they had believed. Deism won many followers. If Epicureanism proved devastating to the idolatrous religion of the pagans, Deism has been no less devastating in our own time to the Judaic notions adopted by our ancestors. The freedom of thought that reigned in England contributed greatly to the progress of philosophy."

From this passage it is clear that Frederick the Great, when he wrote these lines in the middle of the eighteenth century, still looked upon England as the source of irreligious doctrines. And one sees something even more striking: a sovereign among those with the deepest knowledge of humanity and politics seems to have had no inkling that religion might be politically useful – so great was the extent to which the intellectual failings of his teachers had affected the qualities of his own mind.

Page 155, line 29

This progressive spirit, which was apparent in France at the end of the eighteenth century, emerged throughout Germany at the same time, and, as in France, it was everywhere accompanied by a desire to change institutions. Consider this portrait by a German historian of what was happening at the time in his country:

"In the second half of the eighteenth century, the new spirit of the age gradually insinuated itself into the ecclesiastical territories themselves. Reforms were begun. Industry and tolerance spread everywhere. Enlightened absolutism, which had already taken hold of the larger states, made its appearance even here. It must be said that at no time in the eighteenth century were such remarkable and estimable rulers to be found in the ecclesiastical territories as in the last few decades before the French Revolution."

Note how much this portrait resembles that of France, where the improving, progressive movement began at the same time, and where men worthier to govern than any others appeared just as the Revolution was about to devour everything.

Note, too, how clearly this whole region of Germany was drawn into what was happening in French civilization and politics.

Page 155, line 30

How the Judicial Laws of the English Prove That Some Institutions Can Have Many Minor Flaws and Still Achieve the Principal Purposes for Which They Were Established

The ability of nations to prosper despite minor imperfections in their institutions, provided that the general principles and animating spirit of those institutions are sound, is never more apparent than when one examines Blackstone's account of English justice as it was constituted in the last century.

Two striking diversities stand out: 1) diversity of laws and 2) diversity of the courts that apply those laws.

I. Diversity of Laws
A. The laws are different for England proper, for Scotland, for Ireland, for the various European appendages of Great Britain such as the Isle of Man, the Norman islands, etc., and finally for the colonies.

B. In England proper, one finds four types of law: customary law, statute law, Roman law, and equity. Customary law is itself divided into general customs, adopted throughout the kingdom, and customs peculiar to certain manors or towns, or, in some cases, exclusively to certain classes, such as the customs of merchants. Sometimes these customary laws differ strikingly from one another. For instance, there are customs at odds with the general tendency of English law that insist on equal division of inheritances among the children (*gavelkind*) and, what is even more surprising, that grant a right of primogeniture to the youngest child.

II. Diversity of Courts. According to Blackstone, the law established a prodigious variety of courts, as will be evident from the following brief analysis:

A. Courts were established outside of England proper, such as the courts of Scotland and Ireland, which were not always subordinate to the English higher courts, although I believe that all were subject to the House of Lords.

B. As for England proper, assuming I have not forgotten any of Blackstone's categories, we find the following:

1. Eleven types of courts defined by the common law, four of which were already obsolete, however.

2. Three types of courts whose jurisdiction included the entire country, but only in certain types of cases.

3. Ten types of courts having a special character. One of these types comprised local courts created by various acts of Parliament or that existed in virtue of some tradition, either in London or in provincial cities and towns. There were many such courts, and their structure and rules were so different that Blackstone does not even attempt a detailed account.

Thus, in England proper only, according to Blackstone, there existed, at the time of writing, that is, in the second half of the eighteenth century, twenty-four types of court, several of which were further subdivided into distinct subtypes, each with an individual character of its own. If we exclude those types that had apparently already ceased to function, eighteen or twenty still remain.

Now, if we examine this judicial system, we readily discover that it contained all sorts of imperfections.

Despite the multiplicity of tribunals, the system often lacked lower courts located near citizens and designed to judge minor cases locally and at low cost, so that justice was cumbersome and costly. The same cases often fell within the jurisdiction of several courts, which cast a troubling uncertainty over the initiation of proceedings. Nearly all courts of appeal heard certain cases in the first instance, and some of these were common law courts while others were courts of equity. Appellate courts were quite diverse. The only central point in the system was the House of Lords. Administrative cases were not distinguished from ordinary cases, which most of our legal specialists would consider a major flaw in the system. Finally, all of these courts drew grounds for their decisions from four different bodies of law, one of which was based solely on precedent, while another, equity, was based on nothing precise at all since its purpose was most often to counter either customary or statutory law. The idea was that judicial arbitrariness could be introduced as a corrective to whatever was outdated or unduly harsh in customs and statutes.

The system thus had many flaws, and if we were to compare the vast, ancient machinery of English justice with the modern fabric of our judicial system, the simplicity, coherence, and logic evident in the latter with the complexity and incoherence found in the former, the flaws of the English system would seem greater still. Yet there is no country in the world in which the great purpose of justice was as completely achieved as in England, and this was already true in the time of Blackstone. In no other system of courts was every individual, regardless of status, and no matter whether he was pleading against a private individual or a prince, more certain of obtaining a hearing, nor were his fortune, liberty, and life more securely guaranteed than in England: that is what I mean by the great purpose of justice.

This does not mean that the flaws of the English judicial system served that great purpose. It proves only that there are, in any judicial organization, minor flaws that may only moderately impede that great purpose, while there may also be more serious flaws that not only impede but negate that purpose, even when associated with many lesser virtues. The minor flaws of a legal system are easier to see. They are the ones that usually strike untutored minds first. They leap to the eyes, as the saying goes. The greater flaws are often more hidden, and it is not always legal scholars or other professionals who discover them and point them out.

Note, moreover, that specific qualities can be of greater or lesser importance depending on the time and the political organization of society. In aristocratic eras, that is, eras of inequality, anything that tends to diminish the judicial privileges of certain individuals, to protect the weak citizen against the strong, or to increase the dominance of the state, which is by its nature impartial when it is only a matter of a dispute between two subjects, becomes an important virtue, but the importance of these things diminishes as the social state and political constitution become more democratic.

If one studies the English judicial system with these principles in mind, one finds that while tolerant of innumerable defects that sometimes rendered British justice obscure, cumbersome, slow, expensive, and inconvenient, our neighbors across the Channel took infinite precautions to ensure that the strong would never be favored at the expense of the weak, or the state at the expense of the individual. As one delves more deeply into the details of English law, one finds that each citizen was given all sorts of weapons with which to defend himself, and things were arranged so as to provide each person with the maximum number of guarantees against judicial partiality and venality (in the narrow sense), as well as against that more common form of venality, surely much more dangerous in democratic times, to which the courts' servile attitude toward the public authorities gives rise.

In all these respects, the English judicial system, despite the numerous minor flaws it still contains, seems superior to ours, which, to be sure, suffers from almost none of these flaws but at the same time does not share the principal virtues of the English system to the same degree. Our system excels when it comes to the guarantees it offers to each citizen in disputes between individuals but is weak in the one aspect that always needs to be reinforced in a democratic society like ours, namely, the guarantees provided to the individual against the state.

Page 157, line 14
Advantages Enjoyed by the Paris District
This district enjoyed as many advantages with respect to governmental charities as it did for the levying of taxes. An example: a letter from the comptroller general to the intendant of the district of Île-de-France, dated May 22, 1787, informed the intendant that the king had set the sum to be used for works of charity in the Paris district at 172,800 livres for the year. An additional 100,000 livres were set aside for the purchase of cattle to be given to farmers. The letter makes it clear that the sum of 172,800 livres was to be distributed by the intendant alone, in compliance with the general rules communicated to him by the government and upon approval of his allocation by the comptroller general.

Page 157, line 39

The government of the Ancien Régime wielded a broad range of powers created at different times, usually to meet financial needs and not governmental needs per se. These powers sometimes overlapped. Confusion and conflict could be avoided only if each of the various powers was used relatively sparingly or not at all. Whenever the need was felt to overcome this lethargy, the various powers came into conflict and became entangled with one another. Complaints about the complexity of the administrative machinery and the confusion of responsibilities were, therefore, far more acute in the years immediately prior to the Revolution than they had been thirty or forty years earlier. The political institutions had not become worse. On the contrary, they had been greatly improved. But political life had become far more active.

Page 162, line 14

ARBITRARY TAX INCREASE

What the king says here of the taille he could have said with as much justification about the *vingtièmes*, as we can judge from the following correspondence. In 1772, the comptroller general Terray decided on a considerable increase, 100,000 livres, of the *vingtièmes* for the district of Tours. We can see the pain and embarrassment that this measure caused the intendant, M. Du Cluzel, an able administrator and decent man, in a confidential letter in which he wrote that "it was probably the ease with which the 250,000 livres [of the previous increase] was raised that encouraged this cruel interpretation and the letter of this June."

In a highly confidential letter that the director of taxes sent to the intendant at the same time, he said: "If, in light of the general misery, you still find the requested increases as irksome and repellent as you have so kindly indicated to me, it would be desirable for the province, which, but for your generosity of spirit, has no champion or protector, if you could at least save it from the supplementary tax, a retroactive levy that is always odious."

This correspondence also reveals the utter lack of any basic procedure and the arbitrariness that was practiced (even with the best of intentions). Both the intendant and minister wanted to shift the burden of the surtax from industry to agriculture, or in some cases to one sort of agriculture (such as vine growing) rather than another, depending on their judgment as to whether industry or some branch of agriculture needed relief.

Page 163, line 37
On the Way in Which Turgot Spoke of Country People in the
Preamble to a Royal Declaration
"Throughout much of the kingdom," he wrote, "rural communities
are made up of poor, ignorant, and brutish peasants incapable of govern-
ing themselves."

Page 167, line 20
How Revolutionary Ideas Quite Naturally Germinated in
People's Minds at the Height of the Ancien Régime
In 1779, a lawyer petitioned the council for a decree to reinstate a price
ceiling on straw throughout the kingdom.

Page 167, line 23
In 1781, a chief engineer wrote to an intendant about a request for
a supplementary indemnity: "The petitioner seems unaware that the
indemnities that we grant are a special favor to the Tours district and
that people should be quite happy to recover a portion of their losses. If
compensation were awarded in the manner indicated by the petitioner, 4
million livres would not suffice to cover the cost."

Page 171, line 34
The Revolution did not occur because of this prosperity, but the spirit
that was to produce the Revolution – the active, restless, intelligent, innovative ambitious spirit, the democratic spirit of the new societies – had
begun to animate everything and, before briefly turning society upside
down, was already strong enough to spur it on and develop it.

Page 173, line 3
Conflict of Various Administrative Powers in 1787
Example of this: The interim commission of the provincial assembly
of Île-de-France claimed responsibility for the poorhouse. The intendant
wanted to hold on to this responsibility himself, he wrote, "because the
poorhouse is not maintained by provincial funds." During the debate, the
interim commission wrote to the interim commissions of other provinces
seeking advice. Among the responses to its queries we find one from the
interim commission of Champagne, which informed the Île-de-France
commission that it had faced the same challenge, and it, too, had resisted.

Page 175, line 27
In the minutes of the first provincial assembly in Île-de-France, I find
this statement from one committee secretary: "To date, the functions

of syndic, which carry with them far more toil than honor, have surely discouraged anyone whose wealth is coupled with education appropriate to his status."

(Note pertaining to a number of passages in this volume.)
FEUDAL DUES STILL IN EXISTENCE AT THE TIME OF
THE REVOLUTION, ACCORDING TO FEUDAL LAW
SPECIALISTS OF THE TIME

It is not my intention here to write a treatise on feudal dues or to investigate how they might have originated. I simply want to point out which of them were still in force during the eighteenth century. These dues played such an important role at the time, and have ever since retained their force in the imaginations of those who no longer suffer under them, that I thought it would be quite interesting to find out exactly what they were like when the Revolution swept them all away. To that end, I first studied a number of manorial land books or registers, choosing those of most recent date. This method led nowhere, because although feudal dues were governed by laws that were the same throughout feudal Europe, they existed in infinite variety, differing from province to province and even canton to canton. Hence, the only method I thought likely to yield roughly the kind of information I was looking for was the following. Feudal dues gave rise to many types of lawsuits. The resolution of these disputes involved finding out how the dues were acquired, how they could be lost, exactly what their nature was, which ones could be collected only because of a royal patent, which were based solely on a private title, and which needed no formal titles and could be collected on the basis of local customs or even long-established habit. Finally, if the possessor of feudal dues wished to sell them, he needed to know how to appraise their value and what sort of capital each represented. All these points, which affected countless financial interests, were subject to debate, and a whole class of feudal lawyers existed for the sole purpose of elucidating them. A number of these lawyers wrote on the subject in the second half of the eighteenth century, and some were still writing as the Revolution approached. They were not legal scholars per se but rather practitioners whose only purpose was to explain to other professionals what rules to follow in this very specialized and quite unappealing area of the law.

If we study the works of these feudal lawyers closely, we can begin to form a fairly comprehensive and accurate picture of a subject that at first sight is striking for its density and impenetrability. In the pages that follow, I give the most succinct possible summary of what I was able to learn. These notes are based primarily on the work of Edme de Fréminville, who wrote around 1750, and of Renauldon, who in 1765 wrote the *Traité historique et pratique des droits seigneuriaux* (Historical and practical treatise on feudal dues).

The *cens* (that is, perpetual payments in kind and in cash associated with the possession of certain lands under feudal law) still profoundly affected the status of many landowners in the eighteenth century. The *cens* remained indivisible, which meant that the entire amount could be demanded of any one of several owners of real property subject to it. It was always imprescriptible. The owner of property subject to the *cens* could not sell it without being subject to the *retrait censuel*, that is, an option that allowed the owner of the *cens* to claim the property for the price of the sale. This privilege no longer existed, however, except in certain customary codes. The customary law of Paris, which was the most widely recognized, did not allow it.

Lods et ventes. It was a general rule in regions of customary law that the sale of any property subject to the *cens* resulted in *lods et ventes*: these were sums payable to the landlord upon sale of the property. The amount to be paid varied according to the type of customary law, but it was substantial everywhere. The same obligation also existed in regions of written law, where they were called *lods* and usually amounted to about one-sixth of the selling price. In those regions, it was up to the landlord to establish his right, however. In regions of both types, the *cens* created a privilege for the landlord that took precedence over all other claims.

Terrage or *champart, agrier, tasque.* This was a portion of the harvest due to the lord on property subject to the *cens*. The amount varied depending on the contract or custom. This levy was still fairly common in the eighteenth century. I believe that even in regions of customary law, a title was always required for the collection of *terrage*. *Terrage* could be based either on personal obligation to the lord or on land. The conditions that determined this are not worth going into here. Suffice it to say that *terrage* based on land lapsed after thirty years, as did ground rent, whereas *terrage* based on personal obligation was imprescriptible. Land subject to *terrage* could not be mortgaged without the consent of the lord.

Bordelage. This obligation, which existed only in Nivernais and Bourbonnais, involved an annual payment in cash, grain, or poultry due upon inherited land subject to the *cens*. Such obligation had very strict consequences. Failure to pay for three years led to *commise*, or confiscation of the property by the lord. In addition, a person who was in debt for *bordelage* was subject to a variety of impediments on his property. Sometimes the lord could inherit it even though eligible heirs existed. This contract was the most stringent in feudal law, and precedent ultimately limited it to rural property, "because the peasant is like the mule, always ready to accept any burden," according to our authority.

Marciage. This was a special obligation collected in a very few places from the owners of property or land subject to the *cens*, and which was not due until the natural death of the lord of the property.

Feudal tithes. In the eighteenth century there were still a large number of feudal tithes. They were generally the consequence of a contractual obligation, rather than an automatic consequence of a lord's ownership of the land.

Parcière. These were dues collected on the fruit of a property. These were quite similar to *champart*, or feudal tithe, and used primarily in the Bourbonnais and Auvergne.

Carpot. Found in the Bourbonnais, this was to vineyards what the *champart* was to other cultivatable fields, that is, a claim on a portion of the harvest. It amounted to a quarter of the grapes harvested.

Servage. "Servile customs" was the term for dues that still bore some trace of serfdom. There were not many of these. In provinces where such customs were in force, there were few if any parcels of land that did not bear some such traces. (This was written in 1765.) *Servage*, or, as the author also calls it, *servitude*, could be either *personal* or *real*.

Personal servitude was inherent in the person and followed him everywhere. Wherever the serf went, wherever he took his savings, the lord could lay claim to them as his residual due. The authorities mention a number of decrees that established this right, including one of June 17, 1760, in which the court dismissed the claim of a Nivernais lord to the estate of Pierre Truchet, who died in Paris. This Truchet was the son of a serf subject to the customary law of the Nivernais, who had married a free woman in Paris and had died there, like his son. But this judgment was apparently based on the fact that Paris was a place of asylum, in which the lord's residual rights over the son of his former serf did not apply. Although the right of asylum prevented the lord from seizing his serf's property in the place of asylum, it did not prevent him from inheriting any of the serf's property remaining within the boundaries of his estate.

Real servitude was a consequence of landholding and could end if the land in question was vacated or the owner moved to some other place.

Compulsory labor service. Known as *la corvée*, this was a claim that the lord had on his subjects, which allowed him a certain number of days' use, for his own profit, of their labor or that of their oxen or horses. Arbitrary labor service, in which the number of days of service could be set by the lord as he pleased, had been entirely abolished. Compulsory service had long since been reduced to a fixed number of days per year.

Compulsory labor service could be either *personal* or *real*. Personal services were owed by working people who lived within the boundaries of the lord's estate, each according to his trade. Real services were associated with the ownership of certain kinds of property. Nobles, ecclesiastics, clergy, officers of the court, lawyers, physicians, notaries, bankers, and notables were supposed to be exempt from compulsory labor services. The author cites a decree of August 13, 1735, exempting a notary whose lord wanted him to spend three days preparing, for free, contracts pertaining to the estate within whose boundaries the notary resided. Another decree of 1750 declared that when the service obligation could be discharged either by appearing in person or paying in cash, the choice was to be left to the person obliged to perform the service. Every compulsory service obligation had to be justified by a written document. The seigniorial *corvée* had become quite rare by the eighteenth century.

Banalités. The provinces of Flanders, Artois, and Hainault were the only ones exempt from *banalités*, or the lord's right to a monopoly of mills, bread ovens, presses, and other such services within his domain. The custom of Paris was very strict in this regard and prohibited the assertion of this right without an express title. Anyone who resided within the extent of a claim of *banalité* was subject to it, including, in most cases, nobles and priests.

There were many types of *banalité* other than those pertaining to flour mills and ovens:

1. *Banalités* of industrial mills, including those for cloth, cork, and hemp. This right was recognized by the customary laws of Anjou, Maine, and Britanny, among others.
2. *Banalités* of winepresses. Very few customs mention this, but it was recognized in Lorraine and Maine.

3. *Banalité* of the bull. No custom mentions this, but there are titles establishing such a right. The butchering of slaughtered animals could also be subject to a *banalité*.

In general, the less important *banalités*, like those discussed here, were rarer and less well tolerated than the others. They were recognized only if established by a very clear provision of customary law or, failing that, by a very specific title.

Ban des vendanges. This was a charge on the grape harvest and still in effect throughout the kingdom in the eighteenth century. It was a purely regulatory fee associated with the lord's judicial powers. A lord with such powers needed no explicit title to impose this fee, to which everyone was subject. The customs of Burgundy granted the lord the right to harvest his grapes one day before any other vineyard owner.

Droit de banvin. According to the authorities, whether by virtue of customary law or explicit title, a good many lords claimed the right to sell wine originating from their estates for a certain period of time (generally a month to forty days) before anyone else. Among the most important customary laws, only those of Tours, Anjou, Maine, and La Marche established and regulated this right. A decree issued by the Cour des Aides on August 28, 1751, established an exemption authorizing tavern keepers to sell wine during the *banvin*, but only to foreigners. It had to be the lord's wine, made from grapes from his estate. The customs that established and regulated the *droit de banvin* usually required that it be based on an explicit title.

Droit de blairie. This was a right that belonged to the lord with powers of high justice, who could grant permission to residents of his estate to pasture their livestock on land covered by his powers of justice, as well as on empty grazing land. This right did not exist in regions of written law, but it was quite common in regions of customary law. One finds it under various names especially in the Bourbonnais, Nivernais, Auvergne, and Burgundy. The underlying assumption was that all the land was originally the property of the lord, so that after distributing the best parts as fiefs, land subject to the *cens*, and other grants, in exchange for rents, he remained in possession of grazing land to which he could grant temporary access. The *blairie* was established in several customs, but only lords with powers of high justice could lay claim to it, and an explicit title was required, or else ancient affidavits backed by long possession.

Tolls. Originally, according to the authors, there existed a huge number of seigniorial tolls on bridges, rivers, and roads. Louis XIV eliminated many of these. In 1724, a commission was appointed to examine all titles to tolls, and it eliminated 1,200 of them; more were subsequently eliminated every day (1765). In this regard, Renauldon tells us, the first principle is that a toll, being a tax, should not be based on a title but on a title emanating from the sovereign. Such titles bore the inscription "By order of the king." Titles to tolls were accompanied by lists of the fees to be paid by each type of merchandise. This list of tariffs always had to be approved by a council decree. According to the author, the grant of title was invalid unless subsequent possession was uninterrupted. Despite these legal precautions, the value of certain tolls had greatly increased in modern times. The author states that he was aware of one toll that had been let for 100 livres a century earlier but fetched 1,400 at the time of writing. Another, let for 39,000, fetched 90,000. The main ordinances and edicts regulating toll rights were title 29 of the ordinance of 1669 and the edicts of 1683, 1693, 1724, and 1775.

The authors whom I am citing, though in general rather favorable to feudal rights, acknowledge that there were great abuses in the collection of tolls.

Ferries. The ferry right differed markedly from the right to collect tolls. The latter pertained only to merchandise, the former to people and animals. This right could not be exercised without authorization from the king, and the fees collected were set by the Council decree that established or authorized the right.

The right of *leyde* (which went by various other names, depending on the place) was a tax collected on merchandise delivered to a fair or market. Many lords regarded this right as a concomitant of high justice and considered it to be purely seigniorial, according to the feudal law specialists I am following, but they were wrong, because it was a tax that had to be authorized by the king. In any case, it was a right exercised only by lords with powers of high justice, who collected fines due from violation of local regulations. Although the right of *leyde* could in theory emanate only from the king, it appears that, in fact, it was often based solely on a feudal title and long enjoyment.

There is no doubt that fairs could not be established without royal authorization.

A lord did not need a specific title or royal grant to exercise the right to decide what weights and measures his vassals would be obliged to use in fairs and markets within the boundaries of his estates. Custom and unbroken possession were enough to establish this right. The various kings who wished at one time or another to establish uniformity of weights and measures all failed, according to our authors. Things remained as they had been when the customary laws were drafted.

Roads. Rights exercised by lords over roads.

The main roads, called king's highways, were actually the property of the sovereign. Their creation and maintenance, as well as jurisdiction over crimes committed on them, fell outside the competence of lords and their judges. As for private roads within the boundaries of an estate, no one denied that these belonged to lords with powers of high justice. Such lords reserved all rights pertaining to the building, maintenance, and regulation of roads, and their judges had jurisdiction over all offenses committed on them, apart from crown cases. At one time, lords were responsible for maintaining highways that traversed their estates, and in order to compensate them for the cost of such repairs, they were granted the rights of *péage, bornage*, and *traverse*. Later, however, the king reclaimed overall charge of the highways.

Waters. All *navigable* and *floatable* rivers belonged to the king, even if they flowed through a lord's lands and notwithstanding any title to the contrary (ordinance of 1669). If the lord collected fees for fishing, mills, ferries, bridges, etc., he did so by virtue of a grant of authority, which had to be issued by the king. There were some lords who continued to claim rights of justice and regulation over rivers, but only in consequence of a clear usurpation or extorted grant of authority.

That small streams belonged to the lords through whose lands they flowed was not contested. Over such streams lords enjoyed the same rights of property, justice, and regulation as the king enjoyed over navigable rivers. To secure ownership, they had no need of any title other than that conferring powers of high justice. Some customs, such as the custom of Berry, allowed private individuals to construct, without permission from the lord, mills powered by rivers that belonged to the lord but passed through property owned by the individual in question. The custom of Brittany granted this right only to certain nobles. In general law, it was undoubtedly the case that only lords with powers of high justice had the right to allow construction of a mill within the extent of their judicial powers. No one could dam a seigniorial river, even to protect his own property, without permission of the lord's judges.

Fountains, wells, flax-wetting pits, ponds. Rainwater drained from highways belonged to the lords of high justice, who had exclusive rights to its use. A lord of high justice could construct a pond anywhere within the extent of his judicial powers, even on property belonging to his subjects, provided he paid for the land that was submersed. This was a specific provision of certain customs, including those of Troyes and Nivernais. Private individuals could construct ponds only on their own land. Even then, certain customs required the owner to ask the lord for permission. The customs that required the lord's approval insisted that, if granted, it be free of charge.

Fishing. Fishing rights in navigable or floatable rivers belonged exclusively to the king; only he could grant them to others. His judges alone had the right to judge offenses related to fishing. There were, nevertheless, many lords who enjoyed the right to fish in these kinds of streams, but it had either been granted to them by the king or else usurped. As for non-navigable rivers, fishing in them was not allowed, even using a hand line, without permission from the lord having powers of high justice over the territory through which the stream flowed. A decree of April 30, 1749, condemned a fisherman for such an offense. Furthermore, even lords had to abide by general fishing regulations. A lord with powers of high justice could grant the right to fish in his river either as a fief or in exchange for a *cens* (rent).

Hunting. Unlike the right to fish, the right to hunt could not be leased. It was a personal right. Some maintained that it was a royal right, of which even nobles could avail themselves only within the limits of their jurisdiction, or fief, and then only with the permission of the king. This doctrine was set forth in title 30 of the ordinance of 1669. The lord's judges had jurisdiction over all offenses involving hunting, except for those involving the hunting of "red-furred animals" (meaning, I believe, large animals such as deer, both stags and does), which were royal cases.

The right to hunt was more assiduously denied to commoners than any other. It was denied even to freeholders. It was not among the favors granted by the king. So strict was the principle that a lord could not even grant permission to hunt. The law in this regard was very rigorous. Yet it was quite common for lords to grant permission to hunt not only to nobles but also to commoners. A lord of high justice could hunt anywhere within his jurisdiction, but only alone. Within that territory he was entitled to impose whatever regulations, restrictions, and prohibitions on hunting that he wished. Any fief-holding lord, even without powers of justice, could hunt within the boundaries of his fief. Nobles who had neither fiefs nor powers of justice could also hunt on land that belonged to them in the vicinity of their residences. A court held that a commoner with a park in an area of high justice had to open that park if the lord so wished, but the judgment was very old; it dated from 1668.

Rabbit warrens. None could be established at the time of writing without a title. Both commoners and nobles could keep warrens, but only nobles could keep ferrets.

Dovecotes. Certain customs granted the right to keep dovecotes to lords of high justice alone; others granted it to any owner of a fief. In Dauphiné, Britanny, and Normandy, commoners were prohibited from keeping dovecotes, pigeon coops, or birdcages; only nobles could keep pigeons. The punishment for killing a pigeon was quite harsh, often involving corporal punishment.

According to the authors I am following, these were the principal feudal dues and obligations still in force in the second half of the eighteenth century. They write: "Thus far we have discussed only generally established rights. There were a host of others, less well known and less extensively practiced, which existed in only a few customs or even on only a few estates, in virtue of specific titles." The rare and restricted rights mentioned and named by the authors were ninety-nine in number, and most impinged directly on agriculture, by granting lords certain claims on the harvest or establishing tolls on the transport and sale of staples. The authors state that several of these dues had fallen into disuse during their lifetime. Nevertheless, I believe that a substantial number of them were probably still being collected in a few places in 1789.

After studying what the main feudal dues still in effect in the eighteenth century were, according to the feudal law specialists of the time, I wanted to know how important they were in the eyes of contemporaries, including both those who derived income from them and those who were obliged to pay.

One of the authors I have been discussing, Renauldon, provides that information while telling us about the rules that lawyers charged with assessing estate inventories had to follow when evaluating feudal dues still extant in 1765, that is, twenty-four years before the Revolution. Here, according to this lawyer, are the rules to be followed in this realm.

Rights of justice. "Some of our customs," Renauldon writes, "estimate the rights of high, low, and medium justice at one-tenth the revenue of the land. Seigniorial justice was of great importance at the time. Edme de Fréminville thinks that today the rights of justice should be estimated at only one-twentieth of the income from the land. I believe that this estimate is still too high."

Honorific rights. However invaluable these rights may be, Renauldon, a very down-to-earth fellow not unduly impressed by appearances, insists that a prudent expert ought to set a moderately low price for them.

Seigniorial labor services. The author gives rules for estimating the value of these services, which proves that they were still used to some extent. He puts the cost of an ox at 20 *sous* per day and a laborer at 5 *sous*, plus food. This gives us a fairly good idea of the wage level in 1765.

Tolls. In evaluating tolls, the author says: "There are no seigniorial dues for which a lower price should be set than for tolls. They are highly variable. Since the maintenance of the roads and bridges most useful for trade is now the responsibility of the king and the provinces, many tolls today serve no purpose, and more are abolished every day."

Fishing and hunting rights. Fishing rights can be leased and are therefore subject to expert appraisal. Hunting rights are purely personal and cannot be leased. They therefore count as honorific rights rather than remunerative rights and should not be included in expert appraisals.

The author then discusses the rights of *banalité, banvin, leyde,* and *blairie,* showing that these rights were the most frequently invoked and most important of all. He adds that "there are quite a few other seigniorial rights that one still encounters on occasion and that would be tedious if not impossible to enumerate here. From the examples we have just given, however, intelligent experts will be able to define rules for appraising the rights we do not discuss."

Appraisal of the cens. Most customs valued the *cens* at one thirtieth of the land's income. The reason for this high estimate is that the *cens* represented not only itself but other dues calculated as a percentage of income, such as *lods et ventes.*

Feudal tithes, terrage. Feudal tithes were evaluated at a minimum of 4 percent, since this was an asset that required no care, labor, or financial outlay. When *terrage* or *champart* entailed *lods et ventes,* that is, when a field subject to these obligations could not be sold without paying a transfer fee to the lord with a direct claim on it, this variable revenue reduced its value to one-thirtieth; otherwise it was to be appraised the same as the tithe.

Ground rents, which did not yield *lods et ventes* or *retenue* (that is, which were not seigniorial rents), were to be estimated at 5 percent.

ESTIMATE OF VARIOUS FORMS OF PROPERTY HOLDING IN FRANCE
BEFORE THE REVOLUTION

France, the author states, recognizes only three types of property:

1. *Freehold.* This is free tenure, exempt from all charges and not subject to any seigniorial obligations or dues, whether pecuniary or honorific.

There are noble freeholds and common freeholds. A noble freehold has powers of justice, or fiefs subordinate to it, or associated land on which rent is due in the form of the *cens*. It is subject to feudal law in regard to division upon inheritance. A common freehold has neither powers of justice nor fiefs nor dependent lands subject to the *cens*, and its division upon inheritance is subject to the law governing commoners. For the author, only freeholders enjoy full ownership of the land.

Appraisal of freehold property. It should be as high as possible. The customs of Auvergne and Burgundy put it at 2.5 percent. The author believes that 3.3 percent might be correct.

It should be noted that common freeholds located within the jurisdiction of seigniorial justice were subject to it. This was not a form of subjection to the lord but rather submission to a jurisdiction that supplanted the jurisdiction of state tribunals.

2. The second type of property was property held as a *fief*.

3. The third type of property was *property subject to the cens*, or common tenure, in legal parlance.

Appraisal of property held as a fief. The appraisal was to be reduced in proportion to the feudal dues encumbering the property.

1. In regions of written law, as well as in several customs, fiefs owed nothing other than "hand and mouth," that is, homage to the lord.
2. In other customs, fiefs, beyond owing the homage of hand and mouth, were what was called "precarious" (*de danger*), as in Burgundy, and subject to *commise*, or feudal confiscation, if the owner took possession without having sworn an oath and paid homage to the lord.
3. Other customs, such as that of Paris and a good many others, subjected the fief not only to the obligation of oath and homage at the time of purchase but also to the taxes known as *quint* and *requint* (one-fifth and one-twenty-fifth, respectively).
4. In still other customs, such as that of Poitou and a few other places, fiefs were subject to the obligation of *chambellage*, a cash payment at the time the oath of fealty was sworn, as well as the obligation to supply horses on demand.

Property in the first category was to be appraised at a higher value than the other three.

The custom of Paris set the estimate at 5 percent, which seemed reasonable to the author.

Appraisal of land in common tenure, subject to the cens. To arrive at this estimate, it was best to consider three classes of land of this type.

1. Property simply subject to the *cens*.
2. Property subject to other *servitudes* in addition to the *cens*.
3. Property that was in *mainmorte*, subject to the real taille, or subject to *bordelage*.

Of these three forms of common tenure, the first and second were quite common in the eighteenth century; the third was rare. The appraised value should decrease, the author recommended, as one moved from the first to the second and especially the third category. Those in possession of property of the third class were, in fact, not even true owners because they could not sell without the lord's permission.

The *terrier*. Here, according to the feudal law specialists cited previously, are the rules that were followed in establishing and revising the *terrier*, the feudal land registers that I mentioned several times in the text. As is well known, each estate had a *terrier* recording all the titles underlying the various rights associated with that estate, whether as property rights or honorific, real, personal, or mixed rights. It included the declarations of *cens* payers, the customs of the estate, leases, etc. Under the custom of Paris, according to our authorities, lords could revise the *terrier* every thirty years at the expense of the *cens* payers. They add, however, that "you would nevertheless be quite lucky if you found one revision per century." Revision of the *terrier* was an inconvenience for everyone under the estate's jurisdiction, and it could not be done without authorization from the high chancellery (for estates situated within the jurisdiction of more than one parlement) or the parlement; this authorization was known as a *letter à terrier*. A notary was appointed by the court. All vassals, noble as well as commoner, *cens* payers, leaseholders, and others subject to the estate's jurisdiction were required to appear before this notary, and a map of the estate had to be inserted into the *terrier*.

In addition to the *terrier*, estates also kept another record book called the *lière*, in which the lord or his lessees recorded the sums received from the *cens* payers, along with their names and the date of their payment.

Index

absenteeism, and nobility, 87, 113
administration: and conflicts of powers
    in late eighteenth century, 258–9;
    customs of under Ancien Régime,
    62–70; and municipal governments
    of towns as institution of Ancien
    Régime, 47–54, 212–22, 232–4; and
    religious government of ecclesiastical
    provinces, 244–5; revolution in at
    end of eighteenth century, 170–9;
    and village government in Île-de-
    France, 222–5. *See also* centralization
agriculture: and central government
    of Ancien Régime, 45; class and
    societies for, 229; roles of intendant
    and comptroller general in societies
    for, 154. *See also* famine
Aigues-Mortes (district), 190
Algeria, administrative centralization of
    Ancien Régime in Canada compared
    to, 226
America: and English system of
    decentralization, 226, 227; and role
    of religion in society, 140; and rural
    parishes of Middle Ages compared
    to New England townships, 52.
    See also American Revolution
American Revolution, 133–4
Ancien Régime: and administrative
    centralization, 39–46, 59–61,
    225–7; condition of peasants in

eighteenth century compared
    to thirteenth century, 112–24;
    courts and immunity of public
    officials in, 55–8; and customs of
    administration, 62–70; destruction
    of political liberty and separation of
    classes as fatal to, 93–101; divisions
    and uniformity in society, 76–9;
    emergence of French Revolution
    from, 179–85; and irreligion,
    136–42; isolation of social groups
    during, 80–92; kind of liberty
    under, 102–11; and men of letters
    as leading politicians, 127–35; and
    municipal governments of towns,
    47–54; moderating forces on, 246–7;
    and prosperity during reign of Louis
    XVI, 152–9; and revolutionary
    education of people, 166–9;
    sovereign influence of Paris during,
    71–5; Tocqueville on study of, 1–3.
    See also France; monarchy
*The Ancien Régime and the French
    Revolution* (Tocqueville): as
    expression of Tocqueville's personal
    philosophy, xxv–xxviii; and genre
    of history, xiii–xiv; modern editions
    of, xxix; structure of and relation to
    planned second volume, xv–xxv; as
    work of structural analysis and social
    science, xiii–xv

class: and administrative officials of
Ancien Régime, 64; relationship
between middle classes and
aristocracy in England, 86;
separation of as fatal to Ancien
Régime, 93–101. *See also* bourgeoise;
nobility; peasants
clergy: feudal dues owned by, 207–10;
and individual liberty under
Ancien Régime, 106; privileges
of and alienation of people, 207,
247–8; and provincial government
of Languedoc, 195; and public
administration of Ancien Régime,
104–5, 245; and residence of
priests in countryside, 114–15.
See also Church
Colbert, Jean Baptiste, 99, 226
Cologne (electorship), 206
commise, 269
communes, 188
comparative method, and *The Ancien
Régime and the French Revolution* as
work of social science, xv
comptroller general: and administrative
centralization of Ancien Régime, 41;
and customs of administration, 62–3;
role of in 1740 compared to 1780,
61, 153–4
concession, and responses of
governments to crisis, xxi, xxii–xxiii
Constituent Assembly, 73
constitutions: and administrative justice
in postrevolutionary period, 57;
and grievance books of nobility,
241–2; and provincial government
of Languedoc, 193, 195; of towns,
212, 213
council decrees: and administration
of towns, 50; and centralization in
final years of Ancien Régime, 44–6;
and courts, 227–8; and customs
of administration under Ancien
Régime, 63, 66. *See also* King's
Council
Cour des Aides, 108

courts: administrative justice and
immunity of public officials in
Ancien Régime, 55–8; and council
decrees, 227–8; and English legal
system, 254–5; and grievance books
of nobility, 243; legislative power of
in Ancien Régime, 40; and liberty
under Ancien Régime, 108–9; and
royal edicts of Louis XVI, 170–1.
See also criminal justice; law and
legal system
criminal justice: and government
practices during reign of Louis
XVI, 168–9; and grievance books of
nobility, 235–6. *See also* courts; law
and legal system; police

Dauphiné (province), xxiv, 267
Davies, James, xxx
Declaration of the Rights of Man
(1791), 201
democracy: and despotism, 147; and
government of rural parishes in
eighteenth century, 53
Democracy in America (Tocqueville), xv
Department of Bridges and Roads, 44,
58, 97, 167
despotism: democratic form of, 147; and
desire for acquisition of wealth, 5–6
diachronic paradox, xx–xxi
Diderot, Denis, 63, 139
diversity: of administration of Ancien
Régime, 40; of laws and courts in
England, 253–4
draft lottery of 1769, 118
Droz, Joseph, xxx
Duchâtelet, Mme., 162
dynamics, of revolution, xxiv–xxv, xxviii

economics. *See* poverty and poor relief;
price controls; taxation; wealth
Economists, 143–51
Edict of Nantes (1685), 158n1
education: of bourgeois and nobility
during Ancien Régime, 79;
government practices as form of

CAMBRIDGE TEXTS IN THE HISTORY OF POLITICAL THOUGHT

Titles published in the series thus far

Cavendish *Political Writings* (edited by Susan James) 978 0 521 63350 5 paperback

Cicero *On the Commonwealth and On the Laws* (edited by James E. G. Zetzel) 978 0 521 45959 4 paperback

Cicero *On Duties* (edited by M. T. Griffin and E. M. Atkins) 978 0 521 34835 5 paperback

Comte *Early Political Writings* (edited by H. S. Jones) 978 0 521 46923 4 paperback

Conciliarism and Papalism (edited by J. H. Burns and Thomas M. Izbicki) 978 0 521 47674 4 paperback

Constant *Political Writings* (edited by Biancamaria Fontana) 978 0 521 31632 3 paperback

Dante *Monarchy* (edited by Prue Shaw) 978 0 521 56781 7 paperback

Christine De Pizan *The Book of the Body Politic* (edited by Kate Langdon Forhan) 978 0 521 42259 8 paperback

Diderot *Political Writings* (edited by John Hope Mason and Robert Wokler) 978 0 521 36911 4 paperback

The Dutch Revolt (edited by Martin van Gelderen) 978 0 521 39809 1 paperback

Early Greek Political Thought from Homer to the Sophists (edited by Michael Gagarin and Paul Woodruff) 978 0 521 43768 4 paperback

The Early Political Writings of the German Romantics (edited by Frederick C. Beiser) 978 0 521 44951 9 paperback

Emerson *Political Writings* (edited by Kenneth S. Sacks) 978 0 521 71002 2 paperback

The English Levellers (edited by Andrew Sharp) 978 0 521 62511 1 paperback

Erasmus *The Education of a Christian Prince* (edited by Lisa Jardine) 978 0 521 58811 9 paperback

Fenelon *Telemachus* (edited by Patrick Riley) 978 0 521 45662 3 paperback

Ferguson *An Essay on the History of Civil Society* (edited by Fania Oz-Salzberger) 978 0 521 44736 2 paperback

Fichte *Addresses to the German Nation* (edited by Gregory Moore) 978 0 521 44873 4 paperback

Filmer *Patriarcha and Other Writings* (edited by Johann P. Sommerville) 978 0 521 39903 6 paperback

Fletcher *Political Works* (edited by John Robertson) 978 0 521 43994 7 paperback

Sir John Fortescue *On the Laws and Governance of England* (edited by Shelley Lockwood) 978 0 521 58996 3 paperback

Fourier *The Theory of the Four Movements* (edited by Gareth Stedman Jones and Ian Patterson) 978 0 521 35693 0 paperback

Franklin *The Autobiography and Other Writings on Politics, Economics, and Virtue* (edited by Alan Houston) 978 0 521 54265 4 paperback

Gramsci *Pre-Prison Writings* (edited by Richard Bellamy) 978 0 521 42307 6 paperback

Guicciardini *Dialogue on the Government of Florence* (edited by Alison Brown) 978 0 521 45623 4 paperback

Hamilton, Madison, and Jay (writing as 'Publius') *The Federalist with The Letters of 'Brutus'* (edited by Terence Ball) 978 0 521 00121 2 paperback

Harrington *A Commonwealth of Oceana and A System of Politics* (edited by J. G. A. Pocock) 978 0 521 42329 8 paperback

Hegel *Elements of the Philosophy of Right* (edited by Allen W. Wood and H. B. Nisbet) 978 0 521 34888 1 paperback

Hegel *Political Writings* (edited by Laurence Dickey and H. B. Nisbet) 978 0 521 45979 4 paperback

Hess *The Holy History of Mankind and Other Writings* (edited by Shlomo Avineri) 978 0 521 38756 9 paperback

Hobbes *Leviathan* (edited by Richard Tuck) 978 0 521 56797 8 paperback

Hobbes *On the Citizen* (edited by Michael Silverthorne and Richard Tuck) 978 0 521 43780 6 paperback

Hobhouse *Liberalism and Other Writings* (edited by James Meadowcroft) 978 0 521 43726 4 paperback

Hooker *Of the Laws of Ecclesiastical Polity* (edited by A. S. McGrade) 978 0 521 37908 3 paperback

Hume *Political Essays* (edited by Knud Haakonssen) 978 0 521 46639 4 paperback

King James VI and I *Political Writings* (edited by Johann P. Sommerville) 978 0 521 44729 4 paperback

Jefferson *Political Writings* (edited by Joyce Appleby and Terence Ball) 978 0 521 64841 7 paperback

John of Salisbury *Policraticus* (edited by Cary Nederman) 978 0 521 36701 1 paperback

Kant *Political Writings* (edited by H. S. Reiss and H. B. Nisbet) 978 0 521 39837 4 paperback

Knox *On Rebellion* (edited by Roger A. Mason) 978 0 521 39988 3 paperback

Kropotkin *The Conquest of Bread and Other Writings* (edited by Marshall Shatz) 978 0 521 45990 7 paperback

Lawson *Politica sacra et civilis* (edited by Conal Condren) 978 0 521 54341 5 paperback

Leibniz *Political Writings* (edited by Patrick Riley) 978 0 521 35899 6 paperback

The Levellers (edited by Andrew Sharp) 978 0 521 62511 4 paperback

Locke *Political Essays* (edited by Mark Goldie) 978 0 521 47861 8 paperback

Locke *Two Treatises of Government* (edited by Peter Laslett) 978 0 521 35730 2 paperback

Loyseau *A Treatise of Orders and Plain Dignities* (edited by Howell A. Lloyd) 978 0 521 45624 1 paperback

Luther and Calvin on Secular Authority (edited by Harro Höpfl) 978 0 521 34986 4 paperback

Machiavelli *The Prince* (edited by Quentin Skinner and Russell Price) 978 0 521 34993 2 paperback

de Maistre *Considerations on France* (edited by Isaiah Berlin and Richard Lebrun) 978 0 521 46628 8 paperback

Maitland *State, Trust and Corporation* (edited by David Runciman and Magnus Ryan) 978 0 521 52630 2 paperback

Malthus *An Essay on the Principle of Population* (edited by Donald Winch) 978 0 521 42972 6 paperback

Marsilius of Padua *The Defender of the Peace* (edited and translated by Annabel Brett) 978 0 521 78911 0 paperback

Marsilius of Padua *Defensor minor and De translatione Imperii* (edited by Cary Nederman) 978 0 521 40846 6 paperback

Marx *Early Political Writings* (edited by Joseph O'Malley) 978 0 521 34994 9 paperback

Marx *Later Political Writings* (edited by Terrell Carver) 978 0 521 36739 4 paperback

James Mill *Political Writings* (edited by Terence Ball) 978 0 521 38748 4 paperback

J. S. Mill *On Liberty, with The Subjection of Women and Chapters on Socialism* (edited by Stefan Collini) 978 0 521 37917 5 paperback

Milton *Political Writings* (edited by Martin Dzelzainis) 978 0 521 34866 9 paperback

Montesquieu *The Spirit of the Laws* (edited by Anne M. Cohler, Basia Carolyn Miller and Harold Samuel Stone) 978 0 521 36974 9 paperback

More *Utopia* (edited by George M. Logan and Robert M. Adams) 978 0 521 52540 4 paperback

Morris *News from Nowhere* (edited by Krishan Kumar) 978 0 521 42233 8 paperback

Nicholas of Cusa *The Catholic Concordance* (edited by Paul E. Sigmund) 978 0 521 56773 2 paperback

Nietzsche *On the Genealogy of Morality* (edited by Keith Ansell-Pearson) 978 0 521 69163 5 paperback

Paine *Political Writings* (edited by Bruce Kuklick) 978 0 521 66799 9 paperback

Plato *Gorgias, Menexenus, Protagoras* (edited by Malcolm Schofield) 978 0 521 54600 3 paperback

Plato *The Republic* (edited by G. R. F. Ferrari and Tom Griffith) 978 0 521 48443 5 paperback

Plato *Statesman* (edited by Julia Annas and Robin Waterfield) 978 0 521 44778 2 paperback

Price *Political Writings* (edited by D. O. Thomas) 978 0 521 40969 8 paperback

Priestley *Political Writings* (edited by Peter Miller) 978 0 521 42561 2 paperback

Proudhon *What Is Property?* (edited by Donald R. Kelley and Bonnie G. Smith) 978 0 521 40556 0 paperback

Pufendorf *On the Duty of Man and Citizen according to Natural Law* (edited by James Tully) 978 0 521 35980 1 paperback

The Radical Reformation (edited by Michael G. Baylor) 978 0 521 37948 9 paperback

Rousseau *The Discourses and Other Early Political Writings* (edited by Victor Gourevitch) 978 0 521 42445 5 paperback

Rousseau *The Social Contract and Other Later Political Writings* (edited by Victor Gourevitch) 978 0 521 42446 2 paperback

Seneca *Moral and Political Essays* (edited by John Cooper and John Procope) 978 0 521 34818 8 paperback

Sidney *Court Maxims* (edited by Hans W. Blom, Eco Haitsma Mulier, and Ronald Janse) 978 0 521 46736 0 paperback

Sorel *Reflections on Violence* (edited by Jeremy Jennings) 978 0 521 55910 2 paperback

Spencer *Political Writings* (edited by John Offer) 978 0 521 43740 0 paperback

Stirner *The Ego and Its Own* (edited by David Leopold) 978 0 521 45647 0 paperback

Thoreau *Political Writings* (edited by Nancy Rosenblum) 978 0 521 47675 1 paperback

Tönnies *Community and Civil Society* (edited by Jose Harris and Margaret Hollis) 978 0 521 56782 4 paperback

Utopias of the British Enlightenment (edited by Gregory Claeys) 978 0 521 45590 9 paperback

Vico *The First New Science* (edited by Leon Pompa) 978 0 521 38726 2 paperback

Vitoria *Political Writings* (edited by Anthony Pagden and Jeremy Lawrance) 978 0 521 36714 1 paperback

Voltaire *Political Writings* (edited by David Williams) 978 0 521 43727 1 paperback

Weber *Political Writings* (edited by Peter Lassman and Ronald Speirs) 978 0 521 39719 3 paperback

William of Ockham *A Letter to the Friars Minor and Other Writings* (edited by A. S. McGrade and John Kilcullen) 978 0 521 35804 0 paperback

William of Ockham *A Short Discourse on Tyrannical Government* (edited by A. S. McGrade and John Kilcullen) 978 0 521 35803 3 paperback

Wollstonecraft *A Vindication of the Rights of Men and A Vindication of the Rights of Woman* (edited by Sylvana Tomaselli) 978 0 521 43633 5 paperback